The Macrodynamics of Business Cycles

T0327473

For my mother, for her care and affection

The Macrodynamics of Business Cycles

A Comparative Evaluation

Mohammed H. I. Dore

BLACKWELL
Cambridge MA & Oxford UK

First published 1993

Blackwell Publishers
238 Main Street
Cambridge, MA 02139

108 Cowley Road
Oxford OX4 1JF
UK

Library of Congress Cataloging-in-Publication Data
Dore, M. H. I.
    The macrodynamics of business cycles : a comparative evaluation /
Mohammed H.I. Dore.
        p.   cm.
    Includes bibliographical references and indexes.
    ISBN 1-55786-064-5. —ISBN 1-55786-380-6 (pb)
    1. Business cycles—History.   I. Title.
HB3714.D67   1983
338.5'42—dc20

British Library Cataloguing in Publication Data
A CIP catalogue record for this book is available from the British Library.

Typeset in 10½ on 12½pt Plantin by TecSet Ltd, Wallington, Surrey, UK

This book is printed on acid-free paper

Contents

Preface

Some of the ablest minds in the history of economics have written about business cycles, and traditional macroeconomics usually includes some study of steady-state growth, but there was a long period when business cycle theory seemed to have lost favor. The events of the 1970s, however, led to its rediscovery. Indeed, at one time it looked as if macroeconomics would be redefined as the study of business cycles.

The rise of the New Classical school was a purposeful retreat from aggregate income-expenditure categories into microeconomics. For a time macroeconomics, at least in North America, became no more than microeconomic analysis with aggregate data. The problem of index numbers, highlighted by Keynes in the *Treatise*, was quietly forgotten. The representative agent became the central focus of models in the New Classical, as well as the New Keynesian, approaches. It was also forgotten that any recorded price is almost always a kind of average, with some measure of dispersion. This means that the price is a type of index, and the subject matter of macroeconomics – output, employment, inflation, interest rates, capital accumulation – is always represented by an index for each of these variables. The representative agent approach has led to fallacies of composition, a problem that has recently received the kind of attention that it deserves. This, I submit, should lead to a renewed interest in the macro variables listed above, and to an appreciation of their dynamic character which is fundamentally cyclical. In addition to their cyclical nature, some of the macro indices such as real output, real disposable income, and real wages *grow* in a cyclical manner, and decomposing these into trend and cycle components has proved illusory. This also means that concepts such as permanent income, which relied on such decomposition, may have to be abandoned.

Indices that show growth over time are called nonstationary, and nonstationary time series cannot be decomposed except in a purely arbitrary manner. The recognition of the fact that a number of macro time series are nonstationary but exhibit cyclical behavior should lead to a return to business cycles in which trend and cycle are inextricably linked. This means that traditional macro theory must pay more attention to business cycle turning points, and the alternation between expansions and contractions. It is no longer enough to say what must (or must not) be done in a contraction. What macro theorists must do is explain the *alternating* phases of expansion and contraction of the economy. This must be done in *one* integrated, rigorous model. That is the task presently challenging macrotheorists.

This book does not claim to break any new ground in that field. In preparation for the task, however, it may be legitimate to attempt an evaluation of what has been done so far. That is the aim of this book. A clear statement of what one is attempting to evaluate inevitably means bringing different approaches under one cover with full rigor. Without sacrifice of rigor, an attempt has been made to make this work accessible to a wider readership, and consequently more intermediate steps are included in the mathematical derivations than would be customary in a book of this sort. The aim is to join the other Basil Blackwell books in macroeconomics that are lucidly written and enjoy a readership that includes undergraduates.

I believe an advanced undergraduate with a sound background in calculus will find this book comprehensible. The book can be viewed as being completely self-contained: all derivations are fully explained. Chapter 8 provides an introduction to the dynamics of Part III and may be omitted by those readers who are well versed in the dynamics of nonlinear differential equations. The exposition of the models discussed is separate from my assessments, so that readers may evaluate these models themselves, whether or not they accept the criteria proposed in chapters 2 and 3.

I know of no single book that has done what I have attempted here – namely, to evaluate the main approaches to business cycle modeling. I have benefitted by having seen the books by Gabisch and Lorenz (1989) and Sordi (1990). Both books cover some of the same material that is covered in this book, but there are a number of essential differences. For instance, neither Gabisch and Lorenz nor Sordi covers the New Keynesian theory; Sordi does not cover Goodwin's growth cycle model. This is not surprising, as the books do not have the same objectives. When this book was in press, I saw Zarnowitz (1992), which reproduces his excellent *Journal of Economic Literature* survey article, and other papers. While Zarnowitz's work is always interesting, this work does not compete with Zarnowitz (1992).

I have gained much from discussions and cooperative work with Richard Goodwin ever since I met him in 1984. He and the late Sukhamoy Chakravarty taught me what little I know about dynamics. In the summer of 1990 I had important discussions with Serena Sordi in Siena. She was kind enough to let me see a copy of her Ph.D. dissertation for the European University, which formed the basis for Sordi (1990).

I have also benefited from discussions and help from my colleagues at Brock university; in particular, I should like to thank Robert Dimand, Felice Martinello, Zisimos Koustas, Diane Dupont, Hafiz Akhand, Tom Peters, Chuck Masse, Steven Renzetti, and Bill Veloce. Dean Webster made available a very timely research grant that enabled me to finish the project. This research was also made possible by a grant from the Social Sciences and Humanities Research Council of Canada, Strategic Grant # 806–91–0044.

For permission to reproduce tables and diagrams, I should like to express my thanks to the following: the NBER and Chicago University Press for Tables 2.1, 2.2, 2.3, 2.4, and Figure 2.2; the *Quarterly Journal of Economics* and the President and Fellows of Harvard University for Figures 7.1, 7.2, 7.3, 7.4; Wheatsheaf Books for Figures 9.1, 9.2 and 9.3; M. E. Sharpe for Table 11.1; and New York University Press for Figure 11.5.

The book was partly written while I was a Visiting Fellow at Cornell University, Department of Agricultural Economics. There I should like to thank John Conrad and Bill Tomek for their hospitality and for giving me access to the excellent resources of the Cornell libraries.

Successive versions of the book were ably typed by Janet Hastie, who worked long hours at night and on weekends. Finally, as with my other books, Margaret Dore functioned as editor, librarian, and critic; she also did the bibliography and the index. Sophia, Roshan, and Naomi did their bit by not complaining. But all four of them put up with my absences and my preoccupations.

PART I

1

Introduction to Business Cycles

This book is not a survey of all business cycle models. Instead, it is an attempt at a comparative evaluation of the *main* contending approaches, which I have defined to be the New Classical approach, the New Keynesian approach, and the endogenous cycle approach. The New Classical approach is represented by the Lucas misperceptions model and the real business cycle models. The New Keynesian approach is in many ways a direct challenge to the New Classical approach; it is fairly diverse but focuses its attention on the underemployment equilibrium with involuntary unemployment. The endogenous business cycle approach draws its inspiration from Keynes as well as the classical economists, and to some extent Schumpeter. The first two approaches, which explain the business cycle as being caused by exogenous factors, are grouped together in Part II. Business cycle theories that treat the cycle as being endogenously generated are placed in Part III.

The New Classical approach owes much to Milton Friedman, the serious challenger of Keynesian orthodoxy of the 1950s and 1960s. His objective was nothing short of the complete demolition of Keynesian theory and practice, and the rehabilitation, in a modern form, of the classical quantity theory tradition, whose last champion before Friedman was Irving Fisher.

Perhaps Friedman's earliest attempt to break with Keynesianism was his study of the consumption function (Friedman, 1957), where he first proposes a new un-Keynesian concept of *permanent income*. This concept was originally proposed to reconcile the conflicting evidence on the marginal propensity to consume in cross section and time series estimates, where the cross section estimates were very much lower than the time series estimates. A true estimate was very crucial to macroeconomic policy, for the marginal propensity to consume determined the magnitude of the Keynesian multiplier, which in turn determined the effectiveness of countercyclical fiscal policy.

Permanent income as a conceptual innovation should now be considered questionable, as the concept is based on decomposing actual income into a permanent income component and a transitory income component. This is because actual income is a *nonstationary* time series – as it grows cyclically over time – and any decomposition of a nonstationary time series is arbitrary, a subject discussed more fully in chapter 6 and in appendix 6B. If the decomposition is arbitrary, then the concept of permanent income has no *empirical* content. Therefore, in hindsight, permanent income has no theoretical foundation.

Thus Friedman's earliest systematic attempt to break with Keynesian categories has no justification in theory or practice. Other conceptual innovations of Friedman that proved to be indispensable for the articulation of New Classical macroeconomics are discussed in chapter 4. Friedman's presidential address to the American Economic Association, delivered in 1967, is also discussed in chapter 4, as it is an important forerunner to the development of the New Classical approach.

The Lucas misperceptions model of business cycles is essentially a formalization of Friedman's presidential address model – but the formalization makes the required assumptions clear. As shown in chapter 5, a crucial assumption required in the Lucas model is asymmetric information, so that agents confuse movements in the aggregate price level with relative prices and expand output. However, as in Friedman's model, the ultimate cause of shifts in the price level is unanticipated growth of money supply. Thus here again it is the quantity theory equation that determines the price level. This is demonstrated in section 5.3 with a brief exposition of Barro's model.

Although Lucas admits that his 1975 business cycle model is flawed, the account in chapter 5 relies mainly on his 1973 paper (full citations are given in chapter 5). Nevertheless, the misperceptions approach has a major contradiction: misperceptions and rational expectations are incompatible (Okun's and Tobin's argument). By 1985, Lucas had implicitly abandoned his misperceptions approach and was praising the so-called real business cycle theory as being 'progress.' That should not be surprising since real business cycle theory is nothing but a formalization of Lucas's own ideas in the late 1970s. (This is documented in chapter 5). By 1985, Lucas's own position on business cycles was somewhat ambiguous, although he remained opposed to policy activism. While praising real business cycle theory, his Yrjö Jahnsson lectures, given in 1985, suggest that he regards the (American) aggregate business cycle to be a minor problem; smoothing out the cycle would represent a gain of about $8.50 per capita in 1983 constant dollars, or about the price of a good lunch.

The minor utility loss notwithstanding, theorists of the real business cycle have attempted to purge the theory of the defects of the Lucas and Barro models, so that an "equilibrium" account of the business cycle (a long-term objective of Hayek, which Lucas tried to achieve with his formal and informal models) will still be available to counter the efforts of the Keynesian policy activists.

The real business cycle theory is indeed an equilibrium account, and a full account of the model as given by McCallum (1989) is given in Chapter 6; it is also extended to incorporate the influence of money. Although a critique is also offered, the reader must judge how successful the equilibrium account is, because it does achieve some of its objectives, but at a cost. The real business cycle theory is now the *only* New Classical account of business cycles.

As stated above, the most direct challenge to real business cycle theory is provided by the New Keynesian approach, which represents a judicious mix of theory and empirical analysis of aggregate data. An early critique of real business cycle theory was by Mankiw, Rotemburg, and Summers (1985), who tested the intertemporal optimality conditions that are the necessary conditions for an optimum in real business cycle models. Using a more general utility function, they tested whether the conditions for an intertemporal optimum are supported by the data, and they found that they are not. In addition, the rejections occur for almost all possible permutations of utility functions – separable, non-separable, annual data, quarterly data, etc. A convex utility function produces a corner solution; when it is concave, either leisure or consumption becomes an inferior good. The net result is that either markets fail to clear or the intertemporal elasticities of substitution do not exist. Thus there is no empirical support for a theory that claims the economy can be treated as if it were in a continuous intertemporal equilibrium. The same high standards of theoretical and empirical analysis characterize the New Keynesian approach that shows constant departures from the conditions of a competitive equilibrium assumed by the New Classical approach. This makes the New Keynesian approach a wide-ranging inquiry into the nature of the goods market, the labor market, and the credit market. In all three markets, New Keynesians find evidence of constant departures from the competitive norm: price rigidity and excess capacity in the goods market, employment determined by efficiency wages that fail to clear the labor market, and an oligopolistic financial market with credit rationing. Even when the models are explicitly microeconomic with the assumption of the representative agent, the results lead to underemployment equilibria due to coordination failures and aggregate demand externalities. Furthermore, price rigidity is shown to be a logical consequence of optimizing behavior on the part of the agent. A large number of the papers, many collected in Mankiw and Romer (1991), make compelling reading. Chapter 7 proposes a unified framework for a review and assessment of this new and growing body of literature in attempting to explain the business cycle.

The third approach is the endogenous cycle approach. This class of models does not rely on some external shock or stimulus to account for the business cycle phenomenon. The external shock approach has a number of disadvantages, especially when it is recognized that the business cycle is *internationally* synchronized over a large number of countries (chapter 2), over a fairly long period. What exogenous factor can cause cyclical fluctuations in 14 industrialized and industrializing countries at about the same time? It is possible that the cycle is determined by a factor, or factors, endogenous to those economies. Consequently, a large number of endogenous business cycle models have been published; see Gabisch and Lorenz (1989) for a survey. Part III contains three important models in this class.

The two well-known approaches to business cycles, the New Classical and the New Keynesian approaches, both model expansions and contractions as being due to exogenous factors, although the New Keynesian approach does show that an underemployment equilibrium can occur through optimizing *choices*, which makes the underemployment equilibrium or the recession to be caused by *endogenous* factors. However, the expansion is usually caused by exogenous factors, such as an increase in aggregate demand.

The case for studying business cycles that are endogenously generated has been eloquently made by Geoffrey Moore (1977, p. 97), an authority on business cycles:

'My position is that both upturns and downturns in the business cycle are mostly self-generating or endogenous phenomena; that policy reactions are partly reactions to these endogenous developments, in both directions; that 'accidents' like a big strike, a new discovery, an oil embargo, a very poor (or a very good) harvest, or a declaration of war or peace can precipitate both upturns and downturns; and that long-term growth affects the entire cycle.

Part III begins with a chapter on self-sustained cycles (chapter 8), where the fundamental concepts of the theory of self-sustained oscillations are explained with the use of examples; it is shown that the basics are straightforward, requiring no more than a sound understanding of calculus. No background in nonlinear differential equations is necessary to be able to read Part III.

The reformulated Kaldor model (in chapter 9) is a simple introduction to this class of models where the cycles are endogenously generated. As argued in chapter 9, the explanatory power of the Kaldor model is limited; however, it is a good introduction to endogenous cycle theory. In the following chapter, Benassy's non-Walrasian model of business cycles is presented and discussed. It has some very interesting features; it is a generalization of the standard *IS-LM* Model, but with one important difference: it is a representative agent model and therefore has "choice theoretic microfoundations," which should satisfy both the New Classical and the New Keynesian schools, although the former could object to both fundamental equations on which it is based. The two fundamental equations state that the capital stock adjusts to expected demand with a finite speed, and that the wage rate growth depends on a nonlinear Phillips curve. A simpler approach is used to prove the existence of cycles both in the Kaldor and Benassy models; this is done by showing that both models can be formulated as a Liénard equation, a subject discussed extensively in chapter 8.

Chapter 11 is devoted to Goodwin's growth cycle model. After deriving the three coupled partial differential equations that determine the motion of the cycle, the existence of the cycle is shown graphically, essentially replicating Volterra's method, which Goodwin also used in his paper. An assessment of the model is also presented.

Because the objective of this book is to evaluate the main approaches to business cycle modeling, all the models are stated informally and then restated formally. The formal statement contains all the assumptions and the fundamental relationships, so the complete model is presented and all the results are fully derived. This is necessary for a comparative evaluation; without a rigorous statement of each model, the comparative evaluation would be compromised and the reader would not know how a particular model was evaluated.

In order to facilitate the comparative evaluation, chapters 2 and 3 develop the necessary criteria. Chapter 2 contains a brief statistical description of U.S. business cycles, and a set of stylized facts consistent with observation as well as with a simple macroeconomic model is stated. Chapter 3 completes the three main criteria used to evaluate the models. The final chapter summarizes the main conclusions.

Before closing this chapter, the main issue in business cycle theory, as presented in this book, is stated in summary form. Figure 1.1 presents the growth rates of U.S. real GNP for the period 1945 to 1989. It shows the percentage change in a four-year moving average. (The justification for using a four-year moving average is that the average duration of the cycles is four years, as shown in Chapter 2.) It is clear from this figure that output *grows in a cyclical manner*. Figure 1.2 idealizes this as a smoothly rising GNP with peaks and troughs. We can now ask a key question: what is likely to be the most important single variable that drives this cyclical growth? Let this unknown

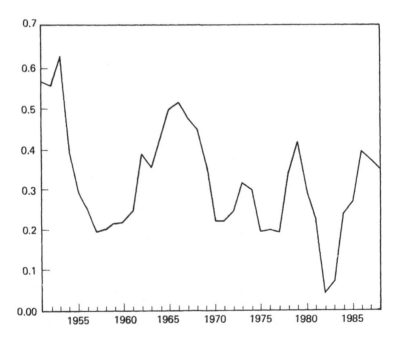

Figure 1.1   U.S. Real GNP Growth Cycles

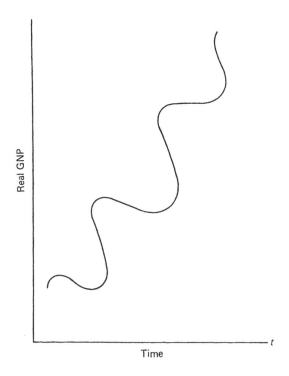

Figure 1.2 Idealized Real GNP

variable be x. Consider a three-dimensional graph of idealized cyclically growing output y, as a function of time t, and x. We thus get a three-dimensional spiral (figure 1.3). Note that the expansionary phase of the business cycle is longer than the contractionary phase.

The main issue in the theory is determining what "x" is in this graph. Three-dimensional graphs are difficult to handle. Take a cross section of this graph; alternatively rotate the time axis 't' through 90 degrees in a clockwise direction and look *down* the spiral. We see a number of closed curves, not perfect circles. All the closed curves seem to be "contained" in some "limiting" closed curve. In terms of economics, what this means is that all business cycles (considering output y over time t) have turning points: one at the peak and one at the trough of the cycle. In other words, the business cycles are irregular but not "explosive" – they do not "run away" to plus or minus infinity. The central objective of business cycle theory is to explain what factor, or factors, *govern* the business cycle. If we can

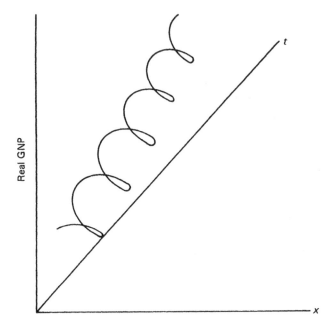

Figure 1.3　Idealized Three-dimensional Spiral of Real GNP

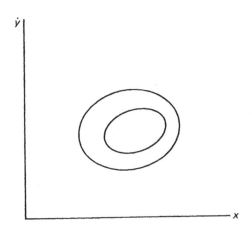

Figure 1.4　The Phase-Diagram for Figure 1.3

discover the "governing mechanism," we then have a *theory*, which we can discuss. Ideally we may even be able to test it.

We can avoid looking down the spiral if we can collapse the time dimension by considering dy/dt, or $\dot{y}$. Then we consider the graph of $\dot{y}$ and x. Technically, this is called a phase diagram. The sketch of the phase diagram of figure 1.3 is given in figure 1.4.

The following two chapters develop the criteria used to evaluate the business cycle models of parts II and III.

2

Stylized Facts of Business Cycles

INTRODUCTION

It would be most unconventional indeed if a book on business cycles
did not begin with the excellent and much quoted definition of
business cycles first given by Wesley Mitchell in 1927 and revised by
Burns and Mitchell (1946, p.3):

Business cycles are a type of fluctuation found in the aggregate activity of
nations that organize their work mainly in business enterprises: a cycle
consists of expansions occurring at about the same time in many economic
activities, followed by similarly general recessions, contractions, and revivals
which merge into the expansion phase of the next cycle; this sequence of
changes is recurrent but not periodic; in duration business cycles vary from
more than one year to ten or twelve years; they are not divisible into shorter
cycles of similar character with amplitudes approximating their own.

According to Moore and Zarnowitz (1986, p. 736), this working
definition of a business cycle is still in use at the National Bureau of
Economic Research (NBER), which has had an enduring interest in
the analysis of business cycle phenomena. When cycles continue to
occur, why is it that much of economic analysis is considered either in
static equilibrium, market clearance framework, or in steady-state
growth and full employment equilibrium? Granted, the enormity of
the task and analytical convenience dictate that economics start with
manageable problems first. With the developments in general equilibrium theory, much has been learned about static equilibria, but the

evolution over time of general equilibrium still eludes us, as Frank Hahn (1982) has readily admitted.

General equilibrium is a good description of market exchange when endowments are given and trade occurs only after a vector of equilibrium prices has been found. Is it possible that when trade (a) is in produced goods and not initial endowments, and (b) occurs in "disequilibrium", or before an equilibrium vector of prices is found, the sort of cycles described in the Burns-Mitchell definition cannot be avoided?

We seem to have at least a 300-year history of business cycles (Ashton, 1959), and much has been learned about the nature of cycles through the efforts of many researchers, among them Wesley Mitchell, Arthur Burns, Geoffrey Moore, and Victor Zarnowitz. Their work has been important in guiding the formulation of the *theory* of business cycles, the subject of this book. Accordingly, section 2.1 below summarizes the descriptive characteristics of the business cycle. Section 2.2 goes beyond description to ask which of the many descriptive characteristics of business cycles should an acceptable theory attempt to incorporate and explain.

No description of economic phenomena is theory-neutral, a lesson that Koopmans (1940, 1941, 1949) attempted to drive home, especially in relation to the study of business cycles. Consequently, it is shown in section 2.3 that all but one of the descriptive characteristics can be viewed as the logical consequence of a particular model, which is simple in the extreme. Any empirical work can then be viewed as *confirmation* of the proposed theory, or it can be seen as independent *corroboration*, and sometimes a weak form of refutation.

In much of the physical sciences, confirmation and corroboration are simpler than in economics, although there are areas such as astrophysics or quantum physics where confirmation and corroboration are just as difficult. Confirmation and corroboration in economics are considered in the next chapter.

2.1 BUSINESS CYCLES: A DESCRIPTION

2.1.1 Output

Although a detailed description is not possible here, some interesting information has been collected by Moore and Zarnowitz, published as appendix A in Gordon (1986). Table 2.1 gives British and U.S.

Table 2.1 Annual reference dates and duration of business cycles in Great Britain and the United States, 1790–1858

Dates of peaks and troughs by years		Duration in years			
				Full cycle	
Trough (T) *(1)*	*Peak (P)* *(2)*	*Contraction (P to T)* *(3)*	*Expansion (T to P)* *(4)*	*(T to T)* *(5)*	*(P to P)* *(6)*
Great Britain					
	1792				
1793	1796	1	3		4
1797	1802	1	5	4	6
1803	1806	1	3	6	4
1808	1810	2	2	5	4
1811	1815	1	4	3	5
1816	1818	1	2	5	3
1819	1825	1	6	3	7
1826	1828	1	2	7	3
1829	1831	1	2	3	3
1832	1836	1	4	3	5
1837	1839	1	2	5	3
1842	1845	3	3	5	6
1848	1854	3	6	6	9
1855	1857	1	2	7	3
1858		1		3	
Mean duration (years)		1.3	3.3	4.6	4.6
Standard deviation (years)		0.7	1.5	1.5	1.8
United States					
1790	1796		6		
1799	1802	3	3	9	6
1804	1807	2	3	5	5
1810	1812[a]	3	1.5	6	4.5
1812[a]	1815	0.5	3	2	3.5
1821	1822	6	1	9	7
1823	1825	1	2	2	3
1826	1828	1	2	3	3
1829	1833	1	4	3	5
1834	1836	1	2	5	3
1838	1839	2	1	4	3
1843	1845	4	2	5	6
1846	1847	1	1	3	2
1848	1853	1	5	2	6
1855		2		7	
Mean duration (years)		2	2.6	4.6	4.4
Standard deviation (years)		1.5	1.5	2.4	1.6

[a]In 1812 there is first a "brief recession," then a revival. The corresponding duration measures are based on the assumption that the recession occurred in the first half of the year, before the outbreak of the war with England. For details, see source material.

Source: Moore and Zarnowitz (1986, table A.2, p. 746).

business cycles between 1790 and 1858. The data cover seven decades of the rise of modern capitalism and industrialization. As the table shows, the average duration of the cycle in both countries is about 4.5 years, with a two-year standard deviation. Table 2.2 gives U.S. cycles from 1846 to 1982, and shows that after World War II, the eight cycles had longer expansions than contractions: the mean duration of complete cycles fell from 59 months to 57 months, while the mean of expansions was four times the mean of contractions.

Considering the cycles in the 1945–82 period, Moore and Zarnowitz find that contractions have become more predictable in length than in earlier times. Taking two standard deviations as the likely range, which is eight months (see Table 2.2), and adding the eleven month mean for contractions, we get 19 months as a practical upper limit for contractions. No contraction in the 1945–82 period lasted more than 17 months, but before 1945 the estimated range was 26 months, yielding an upper limit of 46 months. Even the Great Depression did not exceed this limit, as it lasted for 43 months.

2.1.2 Prices

For some 140 years before World War II, wholesale and consumer prices rose in expansions and fell in contractions so that at the bottom of the Great Depression the price level was about where it was at Independence (1776). But during 1932–82, the record was one of sustained inflation, except for price declines in the recessions of 1937–38 and 1948–49, as shown in Table 2.3. Although this was a long-run secular trend, all price indexes showed procyclical short-term movements – that is, prices rose in expansions and fell in contractions. Since 1949, prices have kept increasing, although every slowdown or recession has been associated with a decline in the inflation rate. Compared to the pre–1949 period, booms have not become more inflationary; it is the contractions that have not cancelled the previous price increases. Thus the average percentage increase per year in wholesale prices is 1.8 for the ten recessions of 1937–82, which is substantially higher than the increase over the previous 200 years before 1937 (Table 2.3).

In short, prices tend to move up when expansions gather steam, particularly when capital and labor utilization rates are high in booms, but they rise very slowly in contractions, particularly in long slumps. To quote Zarnowitz and Moore (1986, p. 531):

In a recession costs are cut, profit margins are pared, and discounts are given to move heavy inventories or prevent their costly accumulation. Failures increase,

Table 2.2 Duration of business cycles in the United States by selected subperiods, 1846–1982

Period (1)	Number of business cycles covered (2)	Duration in Months[a]						Percentage of time in contraction[b]	
		Expansions		Contractions		Business cycles		All (9)	Peacetime (10)
		Mean (3)	SD (4)	Mean (5)	SD (6)	Mean (7)	SD (8)		
All Cycles									
1846–85	8	32	16	27	18	59	28	45	46
1885–1912	8	23	5	17	5	40	4	42	42
1912–45	8	33	24	17	12	51	20	34	47
1945–82	8	45	28	11	4	56	27	20	25
Exclud "marginal recessions"[c]									
1846–85	7	39	21	28	19	68	38	42	
1885–1912	6	36	21	18	5	53	21		33
Summary									
1846–1945	24	30	17	20	13	50	21	41	
1846–1945[c]	21	36	21	21	14	57	27	37	
1846–1982	32	33	21	18	12	51	22	35	
Peacetime cycles[d]									
1846–1982	27	28	13	19	12	46	18		41
1846–1982[c]	24	33	18	19	13	52	25		37

[a]Based on the monthly NBER reference dates, except for the two earliest cycles dated in calendar years (troughs: 1846 and 1848; peaks: 1847 and 1853). Mean = mean duration; SD = standard deviation, in months. Col. (3) + col. (5) = col. (7), except for rounding.

[b]Months of business cycle contractions divided by total months covered, multiplied by 100.

[c]The following phases designated as contractions in the NBER chronology are treated as retardations rather than recessions and included, along with the preceding and following phases, in long expansions: 6/1869–12/1870; 3/1887–4/1888; 6/1899–12/1900. For details, see Zarnowitz 1981, 494–505.

[d]Excludes five wartime cycles (trough-peak-trough dates) associated with the Civil War (6/1861–4/1865–12/1867); World War I (12/1914–8/1918–3/1919); World War II (6/1938–2/1945–10/1945); Korean War (10/1949–7/1953–10/1954); and Vietnam War (2/1961–12/1969–11/1970).

Source: Zarnowitz and Moore (1986, Table 9.1, p. 524).

and going out of business sales at low prices multiply . . . . Wages rise more slowly and are reduced here and there under pressure of increased layoffs and unemployment. Costly overtime work is cut back . . . . Consumers become more economical and cautious, especially about borrowing and spending on durable goods. All of this works in the direction of lower prices or at least lower inflation rates.

2.1.3 Unemployment

The record of unemployment for the United States is summarized in table 2.4. Zarnowitz and Moore classify downturns according to

Table 2.3 U.S. Average Annual Inflation Rates[a] in Percent for Expansion and Contractions

Period	Business cycle expansion	Business cycle contractions
1864–1896	0.4	− 2.3
1896–1920	9.7	− 1.6
1920–1932	2.1	−13.7
1932–1982	6.5	1.8

[a]As measured by the Wholesale Price Index

Source: Moore and Zarnowitz (1986, Table 9.2, p. 527)

Table 2.4 Selected Measures of Duration and Unemployment of Business Cycle Contractions for the United States, 1920–82 (averages only)

		Percentage Decline			Unemployment rate (%)	
	Duration in months	Real GNP	Industrial	Nonfarm	Increase[a]	Maximum[b]
3 major depressions	25	−19.8	−39.4	−17.6	+13.7	18.9
6 severe recessions	12	− 3.3	−13.1	− 3.5	+ 3.8	7.8
4 mild recessions	10	− 1.7	− 7.8	− 1.7	+ 2.3	6.4
14 contractions	14	− 6.6	−19.0	− 6.4	+ 5.4	9.5

[a]From lowest month to highest.
[b]Highest figure reached in the trough

Source: Moore and Zarnowitz (1986, Table 9.7, pp. 544–5.)

severity. The classifications become obvious in Table 2.4. In the 62-year period between 1920 and 1982, there were three major depressions, six severe recessions, four mild recessions, and fourteen contractions. The average duration of the decline in output as well as the average increase in unemployment is shown in the table.

The above description is not meant to be complete in any sense; it is designed to illustrate the Burns-Mitchell definition. It shows that cycles are persistent but that their duration is variable; some cycles lead to mild contractions, while others are more severe. Expansions carry income and output to new heights, but contractions still leave income above the trough of the previous contraction. Thus the cycle displays significant real growth. Indeed, most of the cycles may be properly described as *growth cycles*, as growth and cyclical fluctuations are intertwined (see figure 1.1 in chapter 1, p 8.).

2.2   BUSINESS CYCLE PHENOMENA

The above description, though brief, should suggest that business cycles are complex phenomena, and there may be a number of legitimate ways of looking at them. The theorist will, however, want to distill from the description some enduring empirical regularities that, taken together, will represent the business cycle phenomenon. There is no doubt, of course, that there have been subtle changes in some of the descriptive characteristics of the cycle, and we have hinted at some of these. Nevertheless, the emphasis has to be on the *enduring* regularities, or what Kaldor once called *stylized facts*.

The object of theory is to illuminate and bring to the fore certain interrelations that are not obvious *a priori*, but after the theory has been expounded, the *process* of theorizing must make sense, and the interrelations must also make sense. But before that can happen, the would-be theorist must decide on what needs to be explained. In the physical sciences, what needs to be explained is often very clear: for example, one needs to explain the motion of the pendulum, or to understand why certain crystals form. In economics the task is much more difficult.

In the case of business cycles, one could attempt to explain very specific aspects – for example, the depth of a given cycle, or even the exact factors that determine the number of complete cycles in a decade. These are very hard questions, assuming that they are both interesting questions, which they may or may not be.

It might in fact be much easier to try to explain the general phenomenon of the business cycle first, before tackling harder questions. The general phenomenon of the business cycle may be described as *the increase and subsequent decrease of output*, a phenomenon that recurs, although at irregular intervals. If we are agreed on that as an important feature from the description in section 2.1, then we can ask the next question: what are its concomitants? What else goes with the up and down movement in output and income? The first important feature then leads to a set of related features, through which much sifting will have to be done. Fortunately in the case of business cycles, much of the sifting has already been done by dedicated researchers at the NBER and elsewhere. In this section, a set of these related features (or concomitants) are proposed. Taken together they may be called the stylized facts of business cycles. After listing them, it will be appropriate to discuss them. It could be argued that these facts reflect a theoretical perspective. In other words, the "facts" come from "theories," as Koopmans noted. We must, however, avoid an infinite regress.

2.2.1 The stylized facts[1]

For twentieth-century cycles, especially those observed in market economies after World War II, the most striking stylized facts about business cycles are the following:

1 The fluctuating growth of output is accompanied by a procyclical inflation rate and an inverse relationship between the inflation rate and the unemployment rate; that is, the inflation rate is anticyclical with the unemployment rate (see figure 2.1).
2 The comovement of price inflation with wage inflation, with the latter usually leading the former except during periods of very rapid inflation.
3 Procyclical real wages indicating that the wage share out of national income is also procyclical. Consequently, at cyclical peaks the profit share, defined as one minus the wage share, is generally low.
4 A long-term positive trend rate of growth of real GNP or GDP. This implies each subsequent cyclical trough of GNP(GDP) does not cancel out the "gains" made by the previous cyclical peak. This has led to the growing acceptance of the Schumpeterian view that growth and cycle are inextricably intertwined, and that the cycle is

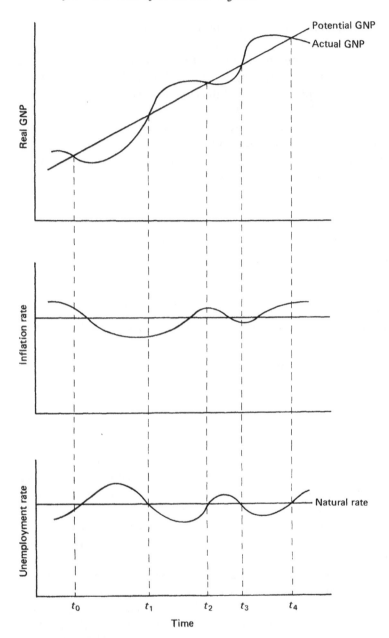

Figure 2.1   Real GNP. Inflation, and Unemployment

growth and cycle are inextricably intertwined, and that the cycle is a necessary condition for growth and vice versa. This view is also associated with Harrod (1936) and Goodwin (1982).

5 Recurrent but nonperiodic cycles. This suggests that although we can compute the average duration of a large number of cycles, as done by researchers at the NBER, no two cycles ever appear to be of equal duration. Consequently, turning points cannot be predicted.

6 A procyclical relationship between labor productivity and output. (Incidentally, this rules out the standard neoclassical aggregate production function, with a declining marginal product of labor, as part of a business cycle theory.)

7 The general procyclical nature of profits. In particular, before sales decline, profits per unit of sales decline.

8 Procyclical nature of investment in fixed capital and inventories. Although this is well established for the typical cycle, there are individual components that either lead or lag behind in the cycle.

9 Procyclical expansion of credit and monetary aggregates. During contractions, both narrowly and broadly defined monetary aggregates show reduced growth rates, but not absolute declines. This implies that the income velocity of money is also procyclical.

10 The synchronization of international cycles, a tendency that may well intensify in the future. Institutional changes such as free capital mobility, floating exchange rates, and the increase in international arbitrage and speculative activities have increased interdependence among the major capitalist nations, which is likely to lead to a further synchronization of cycles.

2.2.2 Stylized facts and theory

The first stylized fact is a relationship between output, inflation, and employment. The second is a relationship between inflation and the growth of money wages. The third relates real wage growth to real output. It could be argued that much of macroeconomics is, or should be, a theory that interrelates output, inflation, employment, and wages.

One simple *microeconomic* approach would be to propose a market for goods and a market for labor. Firms buy labor services and supply goods. In this model, equilibrium is defined as both markets clearing at some positive price vector of goods and a positive price of labor services (wages). Prices and wages thus change in this model only when there are supply or demand imbalances. In particular, prices rise when demand exceeds supply; they fall when supply exceeds demand. This approach reduces all macroeconomics to a special case of Walrasian trading in a so-called general equilibrium model. It is no more than a truism in its generality. In particular, it proposes no testable or even disputable hypothesis.

Next consider a simple *macroeconomic* approach, where the level of aggregation is deliberate. Conceptually, replace *goods* with (aggregate) *output*; prices with the *price level*, and labor services with *employment*. Such a theory is close in spirit to macroeconomists such as Akerlof (1969), Akhand (1991), Blanchard (1986), Davidson (1972), Kaldor (1959), Keynes (1972), Tobin (1972), and Weintraub (1961).

Let the wage bill $W = wN$ where w is the money wage and N is employment. Let total output Z be some multiple of W – that is, let $Z = kW$. We also know that total output is price P times quantity Q – that is, $Z = PQ$. Combining these definitions we have

$$PQ = kwN$$

$$\text{or } P = kw/A, \text{ where } A = Q/N \tag{2.1}$$

Expressing the above equation as proportions gives us

$$\dot{P}/P = \dot{k}/k + \dot{w}/w - \dot{A}/A \tag{2.2}$$

where the left side is the growth rate of the price level, or inflation. Thus inflation rises as the parameter k rises, or the money wage w increases, where the increases are uncompensated by increases in average productivity.

Note that $1/k = W/PQ$, and that $1/k$ is the wage share in total output or total income. If total income is divided between firms, which earn profits, and workers, then the firms' share is $1 - 1/k$.

Suppose now that unions and labor representatives attempt to set the money wage w at time t to achieve a target labor share α, based on their estimate of the price level $p^e(t)$:

$$w(t) = A/\alpha.P^e(t) \tag{2.3}$$

Similarly, let firms set prices $P(t)$, based on their estimate of the current wage-level $w^e(t)$ and a target markup m over wages:

$$P(t) = (1/A)(1 + m)w^e(t)$$

Both labor unions and firms attempt to appropriate productivity gains. Equations (2.3) and (2.4) are, of course, not independent, as the wage share plus the profit share must add up to total output. Hence both equations (2.3) and (2.4) must be consistent with equation (2.1). Consistency requires that $\alpha \leq 1/k$, and that $m \leq k - 1$. Alternatively, the consistency requirement can be expressed as:

$$\alpha (1 + m) \leq 1 \qquad (2.5)$$

When both parties' expectations are fulfilled, then equation (2.5) would be satisfied. Strict inequality would mean firms' profits would be higher than expected, assuming the residual accrues to the firms, or some deflation of prices, or both. When expectations regarding wages and profits are fulfilled, there would then be no inflation, as increases in wages and profits would just cover productivity gains.

However, when the targets of labor unions and firms are inconsistent, then $\alpha (1 + m) > 1$, in which case the conflict over income distribution leads to inflation. The conflict may be avoided if both parties agree *a priori* that inflation is undesirable and make their income claims consistent with equation (2.5). Such an agreement amounts to a social contract, or an "incomes policy." In a decentralized economy, equations (2.3) and (2.4) hold – with workers attempting to bargain or set wages and firms having the right to set prices. Such an economy contains elements of the "prisoners dilemma" (Maital and Benjamini, 1980; Dalziel, 1990). This is because neither party knows what productivity gains will be realized *post factum*. If workers make too low a bid, the residual accrues to profits. Similarly, if the markup is too low, workers will gain at the expense of profits. Consequently, both overstate their claims, which leads to inflation.

It is important to note here that the direction of causation is from wage increases to price increases, as labor cost is typically the largest cost item. This, of course, does not exclude the possibility of one-time supply shocks, such as the oil price shocks of 1973 and 1979, which contribute to inflation. However, such shocks are exceptional. The main underlying cause of price increases is wage-cost increases that exceed productivity gains, as shown in equation (2.2).

The simple model outlined above shows that a *ceteris paribus* increase in wages leads to an increase in the share of labor (equal to $1/k$), which means that the profit share of firms (equal to $1-1/k$) falls. In addition, an increase in wages that exceeds average productivity gains will lead to inflation, through equation (2.2). The theory therefore proposes that both inflation and *money* wages are procyclical. But even real wages are also procyclical, for it is easy to see from equation (2.1) that

$$(\partial Q)/\partial(w/P) = kN > 0 \qquad (2.6)$$

However, whether real wages are procyclical or not has been subject to debate ever since the 1930s. It would seem natural to consider this briefly, and to seek either corroboration or refutation from empirical work.

Following the publication of Keynes' (1936) *General Theory*, it was suggested that the *General Theory* implied that the pattern of real wages and employment over the cycle represents movements along a (fixed) downward-sloping demand curve for labor. This implied a counter-cyclical real wage. Dunlop (1938) and Tarshis (1939) both claimed to have found evidence of a procyclical real wage. Bodkin (1969) claimed that an acyclic real wage could not be rejected by the data. Subsequent to that, Barro and Grossman (1971) formulated a disequilibrium macro model designed, in part, to explain why the real wage could be either countercyclical, procyclical, or acyclic – that is, that the real wage need bear no definite relationship to output and employment. Next, Neftci (1978) claimed to have found new evidence supporting a countercyclical real wage, and Sargent (1978) argued that the evidence was consistent with an economy moving along a labor demand curve subject to dynamic adjustment costs. But Geary and Kennen (1982) claimed that the evidence of Neftci and Sargent was based on a particular time period and a particular price index. Changing either made a difference to the result.

Following this, a number of researchers have found that the real wage is indeed procyclical (e.g. Bils, 1985; Raisian, 1983). This evidence has been further strengthened by another panel data study by Keane, Moffitt, and Runkle (1988). In this study, the authors correct for various biases. We conclude that the empirical evidence corroborates the theoretical conclusion, reached earlier, that the real wage is procyclical.

The simple static macro model is one way of relating the crucial variables. It suggests that the first three stylized facts are consistent with each other in that one does not contradict any of the other two. They can also be viewed as a logical consequence of the model. But the model itself is not geared to explaining cyclical fluctuations in output, employment, and inflation. However, a model capable of explaining cyclical fluctuations must also reflect the three stylized facts as the logical concomitants of fluctuations in output.

The fourth stylized fact suggests that cycles and growth are inextricably linked, that the growth and the cyclical components are nonseparable. It can be shown that any "decomposition" of output into a "trend" and a "cyclical" component will be arbitrary. This subject is discussed more fully in appendix 6B, and is best deferred until the reader has seen examples of such decomposition. Suffice it to say that twentieth-century business cycles are not sinusoidal cycles, in which output (or even real wages) return to a previous level. On the contrary, output and real wages grow so that each business cycle trough represents a higher level of real output over time. A business cycle model that shows cycles but no growth of output will fail to reflect the fourth stylized fact.

The fifth stylized fact reflects the fact that a cycle, taken from peak to peak, or from trough to trough is not constant. If it were constant, we would say that the cycle was *periodic*. If it were *periodic*, downturns and upturns would be perfectly predictable. If it were perfectly predictable, the cycle would not occur because private agents would take actions to offset its effects.

Cycles that are recurrent but nonperiodic make decisions risky and create an exposure to unemployment and bankruptcy (Gordon, 1986, p. 3). Workers cannot predict when a layoff may eliminate the extra income needed to meet some debt obligation (for a mortgage or a consumer durable). Similarly, firms cannot predict whether an expansion to a plant undertaken now will be justified through increased sales due to general prosperity or whether the increased sales will fail to materialize due to the onset of a recession. If a recession does occur, the carrying costs of the expanded plant may exceed the marginal increase in sales revenue. Furthermore, firms cannot shift to other activities because the recession typically affects many economic activities, as the Burns-Mitchell definition makes clear.

The sixth stylized fact, procyclical labor productivity, raises some uncomfortable questions about the treatment of labor in macroeconomics, a subject taken up in chapter 7 (section 7.1.4). The essential fact is that labor is not like any other input that a firm may buy and use as needed. It is a quasifixed factor (Oi, 1962, 1983), and the higher the skilled component of a firm's labor force, the more reluctant the firm is to part with its workers in a downturn. Thus firms tend to shed their least skilled workers first. As a result, there is considerable evidence of labor hoarding in cyclical downturns. When an expansion does occur, firms are able to produce a large increase in output with only a very small increase in the employed labor. This shows up as a strong upturn in labor productivity in an expansion. This fact, and the evidence reviewed in chapter 7, suggest that the treatment of labor as a competitive auction market, with the real wage determined by its marginal product, may be very misleading. A business cycle model that ignores the sixth stylized fact may be subject to criticism.

Finally, it should be noted that from the definition $Q \equiv AN$ it follows that

$$\frac{\dot{Q}}{Q} = \frac{\dot{A}}{A} + \frac{\dot{N}}{N}$$

In other words, labor productivity, which is $\dot{A}/A$, is procyclical – it grows as Q grows. In fact, the above equation states that the growth rate of output is the sum of the growth rates of labor productivity and employment.[2]

The seventh and eighth stylized facts can be considered together, as they both relate to profits. First, recall that $W = wN$, so that W/PQ is the labor share. This means that the higher the W, the higher the labor share. But for a given output, the higher the labor share, the lower the profit share. Therefore, in an expansion, profits can increase only if prices are increasing at a faster rate than wages. However, the real wage w/P is also procyclical, as argued above. Profits can thus be procyclical only as long as real wage increases do not exceed productivity increases. In the late expansion phase, employment is high, with the result that the bargaining power of workers is high. This high bargaining power implies not only rising wages but also a rising wage share, which means declining profits per unit of sales.

The declining profits at the peak of the cycle also signal the end of the expansion phase, for new investments are governed by profit expectations. The poor profit expectations therefore lead to a reduction in investment, which signals the beginning of a contractionary phase in which employment will fall as investment falls. The fall in employment could further reduce demand.

Thus profitability is crucial to an expansion; a decline in profits is indicative of a contraction. The two stylized facts about profits and about investment could play an important role in the upper turning point in a business cycle theory. Indeed, it would seem hard to conceive of a business cycle theory without some role for profits in it.

The above model is a *real* model with no money. It therefore cannot reflect the ninth stylized fact, which states that money growth is procyclical. But there is a simple way of introducing money: let the demand for money M^d be determined by transactions demand alone:

$$M^d = \rho Q$$

Let the supply of money be fixed at M/P. Then in equilibrium

$$M^d = M/P, \quad \text{or} \quad \overline{M}/P = \rho \, Q$$

In this simplified form, the above equation is equivalent to the quantity theory, but it does make money growth procyclical:

$$\dot{Q}/Q = 1/\rho \left[\frac{\dot{M}}{M} - \dot{P}/P \right]$$

It will be recognized that though this sort of formulation is used (e.g. Ball, Mankiw and Romer, 1988, p.5), it is extremely simple. This is a specification of outside money only. A richer model must incorporate inside money, which is by far the largest component of total money. A glance at the statistics of "Bank Debits and Deposit Turnover" published in the monthly *Federal Reserve Bulletin* will make that clear.

The last stylized fact is of descriptive and institutional character. It is not at all clear how it can be incorporated into a business cycle model. It suggests that one cannot 'export' one's way out of a recession, as export demand will be low if the rest of the world is also in a slump. Nevertheless, the degree of synchronization is remarkable, as shown in figure 2.2, taken from Moore and Zarnowitz (1986, pp. 756–17). There is also a similar diagram that shows the synchronization of the growth cycles of the United Kingdom, France, West Germany (as it then was), and the United States. A growth cycle represents fluctuation around the long-run growth trend of the economy of a particular nation. In another table (1986, Table A.8, p. 774–5) Moore and Zarnowitz show the synchronization of growth cycles from 1948 to 1982 for 14 countries: Australia, Belgium, Canada, France, Italy, Japan, South Korea, Netherlands, Sweden, Switzerland, Taiwan, the United Kingdom, the United States, and West Germany.

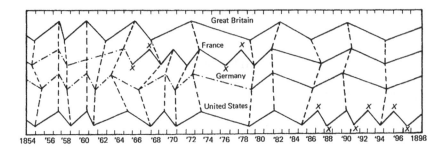

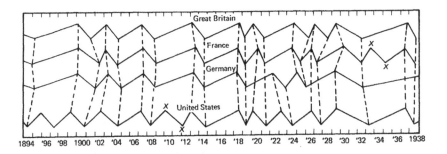

Figure 2.2   The Synchronization of Business Cycles

Timing of reference cycles for four countries and matched turning points, 1854–1938. For each country, the lines connect the dates of business cycle peaks (upper turning points) and troughs (lower turning points). Thus the upward-sloping segments of each country line represent expansions; the downward-sloping segments, contractions. The dashed links between the country lines connect the matched peaks or troughs for two or more countries. The sign *x* denotes an unmatched turn. For France before 1865 and for Germany before 1879, the reference dates are annual. They are plotted at midpoint of the given calendar year and connected with dashed and dotted lines. All other reference dates are monthly and are connected with solid lines.

Source: Moore and Zarnowitz (1986, pp. 756–7)

CONCLUSION

This chapter defined a business cycle and described some of its features. There are also some enduring empirical regularities associated with the typical business cycle, regularities that may be referred to as stylized facts. Ten such stylized facts were then listed. Except for the international synchronization of cycles, all other stylized facts were shown not only to be consistent with a simple macro model but also to be derived properties of the model. The model itself, which consisted of a few definitions and a few assumptions, was deliberately sparse, the guiding principle being the fewer the assumptions the better the model. This guiding principle was once enunciated by Bertrand Russell, when he said that the task of science is to derive more and more from less and less. The stylized facts could, of course, stand by themselves as simply observed regularities. But, as Koopmans has shown, all observation or measurement is theory dependent. It is therefore best to make explicit the simplest kind of model that could generate the stylized facts as properties of the model.

Stylized facts play an important role in economics because replication of experiments is not a feasible research strategy. The stylized facts become bench marks against which models may be judged as to their efficacy. There is probably no 'best' model in economics (and in many other disciplines), only better models and worse models. The degree to which a business cycle model reflects the stylized facts will become the *betterness relation* in judging the merits of particular models.

The proposed betterness relation is in some sense blunt. In an ideal world, the betterness relation would be based on *confirmation, corroboration*, or *refutation*. We will explore this, together with certain criteria for the formation of mathematical models in economics, in the next chapter, before turning to theories of business cycles in Part II.

NOTES

1 This section draws on my contributions to Glasner (1993), forthcoming.
2 The definition $Q = AN$ can also be viewed as a production function, but that is not a *necessary* interpretation. In the definition, A is simply defined as output per worker, Q/N.

3

Validity of Mathematical Models in Economics

INTRODUCTION

In chapter 2, a set of stylized facts were shown to be properties of a very simplified model. The stylized facts could also be treated as empirically observed regularities of business cycles that could stand "on their own." But any two stylized facts that contradicted one another could not be consistently derived from a single model. Because the stylized facts are derived as properties of a single model, we can be satisfied that they constitute a *consistent set*, that they do not contradict one another. It was also stated that the stylized facts will be used as bench marks for judging and assessing the value of the business cycle models covered in parts II and III.

Why is it necessary to use the stylized facts to assess the relative merits of the models in parts II and III? Is there no other way to *confirm* the validity of an explanation offered by a model? Can we not seek *corroboration* from empirical work? This chapter is a brief excursion into the nature of confirmation and corroboration in economics. However, prior to confirmation and corroboration is the issue of mathematical modeling in economics.

Mathematical modeling in economics is frequently derivative in the sense that the modeling exercise draws often on physical analogs: from physics, biology, and applied mathematics. Frequently the economic model is a reinterpretation (in terms of economics) of some known mathematical theorem, or an engineering relationship. When the translation is complete, and arises from first principles *in economics*, then the interpretation is valid and it is useful. Accordingly, the first section considers the question of the validity of an economic interpretation of mathematical structures and their implied theorems. The inquiry develops criteria for assessing the validity of mathematical models, and shows that there must be no 'redundant mathematics' that have no economic content. Then section 3.2 considers the nature of confirmation and corroboration in economics.

3.1   THE OBJECTIVE OF MATHEMATICAL MODELING

Modern mathematics is divided into pure and applied mathematics. Pure mathematics deals entirely with mental constructs defined by certain symbols and operations.[1] The mental constructs range from partial derivatives to such concepts as rings, fields, eigenvalues, matrices, functions, and even differential equations of different orders. In applied mathematics, these abstract entities turn out to be useful in understanding physical reality when the abstract constructs are given empirical content with some specific segment of reality. Actual experiments then often lead to modifications of the mathematical statement of the specific segment, until the theoretical mathematical statement fits the reality as closely as possible, with only the inessential detail thrown out for the mathematical statement.

For a mathematical statement of social reality, this dialectical relationship between theory and experimentation is unavailable. The problem is further complicated by the fact that social reality undergoes structural changes; it is in a constant state of flux, largely through the results of human action. Yet the mathematical statement of the theory has an obvious advantage, for otherwise the undertaking would be useless. The obvious advantage is that the mathematical statement enables the social scientist to derive and discover the crucial interrelationship(s) between the variables. Throughout this book, we shall refer to the derived crucial relationship(s) between variables as the *governing mechanism*. To restate: The object of the mathematization of a theory is to uncover the governing mechanism.

It should be noted that pure mathematics itself is "value neutral"; it is not tendentious by itself. For this reason, the same underlying pure mathematics can be used to make rigorous very divergent or even opposing economic theories. For instance, the mathematical theory of convex sets can be used to make rigorous both the labor theory of value and Walrasian general equilibrium theory. Hence, the mathematization *per se* does not enhance the truth content of a theory. Judging the truth content of a theory requires some process of confirmation and corroboration, a topic deferred to section 3.2. This section is confined to the validity and the appropriate use of mathematical structures for conveying the underlying economic meaning. Accordingly, section 3.1.1 explores this and proposes some criteria for the use of mathematics in economics. It involves certain dimensions of mathematical philosophy and illustrates the mathematization of two diverse approaches to economics, two diverse models – namely Walrasian general equilibrium and the labor theory of value. One is a demand approach, the other is a production approach, but both use the mathematics of convex analysis.

3.1.1   Principles for interpreting mathematics as economics

Although the use of quantitative methods in economics can be traced back to the physiocrats, the first systematic use of theorems and structures of pure mathematics was carried out by John von Neumann (1937), published in translation as John von Neumann (1945). This was a model that generalized both Cassel's growth model and Marx's schemes of extended reproduction. In this mathematical model, goods are produced by using other produced commodities. Even labor is a produced commodity, in which labor is reproduced by a constant bundle of (subsistence) consumption. Von Neumann proved, with some simplifying assumptions, that such an economy can grow at a constant proportional growth rate, and that in such a state, the growth rate is equal to the rate of interest. The novelty of this result was that it was the first rigorous proof of Schumpeter's conjecture that it was growth of the economy that ensured a positive interest rate, and that if the growth rate were zero (a stationary state) then the interest rate would be zero too. Finally, von Neumann also proved the existence of a vector of prices and of quantities.

In order to show the above results, von Neumann reinterpreted an earlier mathematical theorem of his own, namely his minimax theorem, applicable to a two person zero-sum rectangular game.

The essential facts associated with the minimax theorem can be summarized as follows. Suppose there are two players, I and II, with *completely opposite* interests, so that what one wins the other loses. Such a game is called zero sum. Player I's gain, called a *payoff*, in a game depends on the action or choice of player II. Under ordinary circumstances, neither player has any idea of what the other might choose. The key is completely opposite interests. If this assumption holds, what player I does would maximize I's advantage. But what is best for I is worst for II, and vice versa. This however has a tremendous simplifying force. Player II will attempt to minimize I's payoff, so it is clear that I must maximize this minimum. This is called a *maximin* policy.

Reciprocally, player II will expect player I's choice to be the worst possible outcome for player II. Thus player II minimizes the maximum that the latter can expect. This is called a *minimax* policy. If the game is two-person zero-sum, then the maximin and minimax policies mean that the value of the game is the same to both players.

Now enrich the game by introducing probabilities for each player, so that the payoff to each player is weighted by the probability of choosing a particular strategy. This enriched structure can now be interpreted in terms of economics: the probability vectors of the two players can now be *renamed* the vector of prices and the vector of outputs. The value of the game to one player is now renamed the growth rate, and the value of the game to the other player is renamed the interest rate. In equilibrium, the interest rate is equal to the growth rate, because in equilibrium the value of the game to both players is the same. In other words, the economic growth model can be derived by a simple reinterpretation of the minimax theorem. This has been demonstrated mathematically in Dore (1989).

What John von Neumann did was to reinterpret the minimax theorem: each mathematical symbol (be it the value of the game to each player, each probability vector or elements of the matrix game) was renamed, but such renaming remains consistent throughout. In other words, no one symbol is made to represent two different economic entities. Thus a *one-to-one correspondence* between mathematical objects and economic concepts is strictly maintained. With one-to-one correspondence between the mathematical object and an economic entity, there would be *no* mathematical entity without an economic interpretation. If there is such a mathematical entity without a corresponding economic interpretation, then we will call it "redundant mathematics." Redundant mathematics are dictated purely by mathematical considerations.

Then in order to prove the existence of a nonnegative and nontrivial solution (i.e., the existence of prices and quantities, and the growth rate that equals the interest rate), von Neumann proved a generalization of Brouwer's fixed-point theorem, which we know from hindsight to be quite unnecessary overkill to prove the existence of the solution.

As argued by Georgescu-Roegen (1951), convexity and the resulting hyperplanes could be used to establish the existence of the solution.

Quite apart from overkill, there is a more fundamental objection to the use of fixed-point theorems, based on Brouwer's rejection of proof by double negation, a foundation stone of intuitionist and constructivist philosophy of mathmatics.

In classical mathematics, the proof of existence may take the following form: nonexistence of a solution will involve a contradiction. At best, a fixed-point theorem is a negative statement; it indicates that it is impossible that there can be no solution, given the assumptions of compact subspaces and topological mappings. Such a classical proof gives no hint of how the solution may be found. In contrast, a constructive proof of the existence of a solution will give a general outline of how a solution may be found. It may be longer, but it contains more information. Consider a well-known example, the Fundamental Theorem of Algebra. The classical proof of this theorem states that every polynomial with complex coefficients has at least one complex root. In contrast, Brouwer's proof of this theorem indicates how the root may be found.

In 1941, Kakutani published a further generalization of von Neumann's fixed-point theorem to cover point-to-set mappings (Kakutani, 1941). This theorem has now become the standard method of establishing existence of solutions both in the neoclassical school (Arrow, Debreu) as well as the neo-Keynesian school (e.g. Benassy [1976]). Hence an unnecessary bad habit has been acquired by the economics profession from John von Neumann.

However, one of his central objectives – as a mathematician – was to publish the generalized proof of the fixed point theorem. Perhaps for von Neumann economics was merely a convenient vehicle for an essentially mathematical exercise.

What principles can we elicit from von Neumann's reinterpretation of an earlier theorem as an economic model, a model which formalized the insights of both Cassel and Marx?[2]

First, note that a given interpretation must be consistent – that is, it must not be contradictory in two different instances. Consistency is a minimal requirement; it requires that a mathematical object represented say as a price cannot also be represented as a quantity, since price and quantity are conceptually distinct.

Second, there must be a one-to-one correspondence between mathematical objects and real economic entities. In von Neumann's economic model, there are m distinct processes and n distinct goods – all finite. One can make that one-to-one correspondence between the mathematical representation of a process and its *real* counterpart. One can do the same with the n goods, no matter how large, as long as there are n distinct goods, and n is finite.

The first criterion, that of consistency, is usually met by most models worth thinking about. The second, that of one-to-one correspondence may not always be met, as will become clear below.

The third criterion, which von Neumann did *not* meet is of a philosophical nature. In simple words, reliance on a fixed-point theorem for the proof of the existence of a solution means that nonexistence of a solution would involve a contradiction, the implication being that the solution must exist. As pointed out earlier, this is inadequate. The use of a fixed-point theorem to show existence involves embedding a particular problem within a larger mathematical structure, a technique frequently used in mathematics. It is a way of solving a particular problem by embedding it in a family of problems and solving the latter to obtain an implicit solution of the former.[3] Although this technique works well for special problems,[4] it shifts the focus from a particular problem to a larger family of problems. It is no longer clear whether the one-to-one correspondence between mathematical objects and reality has been preserved or lost. The technique of embedding solves the larger mathematical family of problems. The particular problem is solved only implicitly. Naturally, no insight into the nature of the solution of the particular problem is obtained. A constructivist approach would avoid this difficulty.

Thus our third criterion suggests a constructivist proof theory. A constructivist proof is also a proof in classical mathematics, but not all proofs in classical mathematics are constructivist proofs. This third criterion is really related to the second; it has been argued that a nonconstructive proof (of existence) tends to obscure the one-to-one correspondence between mathematical objects and their real counterparts. It has thus been taken for granted that the objective of mathematical formalism in social science, and in economics in particular, is to understand real social phenomena, be they labor unions, oligopolies, or household expenditure patterns.

By examining von Neumann's work, three criteria for judging the validity of a mathematical model in economics were derived. Their use is illustrated in the next subsection.

3.1.2   Two examples of economic interpretations

In section 3.1.1, a concrete example of a mathematical structure and its implied theorems was considered as a basis for understanding the process of production and growth. This example was von Neumann's economic growth model. From this example, three important criteria emerged, which should shed light on what constitutes a legitimate use of the mathematical mode of portraying and understanding social reality. In this section, we apply these criteria to two mathematical models as examples.

One of the most complete mathematical statements of the neoclassical theory of pure exchange is Debreu's (1959) *Theory of Value*. In it he develops a mathematical structure, or rather he restates the part of mathematics known as convex analysis. He also suggests an economic interpretation. The economics is as good as the interpretation given to the mathematical structure; after all, abstract mathematical structures have no empirical content. Debreu recognizes the difference between his exposition of convex analysis and his economic interpretation:

Allegiance to rigor dictates the axiomatic form of analysis where the theory . . . is logically entirely disconnected from its (economic) interpretations. (p. viii)

Hence one would be justified in concluding that Debreu's main objective was the systematic exposition of convex analysis, and the validity of the economic interpretation is very much a secondary question. (For that, further tests would be necessary.) In light of the criterion stated above, is there a well-identified, one-to-one correspondence between the mathematical objects and economic entities? The theory of convex sets states that if two sets are convex, then there exists a separating hyperplane. In Debreu, one of the sets is identified with the consumption set, the other with the production set. The hyperplane is identified with the set of prices. It requires strong continuity assumptions, but there is a one-to-one correspondence between the mathematical entities and the (corresponding) economic concepts. There are no mathematical assumptions that do not have an economic meaning. Thus it contains no **redundant mathematics**. But the strong continuity assumptions mean that there is an infinity of consumption bundles, whereas in the von Neumann model there are m

processes and n goods, where m and n may be large but finite. This clarity of the von Neumann model, which may be seen to be a special case of the more general Debreu model, is obscured in the latter. Just as von Neumann insisted on a nonnegative solution to the system of Walrasian equations, it might be desirable to formulate the Walrasian model with finite commodity bundles, if only for added realism.

Finitary methods thus have an appeal in formulating economic models. It is for this reason that Sraffa (1960) chooses finitary methods, although the Sraffa system can be equally presented by using infinite dimensional linear spaces. Sraffa does not express his results by using matrix methods. A methodological purist, and philosophically inclined towards constructivism, Sraffa could not possibly compromise his inquiry by embedding his theory in a more general mathematical structure that could raise the possibility of additional assumptions, a baggage that he did not need. For instance, expressing the Sraffa system by matrix methods would imply that he was assuming constant returns to scale, an assumption that he did not wish to make. As argued earlier, embedding entails the potential danger of a loss of focus, unless the one-to-one correspondence between mathematical objects and economic entities is carefully preserved, with no loss of economic intuition.

We consider now a second model, that of Brody (1970); *Proportions, Prices and Planning*, which is subtitled 'A Mathematical Restatement of the Labor Theory of Value." It is strongly influenced both by von Neumann and by Sraffa, in spirit and method. Marx's simple as well as extended reproduction are treated using matrix methods. Using an ingenious device that he attributes to Lange, Brody introduces a matrix of capital coefficients and fully exploits the properties of Frobenius-Peron theorems in a consistent manner. Furthermore, the approach is entirely constructivist. If the data were available (i.e., if there were a matrix of input-output coefficients and a matrix of capital coefficients), then the model could be used in planning to determine the equilibrium long-run price system, including the mark-up required for growth. The model also yields a consistent method of investment appraisal and the optimum choice of techniques through an algorithm.

In this reformulation of the labor theory of value, Brody is using the *same* mathematical theory as that used by Debreu. Brody's work is also a consistent use of convex analysis. The only minor difference is that while Debreu has convex sets of the more general kind, Brody uses convex cones – i.e., a convex set with "straight edges." The price and quantity vectors that emerge from the mathematical formulation are left- and right-hand eigenvectors. Mathematically, every eigenvector is also a hyperplane;[5] thus the mathematical objects used in the reinterpretation are essentially the same as those of Debreu. Yet conceptually the two interpretations (of the same underlying mathematical theory) are antithetical: Debreu's is a mathematical reformulation of Walras' model of pure exchange; it is also a celebration of Adam Smith's invisible hand, in which society is better off if the market is allowed to operate unfettered.

Brody's approach, on the other hand, is rooted in commodity production, in which, as in Sraffa (1960), commodities are produced by means of commodities and labor. But unlike Sraffa, Brody does not mind the implied assumption of constant returns to scale.

Brody's book also contains an interesting conjecture about pricing. In the phase of simple reproduction, prices are determined by the labor content in the production process; in extended reproduction, prices are the so-called "production prices" that are determined by capital content – that is, reflecting "reproduction" of plant and equipment. However, as society becomes more technologically sophisticated, larger and larger investments are made for the reproduction of skilled manpower. Hence as the society becomes more technologically advanced and more service oriented, prices will be determined more and more by the labor theory of value. The same mathematical model is used throughout, pointing to this conjecture, which thus has a rigorous basis. This position is close in spirit to Sraffa's reduction of prices to dated labor, but it goes much further in being applicable to planning. In terms of the three criteria, Brody's model is consistent. There is a one-to-one correspondence between the mathematical objects and their economic counterparts. In fact this is not surprising because Brody's model can be regarded, mathematically at least, as a special case of von Neumann. The approach is constructivist; indeed the model can even be used for planning, as indicated earlier. Hence it is a credible formulation; it achieves its objective of formalizing the labor theory of value.

To sum up, both models use the same underlying mathematical structure to produce very divergent economic theories. Both follow the lead of von Neumann, who first introduced convex analysis into economics. Neither has mathematical entities without a sound and credible economic interpretation. Thus all mathematical "objects" (eigenvalues, eigenvectors, separating hyperplanes) have economic interpretations. Consequently there is no *redundant mathematics* – that is, mathematics required purely for mathematical reasons with no economic justification or interpretation. Part II will present examples of redundant mathematics.

We now turn to the truth content of models in economics.

3.2 TRUTH CONTENT, CONFIRMATION, AND CORROBORATION

As noted above, the truth content of many physical theories is often confirmed through experimentation. The truth content of "grand theories" is much more difficult to establish. Newtonian physics "worked" perfectly well to a first approximation, until generalized by Einstein, when Newtonian physics became a special case of Einstein's more general theory. In economics, grand theories such as the Walrasian general equilibrium theory or the labor theory of value are themselves mental constructs whose truth content cannot be confirmed in any meaningful sense. The Walrasian model is the model of an auction; the actual economy does not behave like an auction, although auctions do take place in the economy. The value of general equilibrium theory is that of a counterfactual: *if* an economy were perfectly competitive, with no frictions, and there were complete markets for all contingencies, then all prices would reflect true opportunity costs, etc. It is no more than a thought experiment.

Similarly the labor theory of value is a "grand theory" that is a counterfactual thought experiment: if all goods were produced with other produced goods and labor, then the prices of all goods would reflect their direct and indirect labor content.

We conclude that such thought experiments cannot be confirmed or rejected: their scale is just too grand.

On the other hand, "smaller" hypotheses may be testable. For example, Friedman's proposition (chapter 4) that the growth of money supply is both a necessary and a sufficient condition for inflation is in principle testable. Of course, it is always possible to set up a model in which the proposition is always true. But the truth content of the model can be established only by some attempt to *confirm* or reject it in some economy over a given period of time. Suppose that the Friedman proposition about money causing inflation were confirmed (say) by an econometric analysis of Brazilian data, from 1960 to 1980. If it is found that the proposition also holds for another economy (say Argentina), over a different time period, one could claim that the proposition has been corroborated.

Friedman's empirical work sought both to confirm and to corroborate the general validity of the quantity theory of money. However, as we shall see in chapter 4, David Hendry has reworked the econometrics using Friedman's data and Hendry and his colleagues claim that Friedman's conclusions are unwarranted.

Time and again a number of macroeconometricians have imposed enough *a priori* restrictions on the models they estimate that they have been able to conclude that their "theory" is consistent with the data. Here "theory" could be any one of a number of propositions, for example: "that the Phillips Curve is vertical"; "that money Granger-causes inflation"; "that Ricardian equivalence is consistent with the data"; "that large government debts do not affect the rate of interest"; "that the Central Bank operations do not affect the foreign exchange value of a currency." A number of these are **neutrality propositions** (see Sargent, 1987) designed to show that virtually all government actions are deleterious, or at best ineffective in affecting the private sector economy. All or almost all neutrality propositions are associated with the New Classical school.

Of course, a number of econometricians (e.g. Leamer, 1983; Hendry and Ericsson, 1991; Pagan, 1987) are deeply concerned about the abuse of econometrics. Hendry and Ericsson (1991) in particular have articulated a rigorous econometric methodology (see chapter 4) that pays a great deal of attention to specification testing. They have set down a set of six criteria that must be satisfied in order that a model may capture the salient features of the data and deliver reliable inferences on economic issues; it may however, take a while before that method is adopted by applied econometricians.

With the misuse of econometrics in mind, an interesting paper relevant to business cycles should be cited: Sheehan and Grieves (1982) illustrated the weakness of Granger-causality by demonstrating that fluctuations in the American economy Granger-cause sunspots, rather than the other way round!

This chapter is not meant to be an evaluation of econometric practice (see Darnell and Evans, 1990); it is simply to observe that *current* econometric practice (as opposed to theory) cannot in any way be equated with serious attempts at confirmation, corroboration, or refutation. Perhaps the best one can hope for is that when properly done, econometrics could be used destructively in the sense that no evidence is found to support a particular hypothesis. However, if the objective of confirmation/corroboration is to make a *choice* among competing theories, then it seems to me that that cannot be done adequately with econometrics just yet. But maybe the time will come some day in the future.

The objective of this book is a comparative evaluation of the main theories of business cycles, and I am not qualified to evaluate the main theories through econometric testing. At least one econometrician, Desai (1984), has stated that the econometric testing of nonlinear models with nonlinear differential equations, which may sometimes be coupled, will be extremely difficult and may not be feasible.

For the reasons given above, this book is an attempt to assess business cycles not empirically but logically, *qua* theories. This means that models or theories will be assessed in terms of the criteria developed in this and the previous chapter. First, at the level of economic interpretation, *the one-to-one correspondence requirement will fail if the model contains redundant mathematics*. Second, the explanatory power of the model will be assessed in terms of the derived properties of the model. For example, does it reflect the main stylized facts? How does it explain turning points? Finally, we shall ask whether the model identifies the most important interactions between the most important variables that determine the cyclical motion.

To sum up, the three criteria can be viewed as answers to the following three questions:

1 Does the model contain redundant mathematics? If it does, then it fails to meet the one-to-one correspondence requirement.
2 Do the properties of the model reflect the nine stylized facts, derived and discussed in chapter 2? The merit of the model increases the more of the stylized facts that it can explain.
3 Does the model identify some crucial interaction? If so, what is it? This is the **governing mechanism**, which in principle must be testable and falsifiable.

On the basis of these criteria, it is hoped that one can say which is a *better* model of business cycles.

NOTES

1 This section draws on Dore (1988).
2 See Arrow (1989) in Dore (1989).

3 For example, this is what Richard Bellman (1957) did in developing the fundamental recurrence relation in dynamic programming.

4 Such as intertemporal planning problems; see Arrow and Kurz (1970) or Dore (1977).

5 The converse, of course, does not hold. Consult any book on linear algebra, such as Lang (1958) or Birkhoff and MacLane (1966).

PART II

INTRODUCTION TO PART II

Part II consists of four chapters that deal with the business cycle theories of the New Classical approach and of the New Keynesian approach. The two approaches are placed in one part because both identify the business cycle as being caused by *exogenous* factors. In the New Classical approach, the cyclical component of output is made up of the sum of past exogenous demand shocks (Lucas), or exogenous productivity shocks (real business cycle theory). Chapter 4 discusses the conceptual innovations, introduced by Milton Friedman, on which economists of the New Classical school rely to build their models. These in turn are discussed in chapters 5 and 6.

In the New Keynesian approach, discussed in chapter 7, the underemployment equilibrium or recession is caused endogenously through the profit-maximizing behavior of the representative firm; however, the firm (economy) climbs out of the recession through exogenous increases in aggregate demand. The upper turning point is not explicitly modeled in the theory.

The merits of each model are assessed in terms of the criteria developed in Part I (chapters 2 and 3).

4

The Lead from Friedman

Milton Friedman (1957) had already made his mark by expressing his dissatisfaction with Keynesian macro theory and policy. In his analysis of the consumption function, he proposed the concept of "permanent income," a transcendental concept that even he found difficult to render operational: the empirical estimate of permanent income turned out to be nothing but a weighted average of past income, although it was in spirit meant to be a proxy of *future*, *expected* income. After this first attack on Keynesian orthodoxy (for that is what it was in the 1950s and 1960s), Friedman proposed a general critique of Keynesian activist monetary and fiscal policy in his 1959 book, *A Program for Monetary Stability.*[1]

This critique was continued in Friedman and Schwartz (1963). A few years later, in his presidential address to the American Economic Association in 1967, published as Friedman (1968), he articulated a model that was to prove to be the essential forerunner of the business cycle theory of Lucas, Barro, and Sargent.

4.1 THE DANCE OF THE DOLLAR

Friedman, in cooperation with Anna J. Schwartz, had undertaken a series of empirical studies on the relationship of money to business cycles, in which his intellectual interest went beyond just 'business cycles'; indeed it would be fair to say that his effort had been directed at refuting what he called the Keynesian income-expenditure theory, the bedrock of macroeconomic policy of most Western nations. In this process, he attempted to rehabilitate some form of the classical quantity theory model, which Keynes had attacked. In Friedman and Schwartz (1982), the authors claim that this volume was the culmination of a series of four volumes, one of which was written by Phillip Cagan (1965). The first in the series was *A Monetary History of the United States, 1867–1960* by Friedman and Schwartz (1963), which was devoted to the study of changes in the stock of money over nearly a century to determine how changes in this stock were accompanied by changes in other aggregates. The theoretical framework guiding this study was of course the quantity theory.

The second volume was *Determinants and Effects of Changes in the Stock of Money, 1875–1960* by Phillip Cagan (1965), which was concerned with the cyclical and secular behavior of the different money aggregates, such as the monetary base and the currency deposit ratio.

The third volume was *Monetary Statistics of the United States* by Friedman and Schwartz (1970), which was essentially a statistical source book that *inter alia* also gave the particular definition of money on which the authors settled. According to the authors, it provides raw material for analysis but little economic analysis, a task that was left to their fourth volume, *Monetary Trends in the United States and the United Kingdom: Their relation to Income, Prices, and Interest Rates, 1867–1975* (Friedman and Schwaratz [1982]). All four volumes were done for the NBER, which has had an abiding interest in the analysis of business cycles ever since it was set up.

The fourth volume summarizes the main empirical findings regarding the growth of the money stock, the division of nominal income into changes in prices and changes in real output or income, and the nominal and real yield on assets both for the United States and the United Kingdom. The empirical regularities dealing mainly with changes in the money stock and nominal income over a long period enable Friedman and Schwartz to conclude that the Keynesian theory is a special case, applicable only to the interwar period for the United States, whereas the *general* theory is the quantity theory. Furthermore, the authors claim that the quantity theory is supported not only over the long run for the United States and United Kingdom, but also over many other countries for which references are given (pp. xxix-xxx).

Indeed, the validity of the quantity theory does not stop there; it explains the demand for money, inflation, as well as business cycles.

Friedman's business cycle theory is particularly worth noting, as its deficiencies propelled the business cycle theories of the New Classical school.

Friedman's business cycle theory is given in an article, jointly written with Anna J. Schwartz in 1963 and reproduced in Friedman (1969). In this article, the business cycle is seen as a monetary phenomenon, a "dance of the dollar," quoting Irving Fisher (1923). The authors distinguish between "major fluctuations", – such as 1875–78, 1892–94, 1907–08, 1920–21, 1929–33 and 1937–38 – and the other minor cycles noted by the NBER.

For the major fluctuations, Friedman and Schwartz conclude as follows:

(1) Appreciable changes in the rate of growth of stock of money are necessary and sufficient conditions for appreciable changes in the rate of growth of money income; and (2) this is true for long secular changes and also for changes over roughly the length of business cycles.' (Friedman, 1969, pp. 219–20).

Second, they reject changes in autonomous investment as causes of cycles. They seek to extend the same explanation to cover minor fluctuations. They claim that "if [the minor fluctuations] can be interpreted as less virulent members of the same species as the major [fluctuations] . . . [i]s not a common explanation for both more appealing than separate explanations . . .?" (p. 223).

Hence for Friedman and Schwartz, changes in money stock is the *entire* explanation for major fluctuations; since changes in money stock are both necessary and sufficient, all other explanations are ruled out. But also implicit in the explanation is a stabilization policy: controlling the money stock growth would be necessary and sufficient to eliminate fluctuations.

All these conclusions about business cycles, inflation, or the demand for money rest on one simple equation that appears repeatedly in the work of Friedman:

$$M_d = P_p(Y_p) \qquad (4.1)$$

where M_d is nominal demand for money, P_p is permanent prices, and Y_p is the permanent income. That is the *theory*, which must replace the Keynesian income-expenditure theory. One simple equation is enough to trash Keynes, who had "shunted the car of Economic science on to a wrong line" (Friedman and Schwartz [1982, p. 621]).

For Friedman, stability of prices is an important goal in its own right, a stability that was previously assured by the gold standard. While he does not advocate a return to the gold standard, he argues that the monetary authorities could operate as a surrogate for the gold standard by not stabilizing changes in money supply induced by balance of payments considerations. The discipline of the gold standard can be emulated indirectly only if monetary authorities exercise discipline by rigidly controlling the growth of the money stock. For this conclusion, as well as his business cycle theory, Friedman relies heavily on his empirical work done with Schwartz, referred to above. How robust is this empirical work?

To answer the above question, Hendry and Ericsson have done a series of papers, all referenced in their 1991 *American Economic Review* paper (Hendry and Ericsson, 1991). The latter paper reproduces their major criticism of Friedman and Schwartz (1982), in so far as their work covered money demand in the United Kingdom. The main conclusion is that Hendry and Ericsson are extremely skeptical of the conclusions that Friedman and Schwartz come to about the role of the money stock in the determination of price inflation in the United Kingdom for the period 1878–1970. In view of the confidence with which Friedman and Schwartz (1963) conclude their business cycle theory – that growth in the money stock is both *necessary and sufficient* to explain business cycles – it might be useful to review briefly Hendry and Ericsson's criticism of Friedman and Schwartz's other empirical work, also on the role of money.

To be sure Hendry and Ericsson use sophisticated econometric techniques that were not known to Friedman and Schwartz when their book went to press in 1982. However, the fundamentals of this econometric methodology were published by Sargan as early as 1958, with a major statement in Sargan (1964), a methodology that later became known as the LSE econometric method.[2] Although a full description of the method is outside the scope of this book, a fundamental idea in the LSE method of modeling is an attempt to characterize properties of data in *constant* parametric relationships that are then interpretable in the light of economic theory. But these parametric relationships must use explanatory variables that are at least weakly exogenous and must account for earlier results as special cases – in other words, the method must yield better and better results.

Such a method is dedicated to "learning from the data," whereas Friedman and Schwartz use their regression results to corroborate an *a priori* economic theory. In particular, Hendry and Ericsson find, using the data used by Friedman and Schwartz, that the money demand function is not a constant (parametric) relationship, and that money, the main explanatory variable in Friedman and Schwartz, is not weakly exogenous. Hendry and Ericsson (1991, p. 30) also question the use by Friedman and Schwartz of averaging over the (predetermined) business cycle periods. To quote their main conclusion:

[Friedman and Schwartz's] . . . evidence is inconsistent with the hypothesis that over the period 1878–1970, exogenous money determined prices in the United Kingdom via a stable money demand function . . .

Although Lucas (1977, 1981a, 1981b) has repeatedly acknowledged the debt the New Classical school owes to Friedman, and although it is recognized that the New Classical school took over Friedman's concepts of the natural rate of unemployment and the vertical Phillips curve, there are at least three other concepts that also come from Friedman. These do not appear to have been recognized.

These three important conceptual innovations in Friedman's work served as the basis for future analysis, carried out by the New Classical school:

1 The "representative" agent approach, which stands for aggregates
2 The emphasis on "anticipations" in Friedman
3 The use of Walrasian general equilibrium

4.1.1 The representative agent

The representative agent approach in macroeconomics was a sharp break with the aggregate income expenditure approach of Keynes. In spite of the horrendous aggregation problems, the representative agent approach was used by Friedman in his earlier study of consumption. It appears also in his (1969) "Optimum Quantity of Money." Indeed, there appeared no other way of beginning if the Keynesian income-expenditure categories were rejected. Dressing it up as "microfoundations" is a *post factum* rationalization, making a virtue out of a necessity. It is worth emphasizing that Friedman was using the representative agent approach long before the debate on "microfoundations" became a major concern.

According to Hoover (1988), Friedman's methodological position is not to deny the validity of the Walrasian system of interdependent equations but to construct "an engine for analyzing concrete economic problems" (Friedman, 1955, p. 904), as suggested by Cournot (1938, 1927, p. 127). Hence Friedman, along with Cournot and Marshall, is concerned with the *first order* impacts of variables, which does not mean that second, third, or higher order impacts (of a general equilibrium) nature do not exist. On this basis, Hoover concludes that Friedman is a Marshallian, which would justify, perhaps, the use of a representative agent. This may be plausible, but the Marshallian method involves invoking the "*ceteris paribus*" assumption by which everything else is locked up in the *ceteris paribus* pound (see Dore, 1984–85). This is valid for short period analysis only. But, as Hoover notes correctly, Friedman's analysis is of a long period nature: from 1867 to 1975, or some 108 years! Thus the validity of the Marshallian method for Friedman's work is debatable.

Without detailed argument, one may note that Friedman's main concern was operationally useful results with some predictive success, which can hardly be described as methodological purism. Thus the use of the representative agent in Friedman does not spring from a commitment to Marshall's method, but from a conscious decision to break with the Keynesian income and expenditure categories, just as he had earlier attempted to break with the Keynesian consumption function by inventing a transcendental and nonobservable concept of permanent income, already discussed in chapter 1.

4.1.2 "Anticipations"

Having invented the nonmeasurable and nonobservable concept of permanent income, Friedman had to find a proxy for it in his empirical work on the quantity theory of money. The first proxy that he used was called *anticipated income*, another nonobservable concept. Friedman then replaced anticipated income with a weighted average of past incomes. But in Friedman, *anticipations* and realizations do not necessarily coincide. That is, anticipations need not necessarily be of the rational expectations type, and Friedman and Schwartz (1982, p. 629) give historical examples that illustrate cases when anticipations were not in fact realized. However, although anticipations of inflation are not always realized, in their earlier work (1963, ch. 12) the authors explain postwar movements in the velocity of money by changing expectations about economic stability. Presumably, the anticipations about expansions and contractions in output in the postwar United States were in fact realized.

If one starts with a representative agent model, some behavioral rule must be adopted to describe the agent's actions. Because micro-economic theory assumes that agents optimize, that is a very natural behavioral rule and Friedman has no objection to it, which must be implicit in the explanations about the changes in the velocity of money. The New Classical school later simply extended the behavioral rule to *consistent* optimization over time as well as over all available informa-tion. That means anticipations will in general be *realized*, barring random errors.

Hence it is clear that although Friedman and Schwartz (1982, p. 630) object to rational expectations, except in the very long run, the roots of rational expectations lie in the adoption of optimizing repre-sentative agent models for macroeconomic analysis.

4.1.3 Walrasian general equilibrium

Finally, a case can be made that the New Classical passion for Walrasian general equilibrium, and not Keynesian categories, also orginates in Friedman's work. In his *Optimum Quantity of Money*, Friedman (1969, p. 3), begins the analysis of his important essay by assuming that all ". . . [R]elative prices are determined by the solution of a system of Walrasian equations. Absolute prices are determined by the level of cash balances desired relative to income."[3]

Again, in his 1967 AEA presidential address, which is discussed in detail in the next section, Friedman (1968) speaks of the natural rate of unemployment as being the "level that would be ground out by the Walrasian system of general equilibrium equations, provided there is embedded in them the actual characteristics of labor and commodity markets, including market imperfections, stochastic variability in demands and supplies, the cost of gathering information . . . and so on."

Now, it is very doubtful that under the conditions stated by Friedman – namely market imperfections, positive transactions costs, etc. – that a Walrasian general equilibrium can be shown to exist. But at least Friedman explicitly states these conditions, presumably because they are important characteristics of actual economies. But in the New Classical approach these conditions are *explicitly* assumed away (for example, see Barro [1987]) in order to establish the market-clearing approach, which is fundamental to the New Classical macroeconomics. Market clearance means that each market is *continuously* in equilibrium, by assumption; that a state of general equilibrium exists continuously, with its usual properties – namely, optimality, stability, and so on.

Friedman used Walrasian general equilibrium as a convenient backdrop, which enabled him to avoid the Keynesian aggregates; but the New Classical school invokes it in order to assume market-clearance. Although Friedman professes faith in the inherent long-run stability of the market mechanism, he is nevertheless aware of market imperfections, where the imperfections are not *all* created by government policy.

Next, while Friedman relies on Wicksell for the concept of the natural rate of interest, there is in fact no counterpart to Wicksell's model for the existence of the natural rate of unemployment. That is, there is no theoretical model from which the natural rate of unemployment emerges as a valid concept. According to Friedman, the natural rate of unemployment is defined by the Walrasian system of general equilibrium equations in which institutional characteristics of particular markets and other imperfections are embedded. It was argued above that this cannot be done because Walrasian general equilibrium is incompatible with the kind of nonconvexities like transactions costs, market imperfections, such as oligopolistic markets, and so on that Friedman wishes to take into account in the definition of the natural rate of unemployment.

In the New Classical school the concept of the natural rate of unemployment is not faithful to Friedman's definition, perhaps for the reason stated above – namely, the incompatibility of Walrasian general equilibrium with nonconvexities. Instead in the New Classical school, the natural rate is assumed to "exist," an assumption for which no justification is given. Presumably, the amount of labor supplied by the representative agent is an optimizing *choice*; choice, however, rules out involuntary unemployment. Consequently whatever employment is observed is "natural," as it arises from choice. After all, the representative agent is assumed to be rational, and rationality implies consistent choices over time.

Notwithstanding the strict definition given by Friedman, the natural rate of unemployment in Friedman is simply posited by analogy to Wicksell's natural rate of interest. If the natural rate of interest cannot be set by monetary policy, neither can it set the natural rate of unemployment. In both cases monetary authorities can set only the "market" rates: the "market" rate of interest and the "market" rate of unemployment (Friedman, 1968, p. 9). But the market rates can be set only in the short run, as will be shown in section 4.2.

Before concluding this section, a further observation made by Friedman on the natural rate of unemployment is worth comment. The natural rate need not correspond to equality between the number of unemployed and the number of job vacancies; there may be some equilibrium relation between the two, but "there is no reason why it should be one of equality" (Friedman, 1968, p. 8n). There is therefore a distinct possibility that an economy may have too many people. Perhaps it is implicit in this notion that there must also be a natural rate of population growth, and when the actual exceeds the natural, then equilibrium between the number unemployed and the number of job vacancies can be one of inequality, where the former will exceed the latter.

4.2 THE PRESIDENTIAL ADDRESS

Although the above section drew substantially from Friedman's 1967 presidential address (Friedman 1968), the full model articulated there is now summarized. It will be shown that this model is an essential bridge to the models of the New Classical school.

Suppose there is a Wicksellian natural rate of interest, which for a variety of reasons is not known to the monetary authorities, who increase the money supply, thereby lowering the market rate of interest below the natural rate, for a time. Friedman distinguishes between an immediate impact and the impact in a year or two.

The immediate impact is that the lower market interest rate stimulates both investment and other spending, which raises income, which in turn raises the liquidity preference schedule. The low interest rate will also increase the demand for loans. The general demand stimulus will now put upward pressure on prices, and rising prices will cancel the initial increase in nominal money supply; that is, the *real* money supply will fall as prices rise, so that, 'within a year' (Friedman, 1968, p. 6) the rate of interest rises to what it was before the increase in the money supply. Thus lowering the market rate below the natural rate of interest is possible only for a very short period. The length of this period depends on how fast price expectations adjust. Friedman assumes that "[t]his price expectation effect is slow to develop and slow to disappear."

However, if money expansion becomes sustained, so that the public expects prices to continue to rise, then the higher rate of money expansion will *raise* the rate of interest, not lower it. Every attempt to maintain low interest rates entails high and rising nominal interest rates, as the experience of Latin America confirms. Thus Friedman concludes that the monetary authorities can lower the market rate of interest below the natural rate only by inflation.

The changes in money supply also affect the real side of the economy, so we must look at the output and labor markets to trace out the consequences of the changes in money supply.

In a steady state, real wages rise at the rate warranted by capital formation and technological improvement. The increase in money supply lowers the level of unemployment below the natural rate, which puts upward pressure on wages, so that wages rise faster than the rate warranted in a steady state. It is this higher real wage that induces labor to take jobs, which pushes the "market" rate of unemployment below the natural rate. The high employment also raises real output for a time. Recall that real magnitudes are increased because prices are slow to rise, as long as "anticipations" of price changes have not changed.

But that is only the initial impact on the real side. Selling prices of products typically respond to an unanticipated rise in *nominal* demand faster than prices of factors of production (wages). As prices rise, real wages received have gone down although real *anticipated* wages have gone up. This occurs because employees evaluate the wages at an earlier price level. In fact, it is the simultaneous fall *ex post* in real wages to employers and rise *ex ante* in real wages to employees which enables employment to rise in the first place. In other words, workers do not have the latest information on the price level: they were fooled into accepting a nominal wage that was not high in real terms. The *ex post* decline in real wages eventually changes the employee's "anticipations." They then demand higher nominal wages, which in the end raises the unemployment level back to the natural level. Thus the monetary authorities cannot peg the unemployment rate below the natural rate.

It is worth emphasizing that in this model, there is asymmetric information about prices, and "anticipations" are slow to change in either direction.[4] Apart from this statement, there is no attempt to treat "anticipations" in any formal manner, except to indicate that anticipations are important. It goes without saying that these anticipations have no statistical properties. But whereas in Friedman and Schwartz (1982) anticipations may be sometimes wrong, anticipations in Friedman (1968) are about inflation only and these anticipations are *eventually* always right.

CONCLUSION

The entire corpus of Friedman's empirical work surveyed here can be seen as an attempt to reject the Keynesian income-expenditure approach and to rehabilitate the classical quantity theory that Keynes had attacked. Friedman argued that the Keynesian theory is a special case; the general theory, he argued, is the quantity theory. The quantity theory as modified by Friedman is simple and can be represented by a single equation: the demand for real money is a function of permanent income. But permanent income is nonobservable and therefore nonmeasurable; it is a transcendental concept that he invented when he was trying to refute the Keynesian consumption function. Its empirical estimate is also arbitrary.

It is his rejection of Keynesian activist monetary and fiscal policy that had led Friedman to reject Keynes's income-expenditure categories. Having rejected them, he replaced them with an analysis of the representative agent. He also asserted that he was working within the Walrasian general equilibrium paradigm, even though in the strict sense the Walrasian general equilibrium is incompatible with any version of the quantity theory of money (Patinkin, 1965).

His work also emphasized anticipations, and although Friedman had argued that anticipations need not necessarily be realized always, according to his presidential address model, anticipations about inflation are always realized eventually, even though these anticipations are not perfect.

The New Classical school has acknowledged its debt to Friedman. In the New Classical models the price level is determined by the money supply; as in Friedman, the New Classical models adopt the concept of the natural rate of unemployment and deny that there is any trade-off between inflation and unemployment in the long run. In addition, this chapter has drawn attention to three other conceptual innovations that Friedman used and which became adopted by the new classical school.

NOTES

1 M. Friedman, 1959.
2 This method has been developed further by Hendry and others. See Hendry and Ericsson for references; see also Spanos (1986).
3 The fact that a Walrasian system, in which demand curves are homogeneous of degree zero, is inconsistent with a quantity theory of money has been known since 1956, when Patinkin (1956, 1965) demonstrated this inconsistency.
4 But the speed of change in anticipations has been observed to be a function of the magnitude of inflation rates. However, this is a paragraph in which Friedman is venturing a personal judgment.

5

Business Cycles with Misperceptions

INTRODUCTION

Lucas considers much of the traditional territory of macroeconomics to be "business cycle" theory. He has collected 14 of his articles (Lucas, 1981a) in a volume entitled *Studies in Business Cycle Theory*. His Yrjö Jahnsson lectures (Lucas, 1987) are called *Models of Business Cycles*. In the former, Lucas has republished his 1975 article (Lucas, 1975), which is entitled "An Equilibrium Model of the Business Cycle," which, he claims in the introduction, "does not quite work" (p. 15); in that model, "there is "too much" information in the hands of traders for them to be "fooled" into altering real decision variables . . . [that may] induce the sort of responses in real and nominal variables which occur during the observed business cycle' (Lucas, 1981a, p. 186). Consequently there is no *single* candidate that can be presented as *the* Lucas model of the business cycle.

On the other hand Lucas's paper entitled "Understanding Business Cycles"[1] is a very clear exposition of the central questions, as he saw them, as well as the most satisfactory way of formulating an equilibrium model of the business cycle (Lucas, 1977). In fact, this paper can also be seen to be the progenitor of the "real business cycle" school, as all the crucial ideas are there. All that occurred later was that proponents of the real business cycle theory took the lessons of the Lucas critique to heart and proposed Cobb-Douglas utility and production functions, the latter with shocks, and produced synthetic time series that cannot be distinguished from an actual GNP time series. This clue also came from Lucas, as is shown below.

In Lucas (1977), the objective of business cycle theory is made clear. First, citing Hayek (1933, p. 33n), he makes clear that the major unresolved problem was to incorporate cyclical phenomena into an 'equilibrium' theory described by a system of Walrasian general equilibrium theory, which has a logical *a priori* policy consequence:

> By seeking an equilibrium account of business cycles, one accepts *in advance* rather severe limitations on governmental countercyclical policy which might be rationalized by the theory (Lucas, 1981, p. 234; emphasis as in the original). [2]

Thus the theory would provide an *a priori* rationalization for non-intervention if there were any adjustments to be made in the light of cyclical fluctuations. These adjustments were best left to decentralized agents themselves rather than to government. In fact, if the cyclical fluctuations themselves reflect agents' optimal responses to (unexplained) changes or shocks, then there would be nothing left for government to do, except not to aggravate the fluctuations by the actions of the government itself.

Second, the equilibrium business cycle should be clearly defined in a way that does not reinvite governmental action. The business cycle is thus defined exclusively to have the following characteristics. The cycle is *fluctuations in GNP about trend*, where the fluctuations show no uniformity in either period or amplitude. Accompanying these fluctuations are *comovements* among different aggregate time series:

1 Output movements of broadly defined sectors move together.
2 Production of producer and consumer durables exhibits greater amplitude than the production of nondurables.
3 Production and prices of agricultural goods and natural resources fluctuate less than average.
4 Business profits are highly procyclical with much greater amplitude than other series.
5 Prices in general are procyclical.
6 Monetary aggregates and velocity measures, as well as short term interest rates, are procyclical, whereas long-term rates are slightly less so.

These are the *only* comovements that characterize a business cycle. It is worth emphasizing that this is the *complete* definition of the business cycle; there is nothing more. In particular, nothing is said about the labor market; no statement about unemployment or changes in the real wage is included in the definition of a business cycle. We return to that below.

Third, an odd conclusion is drawn from the successful simulation by Adelman and Adelman (1959) of the Klein-Goldberger model of the U.S. economy, which showed that time series generated by applying random shocks to it could not be distinguished from time series produced by an actual economy. Lucas admired the predictive success of shocks to this Keynesian model, although he pointed out that it was not an "equilibrium" model. However, mimicking actual time series by some 'analog' or 'artificial' model with shocks became an important criterion of the value of a model, provided it was an "equilibrium" account.

Indeed, the main reason for rejecting Keynes's model was that it was not an equilibrium account. According to Lucas, Keynes explained unemployment not as a consequence of individual *choices*, as desired states, but as "involuntary." But involuntariness cannot be a consequence of a choice theoretic model – it is in fact a contradiction. Similarly, Keynes gave up Classical theory too readily when wages failed to move as predicted by the Classical theory. According to Lucas, (1981 p. 220), Keynes's analysis of the labor market is unsatisfactory for two reasons. First, the involuntary nature of unemployment is not derived theoretically – he attempted to verify it by "direct observation." Second, instead of explaining why households *choose* to supply labor at sharply irregular rates through time, Keynes sidestepped the problem by postulating rigid nominal prices, which are again not derived. In fact, the derivation is impossible, as it contradicts Walrasian general equilibrium theory characterized by zero-degree homogeneity of demand and supply functions.

Finally, the model must not only be an equilibrium account that generates time series that look like actual GNP data; in addition, it must also have an *invariance* property. This property was first proposed in the Lucas critique (Lucas 1976). According to the Lucas critique, demand and supply responses depend upon the expectations of a particular "policy regime," and demand or supply parameters estimated in one regime will not remain constant in another regime. The invariance property requires that the structure of a model remain unchanged under policy variations being studied. In general, this requires going "behind" demand and supply functions to the primitive parameters of taste and technology. While Lucas admits that invariance is not a property of models that can be assured in advance, he asserts that tastes and technology are less likely to vary systematically with variations in countercyclical policy. In contrast, an agent's decision rules will change with any change in the environment triggered by changes in government policy.

5.1 THE LUCAS MODEL: AN INFORMAL STATEMENT

First note that, given the above definition of a business cycle, *all* business cycles are alike, the only exception being the Great Depression. The recurrent nature of the cycle enables agents to form subjective probabilities about outcomes. This recurrent nature also enables the agent to treat business cycles as being analogous to situations of risk, as opposed to 'uncertainty' in Knight's sense. In situations of risk, the agent can form rational expectations in the sense of Muth (1961).

Now consider a *representative agent*, who is a single worker-producer. In each period, she is confronted with a given market price for a good which she then makes to order. Thus she comes to her place of work, observes her current selling price, determines how many hours to work that day, in accordance with her tastes, produces and sells her output, 'then goes home to relax' (p. 224). In exchange for her goods, she receives money that she spends on a variety of goods each day.

Next consider some thought experiments. Suppose the agent faces an unexplained 10 percent increase over the past average selling price of goods. If this is a *permanent* increase, she will work no harder, in fact she may work a little less. This is rational and in accordance with long-run labor supply elasticities that are zero or negative. But if the price increase is transitory, and if leisure is substitutable over time, then she will supply more labor on high price days and work less on low price days. We can see already that employment and price are procyclical, as we observe the data over actual business cycles. But the explanation is in terms of substitution effects, not based on some unintelligible disequilibria. However, so far the story is consistent with only the movement of output and *relative* prices. The business cycle shows comovement of output and the *price level*.

Next suppose that the good is storable and the agent can buy a machine that will increase her output per hour, for all future periods. Suppose now that the price increase is a mix of temporary and permanent price increases, but only a single price variable can be observed and the agent does not know how much of it is permanent and how much is temporary. Based in part on past experience, she "imperfectly" infers the movements in the two components, and makes a decision, which is based on some average of the permanent and transitory price change. Thus in response to an unforeseen price increase, the representative agent will increase labor supply, reduce her finished goods inventory, and to the extent that she believes the price increase is permanent, she will also increase her capital stock.

Although the relative price increase considered above was exogenous, changes will in general be due to changes in tastes and technology. A new technology reduces costs of producing an existing good, or makes it possible to produce a new good. This will require a shift of resources; such resource shifts will occur through price signals. Similarly, shifts in taste will also be signaled through prices. If there are many goods some relative prices will rise and some will fall.

Next suppose that *all* prices now change. The representative agent, who could not separate out permanent from transitory changes in prices, now faces the same difficulty: she will find it difficult to sort out with certainty the *relative* price change from general price level changes. When tastes and technology change, relative prices change, and there is some "cancelling out" as some prices rise and others fall.

Suppose there are many agents, like the representative agent who produces goods. When there is a general price increase more producers will observe increases in prices – that is what a general price increase means. As the general price increases, more producers will expand output, although some output may be contracting. But in the aggregate, output will be expanding. Hence we get comovement of output, prices, employment, and investment. This process works as long as each producer thinks that that producer's relative price has risen in comparison to the general price level.

If all agents have rational expectations, then a sustained inflation, which is continuous increase in the general price level, will eventually not affect the agents' decisions, although there may be a brief learning period.

A period of general price increases, as long as it is not sustained inflation, will also distort investment decisions, because current investment affects future capacity. If a general price movement is mistaken for a relative price increase, then producers add to capacity through investment. When the mistake is realized, investment will be below normal while capacity readjusts downward. This will make investment more volatile, as observed in actual data over the business cycle.

The entire explanation is based on the confusion on the part of the agents between relative and general price movements. But from the point of view of each individual agent, it is an optimal and rational response to observed price movements. So far nothing has been said about the *source* of the price movement. The source is nothing but increases in the money stock over and above that required by the economy. Thus the monetary shock is the force that triggers the business cycle.

To sum up, excessive increases in the money supply lead to a rise in the general price level. However, agents misperceive the general price increase as an increase in their own relative price and so expand output and investment. When it becomes clear that it was only a general price increase, investment falls as there is excess capacity, until capacity has adjusted to the required level. Thus although agents have rational expectations, they do not have full information about general price increases.

5.2 THE LUCAS MODEL: A FORMAL STATEMENT

The model that is formalized has an approach that is common to Lucas (1973, 1975, 1976) and Barro (1976, 1980, 1981). Suppose goods and services are traded in a large number of localized markets, so that traders in each market z know the price of their own good $p_t(z)$, but have only lagged information on prices in other markets. Therefore, they can calculate the economy-wide average price only on the basis of this lagged information. However, traders are willing to supply a normal or permanent level of output y_t^p. If the relative price on the market were to rise temporarily, the traders would be willing to supply an additional amount. Let us call that the *cyclical component*, $y_t^c (z)$ on market z. (In the case of the permanent component a market index z is not necessary since each market has a permanent output that traders are willing to supply.) Therefore the log of total output in market z is

$$y_t(z) = y_t^p + y_t^c (z) \tag{5.1}$$

where the cyclical component depends on the extent to which the price on market z exceeds the general price as well as the cyclical component last period, $t - 1$. Thus

$$y_i^c(z) = b \{p_t(z) - E[p_t|I_t(z)]\} + \lambda y_{t-1}^c \qquad (5.2)$$

$$with \ b > 0, \quad 0 < \lambda < 1$$

where $p_t(z)$ is the actual price in market z at time t and $E[p_t|I_t(z)]$ is the mean current general price level based on information available in z at time t, $I_t(z)$. Note that λ is less than one because the cyclical component is a deviation from trend, according to Lucas (1981a, p. 133). However, the last term in equation (5.2) is added to maintain persistent effects, by making the cyclical component serially correlated.

The information set available in z is

$$I_t(z) = [p_t(z), I_{t-1}] \qquad (5.3)$$

where I_{t-1}, common to all markets, is the information on past demand shifts, output and prices.

Suppose the current price in market z, which is observed by traders in that market is

$$p_t(z) = p_t + u_t(z) \qquad (5.4)$$

where p_t is the current general price and $u_t(z)$ is the deviation of the market price in market z from the general price, and $u_t(z)$ is a random demand shock such that the mean of $u_t(z)$ is zero – that is, $Eu_t(z) = 0$ – with constant variance σ_u^2.

Next assume that the general price, based on past information I_{t-1}, is known to be normally distributed with mean $Ep_t = \overline{p}_t$ and constant variance σ^2. Hence, the variance of $p_t(z)$ is $\sigma^2 + \sigma_u^2$.

Therefore the general price level can be written as:

$$p_t = E[p_t|I_{t-1}] + \xi_t = \overline{p}_t + \xi_t \qquad (5.5)$$

where $\overline{p}_t$ is the mean and ξ_t is a normally distributed random variable with zero mean and a constant variance.

Substituting equation (5.5) into (5.4) gives:

$$p_t(z) = \bar{p}_t + u_t(z) + \xi_t \tag{5.6}$$

However, the general price is not observable to the agent in market z; the agent must use the information of the distribution of its *own* price to estimate the minimum-variance, unbiased estimate of $\bar{p}_t$. Therefore the agent must estimate coefficients α and β in the equation

$$p_t = \alpha + \beta p_t(z) + w_t \tag{5.7}$$

where w_t is a random error term with mean 0 and constant variance. Let the fitted value of β be $\hat{\beta}$. However, we know that

$$\hat{\beta} = \frac{cov[p_t, p_t(z)]}{var[p_t(z)]} \tag{5.8}$$

$$= \frac{\sigma^2}{\sigma^2 + \sigma^2_u}$$

The numerator in equation (5.8) follows from the fact that the general price level does not vary with the demand shock in market z – i.e., $cov[p_t, u_t(z)] = 0$. Therefore the only variance between $\bar{p}_t$ and $p_t(z)$ is the variance of their common element, p_t. And it has already been shown that the variance of $p_t(z)$ – i.e., the denominator – is $\sigma^2 + \sigma_u^2$.

The line fitted to equation (5.7) must pass through the intersection of the mean values of p_t and $p_t(z)$, which is $\bar{p}_t$. Therefore

$$\hat{\alpha} = \bar{p}_t - \hat{\beta}\bar{p}_t(z) = (1 - \hat{\beta})\bar{p}_t \tag{5.9}$$

Substitute (5.9) into (5.7) to get:

$$p_t = (1 - \hat{\beta})\bar{p}_t + \hat{\beta}p_t(z) \tag{5.10}$$

which is the expected value of the general price. We may therefore write equation (5.10) as:

$$E[p_t|I_{t-1}] = (1 - \hat{\beta})\bar{p}_t + \hat{\beta}p_t(z) \tag{5.10a}$$

where $\hat{\beta} = \sigma^2/(\sigma^2 + \sigma_u^2)$.

To repeat, σ^2_u measures the variability of agent z's own relative price, and σ^2 measures the variability of the general price. The higher the latter, the less likely would be the agent to interpret an increase in her own price as indicating a shift in her own relative price. If inflation were held at some constant level, say at zero, then σ^2 and $\hat{\beta}$ would fall to zero, and any change in $p_t(z)$ would be taken as a change in relative price of the good in market z. On the other hand if the general price were *extremely* variable, then its variance σ^2 would approach infinity and the ratio in equation (5.8) would approach unity – that is $\hat{\beta}$ would approach 1. In that case, any change in $p_t(z)$ would be considered just more inflation, so that the output response of the agent in z would be nil.

Now substitute equation (5.10a) into equation (5.2) and then (5.2) into equation (5.1) to get the agent's supply response:

$$y(t) = b(1 - \hat{\beta})[\,p_t(z) - \overline{p}_t] + \lambda y^c_{t-1}(z) + y^p{}_t \qquad (5.11)$$

Next note that equation (5.1) can also be written, in aggregate terms, i.e. dropping z:

$$y_{t-1} = y^p_{t-1} + y^c_{t-1} \quad \text{or}$$

$$y^c_{t-1} = y_{t-1} - y^p_{t-1} \qquad (5.1\text{a})$$

Now aggregate equation (5.11) over all markets and utilize (5.1a) to get:

$$y_t = y^p_t + b(1 - \hat{\beta})(p_t - \overline{p}_t) + \lambda(y_{t-1} - y^p_{t-1}) \qquad (5.12)$$

Equation (5.12) is the aggregate (Lucas) supply equation in which output is a sum of

1 the permanent component,
2 the price surprise, where the price is in *excess* of the general price, and where this surprise is weighted by agents' experience with relative versus general price variability, and
3 last period's deviation of output from permanent output last period.

The weight λ is *less than 1*, on which more later.

Having considered the supply side, consider the equation of (aggregate) demand, which in log terms is [Lucas, 1981a, p. 135]:

$$y_t + p_t = x_t \tag{5.13}$$

In equation (5.13) on the left-hand side is the log of nominal income PY, and on the right-hand side is exogenous demand, which is a nonobservable random-shock but it is assumed that agents know that it is normally distributed with

$$E(\Delta x_t) = \delta \text{ and } \text{Var}(\Delta x_t) = \sigma^2 \tag{5.14}$$

where

$$\Delta x_t = x_t - x_{t-1}$$

In equilibrium, demand must equal supply:

$$x_t - p_t = y_t^p + b(1 - \hat{\beta})(p_t - \bar{p}_t) + \lambda(y_{t-1} - y_{t-1}^p) \tag{5.15}$$

Suppose that the permanent component of output grows at a trend growth rate γ, so that in log terms,

$$y_{t-1}^p + \gamma = y_t^p \quad \text{or}$$

$$y_{t-1}^p = y_t^p - \gamma$$

Letting $(1 - \hat{\beta}) \equiv \theta$, we get from equation (5.15),

$$y_t^p + b\theta(p_t - \bar{p}_t) + \lambda(y_{t-1} - y_t^p + \gamma) + p_t - x_t = 0 \tag{5.16}$$

From equation (5.16), it is possible to find the solution of both prices and output using Wold's decomposition method, shown in the Appendix to this chapter. Solving equation (5.16) shows that the cyclical component y_t^c is nothing but an infinite sum of past demand shocks that deviate from the average. Hence this business cycle model shows that the cycle is due to unanticipated demand shocks, an explanation that is not too different from the Keynesian explanation, which identified the cause of the cycle as exogenous shifts in the *IS* curve, due mainly to shifts in investment expenditures.

This model relies on the assumption that cyclical growth is decomposable into a trend and cyclical component, an assumption that is unwarranted and has no basis in theory. The indecomposability of trend and cycle can be traced to Harrod: there can be no growth without cycles and no cycles without growth. As Hahn (1971) points out, this would indeed be the main thrust of Harrod's contribution. It is also quintessentially Keynesian. Further discussion of this important issue is deferred to the next chapter, especially appendix 6B.

The model depends crucially on the assumption that the weight λ is less than 1. It is imposed understandably to display serial correlation in output, but it is not *derived* from any theory. In fact, without the assumption that $0 < \lambda < 1$, there would be no cycles. If λ were equal to 0, output would be at the steady-state level, with the cyclical component having a mean value of zero. Thus the imposition of the weight λ is arbitrary and without justification. In terms of the criteria of chapter 3, λ here is redundant mathematics.

To summarize the model, the mechanism generating cycles is as follows: exogenous demand shocks transmit imperfect price signals to firms; the firms are handicapped in not having any information except on their own local markets. The exogenous demand shock leads to an increase in price, which leads to an increase in output – that is, the cyclical component y_t^c. The lower the general price variability, the greater the y_t^c. In this model the *source* of the demand shock does not exist. However Lucas (1977; 1981a, pp. 232–33) identifies the source as being increases in the money supply. If the price level is determined by the quantity theory, then increases in money supply must lead to increases in the price level, where firms, who have no information except prices in their own markets, *misread* a general price level increase as an increase in their own relative price. Without this misperception, there would be no increase in output, no cyclical component. But this misperception occurs even though all agents, including firms, are supposed to have rational expectations.

In the model that follows, the exogenous demand shock is replaced with money shocks, but the limited information assumption is maintained (Barro 1980, 1981).

5.3 A MODEL WITH MONETARY MISPERCEPTIONS

Consider an equilibrium model in which both demand and supply depend on perceived excess of observed prices over normal anticipated values, as well as on unanticipated growth of money supply. In terms of logs, the demand in market z is $y_t^d(z)$ and supply is $y_t^s(z)$:

$$y_t^s(z) = a_s[p_t(z) - E_z p_{t+1}]$$

$$- b_s(m_t - E_z m_t) + \varepsilon_t^s(z) \tag{5.17}$$

$$y_t^d(z) = -a_d[p_t(z) - E_z p_{t+1}]$$

$$+ b_d(m_t - E_z m_t) + \varepsilon_t^d(z) \tag{5.18}$$

where the coefficients a_s, a_d, b_s, and b_d are all positive; $p_t(z)$ is the price in market z at time t; $E_z p_{t+1}$ is the expectation formed at time t in market z of the general price level in the *following* period, $t + 1$; m_t is the growth rate of money at time t; $E_z m_t$ is that part of money growth expected and anticipated by agents in market z. Hence $(m_t - Em_t)$, which may be positive or negative, is the unanticipated growth of money. Similarly, the term $p_t(z) - Ep_{t+1}$ is the unanticipated increase (or decrease) in the relative price in market z. Finally $\varepsilon_t^s(z)$ and $\varepsilon_t^d(z)$ are error terms.

Assume that all local markets are isolated, so that in each market z, market clearance means the equality of demand and supply:

$$y_t^s(z) = y_t^d(z) \quad \text{or} \tag{5.19}$$

$$p_t(z) - E_z p_{t+1} = (1/a)[b(m_t - E_z m_t) + \varepsilon_t(z)] \tag{5.20}$$

where $a = a_d + a_s$; $b = b_d + b_s$; $\varepsilon_t(z) = \varepsilon_t^d(z) - \varepsilon_t^s(z)$. Assume that $\varepsilon_t(z)$ has mean 0, and a constant variance. Now equation (5.20) can be substituted into either (5.17) or (5.18). After some simplification, we obtain:

$$y_t(z) = 1/a[(a_s b_s - a_d b_s)(m_t - Em_t) + a_s \varepsilon_t^d(z) + a_d \varepsilon_t^s(z)] \tag{5.21}$$

In principle, equations (5.20) and (5.21) can be used to solve for $p_t(z)$ and $y_t(z)$ by the decomposition method used in the Appendix to solve the Lucas model. However, note that in this model 'money surprises' (i.e. the growth of money supply in excess of the expected growth) trigger both price increases and output increases. But monetary misperceptions are crucial here; as Barro (1981, p. 49) himself notes, if all agents had full information, so that $m_t = Em_t$, then $p_t(z) = Ep_{t+1}$. In other words, increases in money supply lead to proportional increases in prices, and output would be unaffected. Thus in order for fluctuations in output to occur, there must be unanticipated changes in money supply. The model is close in spirit to Friedman's approach, reviewed in chapter 4.

In what sense is this simplified version of Barro's model a business cycle model? First, it displays comovement of prices and output; there is also comovement of output and money, but there is no serial correlation in output. Hence in this model cycles are not persistent.

CONCLUSION

In this chapter two New Classical business cycle models were reviewed. Both relied on rational expectations but with asymmetric information. The Lucas model has a permanent and a cyclical component of output. It was shown that the cyclical component is due to the effects of past demand shocks that are made to persist by a lag structure of these shocks, a procedure for which no rationale is provided.

One could argue that the ultimate source of these demand shocks is unanticipated growth in money supply. Here, too, it is important to restrict arbitrarily the amount of information available to agents. Without the restriction on information, there would be no departure from steady-state output, and no cycles.

As is argued in the next chapter, the informational asymmetries were the main weaknesses of the New Classical models of business cycles, which led to the so-called "real" business cycle model, in which this defect was corrected.

NOTES

1 Reprinted in Lucas, 1981.
2 .Lucas (1981a p. 235) then asks the appropriate question: if it is a "do-nothing" theory, why do we need the theory? He then answers the question by saying that in a "democratic" society, it is not enough to believe one is right, but one must be able to explain why one is right.

APPENDIX 5A

In this appendix, the use of Wold's decomposition method is illustrated, as many New Classical models use it to derive the solution, following its introduction into economics by Muth (1961). According to Wold's theorem, the solution of any linear stochastic model may be written as a sum of a deterministic component y_t and an infinite moving-average term (Sargent, 1979, p. 257–62):

$$\sum_0^\infty m_i \varepsilon_{t-1}$$

Hence any y_t can be written as

$$y_t = \bar{y}_t + \sum_0^\infty m_i \varepsilon_{t-i}$$

where the m_i coefficients are unknown. Muth's solution method was to equate the unknown coefficients with the known coefficients of the economic model. In this way a solution could be obtained. In the Lucas model, price is a function not only of demand but also of output. Therefore price can be written as the sum of the permanent component of output and an infinite moving average of past output, and an infinite moving average of past demand shocks, as the permanent component of demand is *zero* by assumption. [1].
Hence

$$p_t = a_0 + a_1 x_t + a_2 x_{t-1} + a_3 x_{t-2} + \ldots$$
$$+ c_0 y_t^p + b_1 y_{t-1} + b_2 y_{t-2} + \ldots \qquad (A5.1)$$

where $c_0 y_t^p$ is the deterministic component.

But the same is true of the expected price, which can also be written in a similar manner. Recall that we defined $\Delta x_t = x_t - x_{t-1}$. Let us use it here:

$$E[p_t | I_{t-1}] = a_0 + a_1 E[(\Delta x_t + x_{t-1}) | I_{t-1}] + a_2 x_{t-1} + a_3 x_{t-2}$$
$$+ \ldots + c_0 y_t^p + b_1 y_{t-1} + b_2 y_{t-2} + \ldots$$
$$= c_0 y_t^p + b_1 y_{t-1} + b_2 y_{t-2} + \ldots$$
$$+ a_0 + a_1 (\delta + x_{t-1}) + a_2 x_{t-1} + a_3 x_{t-2} + \ldots$$
$$\qquad (A5.2)$$

Following Muth (1961), we may substitute (A5.1) and (A5.2) into equation (5.16):

$$y_t^p + b\theta[a_0 + a_1x_t + a_2x_{t-1} + a_3x_{t-2} + \ldots$$
$$+ c_0y_t^p + b_1y_{t-1} + b_2y_{t-2} + b_3y_{t-3} + \ldots]$$
$$+ b\theta[-a_0 - a_1(\delta + x_{t-1}) - a_2x_{t-1} - a_3x_{t-2} - \ldots$$
$$- b_1y_{t-1} - b_2y_{t-2} - \ldots - c_0y_t^p]$$
$$+ \lambda[y_{t-1} - y_t^p + \gamma]$$
$$+ [a_0 + a_1x_t + a_2x_{t-1} + a_3x_{t-2} + \ldots$$
$$+ c_0y_t^p + b_1y_{t-1} + b_2y_{t-2} + \ldots] - x_t = 0$$

$$(A5.3)$$

Now collect like terms in the above equations:

$$\therefore [1 - \lambda + c_0]y_t^p + a_0 + [b\theta a_1 + a_1 - 1]x_t - b\theta a_1\delta$$
$$+ [b\theta a_2 - a_1b\theta - b\theta a_2 + a_2]x_{t-1} + a_3x_{t-2} + \ldots$$
$$+ \lambda y_{t-1} + b_1y_{t-1} + b_2y_{t-2} + \ldots$$
$$+ \lambda\gamma = 0$$

$$(A5.4)$$

The variables are y_t^p, x_i, y_j. The above equation is zero if and only if (1) all coefficients of the variables are zero; and (2)

$$a_0 - b\theta a_1\delta + \lambda\gamma = 0 \qquad (A5.5)$$

A5.5 implies that

$$1 - \lambda + c_0 = 0 \Rightarrow c_0 = \lambda - 1 \qquad (A5.6)$$

$$b\theta a_1 + a_1 - 1 = 0$$

$$a_1(b\theta + 1) = 1 \Rightarrow a_1 = \frac{1}{1 + b\theta} \qquad (A5.7)$$

$$[b\theta a_2 - a_1b\theta - b\theta a_2 + a_2] = 0$$
$$- a_1b\theta + a_2 = 0 \quad \text{or} \qquad (A5.8)$$

$$a_2 = a_1b\theta \Rightarrow a_2 = \frac{b\theta}{1 + b\theta}$$

Next note that

$$a_0 - b\theta a_1\delta + \lambda\gamma = 0$$

$$a_0 = b\theta a_1 \delta - \lambda\gamma \tag{A5.9}$$

$$a_0 = \frac{b\theta\delta}{1 + b\theta} - \lambda\gamma$$

and

$$(\lambda + b_1) = 0 \Rightarrow b_1 = -\lambda \tag{A5.10}$$

Finally,

$$\left.\begin{array}{l} a_3 = a_4 = a_5 \ldots = 0 \\ \text{and } b_2 = b_3 = b_4 \ldots = 0 \end{array}\right\} \tag{A5.11}$$

Inserting these values of the coefficients into (A5.1) enables us to solve for p_t, and having solved for it, we can find the equilibrium solution as well as the cyclical component y_t^c. To find price p_t in (A5.1):

$$p_t = \frac{b\theta\delta}{1 + b\theta} - \lambda\gamma + \frac{x_t}{1 + b\theta} + \frac{b\theta}{1 + b\theta}x_{t-1} + (\lambda - 1)y_t^p - \lambda y_{t-1}$$

Let $b\theta/(1 + b\theta) = \pi$, so that

$$p_t = \pi\delta - \lambda\gamma + \frac{1}{1 + b\theta}x_t + \pi x_{t-1} + (\lambda - 1)y_t^p - \lambda y_{t-1} \tag{A5.12}$$

Recall that $y_t = y_t^p + y_t^c$, but $y_t = x_t - p_t$. Hence in equilibrium,

$$x_t - p_t = y_t^p + y_t^c \tag{A5.13}$$

$$y_t^c = x_t - p_t - y_p^t$$

Substitute (A5.12) into (A5.13):

$$y_t^c = x_t - \left[\pi\delta - \lambda\gamma + \frac{1}{1 + b\theta}x_t + \pi x_{t-1} + (\lambda - 1)y_t^p - \lambda y_{t-1}\right] - y_t^p$$

$$= -\pi\delta + \lambda\gamma + \pi x_t - \pi x_{t-1} - (\lambda - 1)y_t^p + \lambda y_{t-1} - y_t^p$$

$$= -\delta\pi + \lambda\gamma + \pi\Delta x_t - \lambda y_t^p + \lambda y_{t-1}$$

$$\therefore \quad y_t^c = -\delta\pi + \lambda\gamma + \pi\Delta x_t + \lambda(y_{t-1} - y_t^p)$$

(Note that $x_t - \dfrac{x_t}{1 + b\theta} = \pi x_t$.) Also, we know by definition that

$\gamma \equiv y_t^p - y_{t-1}^p$, so that:

$$y_t^c = \pi(\Delta x_t - \delta) + \lambda(y_t^p - y_{t-1}^p) + \lambda(y_{t-1} - y_t^p)$$

$$= \pi(\Delta x_t - \delta) - \lambda y_{t-1}^p + \lambda y_{t-1}$$

$$y_t^c = \pi(\Delta x_t - \delta) + \lambda y_{t-1}^c \qquad (A5.14)$$

But A5.14 is an autoregression process of order 1, it can be written as:

$$y_t^c = \frac{\pi}{1 - \lambda L}(\Delta x_t - \delta)$$

$$(A5.15)$$

$$y_t^c = \pi \sum_{j=0}^{\infty} \lambda^j(\Delta x_{t-j} - \delta)$$

This final equation states that the cyclical component is nothing but an infinite series of demand shocks that deviate from the average demand. Hence the cyclical component is nothing but exogenous demand shocks.

NOTES FOR APPENDIX 5A

1 Clearly an unsatisfactory assumption.

6

Tobin, Okun, and the Rise of Real Business Cycle Theory

Among the most cogent critics of the Lucas-Barro approach to business cycles caused by informational asymmetries and misperceptions about price changes were Tobin (1980) and Okun (1980). In fact, one can find in their work not only the germs of the research of the New Classical "real" business cycle theorists but also the theories of implicit contracts and other approaches that later were called "New" Keynesian. The object of this chapter is not to trace ideas; however, the first section draws attention to the critique of the misperceptions view and its demise, which left the New Classical approach without a satisfactory theory to explain business cycles. This critique also implicitly justified policy activism. The real business cycle theory was a response to this critique, an attempt to rescue the policy ineffectiveness proposition of Lucas (1972), Sargent (1973) and Sargent and Wallace (1975), and also to provide an equilibrium account of the business cycle free from the defects of the misperceptions approach.

6.1 Tobin and Okun on the Misperceptions Model

To quote Tobin (1980, p. 789):

Continual equilibrium with rational expectations and fully informed agents makes the model too good to be true. Why would real variables (then) fluctuate, generating the observations that lent credence to Keynesian diagnoses and remedies? ... Of course the real equilibrium of a full information model could move around, driven by fluctuations of natural endowments (like weather), *technologies (and their marginal productivities) and tastes (e.g. leisure versus work). If these fluctuations are serially persistent random processes, the observations they generate may look like business cycles in certain variables.* Theories of this genre . . . explain cycles not as economic mechanism but as the reflection in an intrinsically stable structure, of exogenous shocks [emphasis added].

Thus in his critique of the misperceptions view of cycles, Tobin offered what in his view was an absurd escape hatch, which is precisely what the real business cycle theorists took to heart and later formalized (see below). But we are getting ahead of the story. The model that was "too good to be true" had to be muddied with misperceptions of the sort Friedman (1968) postulated, through informational shortcomings about prices in *other* markets. But as Okun (1980) argued, this implies that there are positive transactions costs in a general equilibrium model. Information therefore has a positive value. In a contingent claims Arrow-Debreu economy, there are billions and billions of goods and services for *every* date and *every* contingency. So why is there no market in the missing information? Why doesn't some rational agent perceive this profit-making opportunity? If a profit-making opportunity exists, then it is *not* an equilibrium account. Hence misperceptions are fundamentally incompatible with rational expectations; if agents have rational expectations, systematic misperceptions cannot occur.

In Friedman's (1968) account, this contradiction does not exist, as agents in his model do not have rational expectations. On the contrary, in his model expectations are very "sticky"; it takes decades to reduce inflationary expectations. Friedman gives a role to monetary policy: the optimal policy is to *disclose the money supply rule and stick to it.* In the absence of the gold standard, the central bank must act as its surrogate and impose the discipline of the erstwhile gold standard. But an equilibrium account explains the business cycle as agents' optimal responses thus requiring *no* policy action, monetary or fiscal. Hence it is clear why Friedman cannot agree with the New Classical school, although he spawned it.

Finally, as Tobin (1980) argues, the informational asymmetry is also of a special kind. The Barro account briefly reviewed in chapter 5, or the Lucas account that identifies the *source* of price surprise as being due to money surprises (i.e., unanticipated increases), assumes an invariant link between money M and nominal income PY. The lack of information on a local island (or market) leads workers to make mistakes in estimating the one period real rate of return on money. The mistake then distorts workers' intertemporal choices between work and leisure. A positive money and price shock is perceived as an opportunity to spend more tomorrow by working hard today. Only later the workers learn that the price shock that raised their wages was just a general price increase. Tobin's argument runs as follows.

Suppose we distinguish employers from employees, buyers from sellers. Suppose sellers are fully informed, but buyers being unaware of money surprises must estimate – rationally – their buying prices. As buyers do not know the "true" prices, they will buy too much, and firms as buyers will now buy too much labor, and workers will work more than they wish to (Tobin 1980, p. 790). The surprises will now induce changes of the same sign in P and Y – i.e. rising prices will be accompanied by rising real output, as observed in actual business cycles.

Suppose now that the informational asymmetry is reversed: let buyers be fully informed, and let sellers be rational but without the information on money surprises. (Tobin argues that this kind of asymmetry is also equally plausible.) In this situation when prices rise due to a money surprise, the fully informed buyers will buy *less* labor and produce lower output. Consequently P and Y will be negatively correlated. Hence Tobin's argument implies that the informational asymmetry has to be special – it must be of the kind that leads to positive correlation between P and Y.

The internal inconsistencies of the misperceptions view led to its early demise – Lucas (1987) in his Yrjö Jahnsson lectures given in May 1985, implicitly acknowledges the vacuity of the misperceptions approach by concentrating his lectures on business cycles entirely on the real business cycle approach of Kydland and Prescott. However, Lucas remains against policy activism: he estimates that for a plausible range of parameter estimates of risk-aversion, the cost of business cycles, as measured by the instability of consumption of the representative U.S. consumer, is exceedingly small. He argues that eliminating the aggregate consumption variability would be equivalent in utility terms to an increase in average consumption of something less than one-tenth of 1 percent (Lucas, 1987, p. 27), or about $8.50 per person in 1983. Hence Lucas concludes that economic instability experienced in the United States since World War II is a "minor problem" (p. 30).

Thus instead of accounting for cyclical fluctuations, Lucas's most recent approach has been partly to dismiss the business cycle as a phenomenon, and partly to assert that the real business cycle theory is a plausible equilibrium account of a minor phenomenon.

Finally, we close this section with a quote from Lucas:

> Kydland and Prescott have taken macroeconomic modelling into new territory that combines intelligible general equilibrium theory with an operational, empirical seriousness that rivals . . . Keynesian macroeconomic models . . . I would like to call this progress. (Lucas, 1987, pp. 46–47)

6.2 REAL BUSINESS CYCLE THEORY

In this section a prototype real business cycle (RBC) model is developed, following McCallum (1989) and Prescott (1986). It will be shown that the RBC model is free of the defects and contradictions of the misperceptions approach of Lucas and Barro. There are however other problems and shortcomings that make the RBC model no better than the models it sought to supplant. It will be shown that a cyclical component is superimposed by an arbitrary autoregressive process in the exogenous and unexplained technology shock. Thus in essence the RBC approach is not fundamentally different from the Lucas misperceptions approach.

Consider an economy made up of a large number of identical, infinitely lived households, each of which maximizes a utility function at time t:

$$E_t\left[\sum_{j=0}^{\infty} \beta^j u(c_{t+j}, \ell_{t+1})\right] \tag{6.1}$$

where c_t and ℓ_t are consumption and leisure at time t for each household; β is a subjective discount factor, $(0 < \beta < 1)$, which represents a preference for current consumption over future consumption-leisure combinations. The operator E_t represents mathematical expectation based upon complete information for period t and earlier. Leisure is time not spent on working, so that $\ell_t = 1 - n_t$, where the total number of hours in a day has been normalized to be 1. Then n_t is the labor supplied during t. It is assumed that the utility function is well behaved – that is, $\forall\, i = 1, 2, \ldots, u_i > 0, u_{ii} < 0$, $u_i(0) = \infty$ and $u_i(\infty) = 0$.

Each household has access to a production function of the form:

$$y_t = z_t \cdot f(n_t^d, k_t^d) \qquad (6.2)$$

where y_t is the output of the economy's single good during t, and n^d and k^d are labor and capital inputs used during t by the household. The variable z_t is a random technology shock. The process generating z_t is a first order autoregressive process, by assumption (see below). The production function f is homogeneous of degree one and is also well behaved with diminishing marginal products. The household's output may be consumed or stored and added to the household's stock of capital in the following period. During each period, a fraction δ of the capital is used up as depreciation.

There are competitive markets for labor and capital services that determine the wage rate w_t and the rental rate r_t . Thus the budget constraint faced by the typical household in period t is:

$$c_t + k_{t+1} = z_t f(n_t^d, k_t^d) + (1 - \delta)k_t - w_t(n_t - n_t^d) - r_t(k_t - k_t^d) \qquad (6.3)$$

At t, the household maximizes equation (6.1) subject to the constraint (6.2). As u and f are well behaved, there are no corner solutions, and the first order conditions for a maximum are

$$E_t u_1(c_{t+j}, 1 - n_{t+j}) - E_t \lambda_{t+j} = 0 \qquad (6.4a)$$

$$E_t u_2(c_{t+j}, 1 - n_{t+j}) - E_t \lambda_{t+j} w_{t+j} = 0 \qquad (6.4b)$$

$$E_t z_{t+j} f_1(n_{t+j}^d, k_{t+j}^d) - E_t w_{t+j} = 0 \qquad (6.4c)$$

$$E_t z_{t+j} f_2(n_{t+j}^d, k_{t+j}^d) - E_t r_{t+j} = 0 \qquad (6.4d)$$

With respect to the period $t+j$, the household faces the same constraint as equation (6.3) with the Lagrange multiplier λ_{t+j}. Then with respect to $t+j$, there is a further necessary condition for an intertemporal optimum[1]:

$$-E_t \lambda_{t+j} + E_t \beta \lambda_{t+j+1} [z_{t+j+1} f_2(n_{t+j+1}^d, k_{t+j+1}^d) + 1 - \delta] = 0 \qquad (6.4e)$$

In addition to the above, for an intertemporal optimum, there must be a terminal condition such that the value of the household accumulated capital should approach zero as time approaches infinity:

$$\lim_{j \to \infty} E_j \beta^{j-1} \lambda_{t+j} k_{t+j+1} = 0 \tag{6.5}$$

Then the conditions given in equations (6.3), (6.4), and (6.5) are necessary and sufficient for an intertemporal optimum. The conditions determine the household's choice at t of c_t, n_t, n_t^d, k_t^d, and k_{t+1} in response to the given market prices of w_t and r_t.

For an equilibrium in the market at each t, the total demand for labor must equal the total supplied, and the total capital demanded must equal total supplied. As all the households are alike and they all experience the same shocks,

$$\sum n_t = \sum n_t^d \text{ and } \sum k_t = \sum k_t^d$$

where the quantities are summed over all households. As the households are all alike, it is also legitimate to write $n_t = n_t^d$ and $k_t = k_t^d$.

Next note that, as expectations are rational, households will predict what the "true" structure of the model of the economy would yield (barring random errors). Therefore market equilibrium will be characterized by the following set of equalities for each period $t = 1, 2, 3, \ldots$ and so on:

$$c_t + k_{t+1} = z_t f(n_t^d, k_t^d) + (1 - \delta)k_t \tag{6.6}$$

$$u_1(c_t, 1 - n_t) - \lambda_t = 0 \tag{6.7}$$

$$u_2(c_t, 1 - n_t) = \lambda_t z_t f_1(n_t, k_t) \tag{6.8}$$

$$\lambda_t = E_t \beta \lambda_{t+1}[z_{t+1} f_2(n_{t+1}, k_{t+1}) + 1 - \delta] \tag{6.9}$$

Equation (6.6) states that in equilibrium (when $n_t = n_t^d$ and $k_t = k_t^d$), the budget constraint is respected: consumption plus net additions to capital stock in period y cannot exceed output; (6.7) and (6.8) state that the ratio of marginal disutility of labor to the marginal utility of consumption is just equal to the marginal product of labor; and finally (6.9) states that the intertemporal marginal utility of consumption net of depreciation is just equal to the marginal product of capital.

It can be shown that in a full competitive equilibrium with random stochastic shocks [Brock and Mirman (1972), and Lucas and Prescott (1971)], there is a sequence-of-markets' equilibrium in which firms and households take prices as given, as there exist time-invariant functions of the wage $w_t = w(k_t, z_t)$ and the rental price of capital $r_t = r(k_t, z_t)$, where these prices are relative to the date t consumption good. In fact, the state of the economy at time t is *fully* determined by the current values of k_t and z_t. Consequently, solutions of equations (6.6) to (6.9) can be written as functions of k_t and z_t:

$$k_{t-1} = k(k_t, z_t) \tag{6.10}$$

$$c_t = c(k_t, z_t) \tag{6.11}$$

$$n_t = n(k_t, z_t) \tag{6.12}$$

$$\lambda_t = \lambda(k_t, z_t) \tag{6.13}$$

This conclusion holds not only when the z_t are serially uncorrelated stochastic shocks but also if the z_t are generated by a stationary Markov process, because such a process contains enough information to determine the shock at time $t + 1$.

Next we ask the question, are there functional forms of u and f that yield explicit solutions of the variables k_{t+1}, c_t, and n_t in terms of k_t and z_t alone, as in equations (6.10) to (6.13)? Long and Plosser (1983) use the special case of Cobb-Douglas utility and production functions. Such a utility function can be written as

$$u(c_t, 1 - n_t) = \theta \log c_t + (1 - \theta)\log(1 - n_t) \tag{6.14}$$

and a Cobb-Douglas production function is

$$z_t f(n_t, k_t) = z_t n^\alpha k_t^{1-\alpha} \tag{6.15}$$

But this Cobb-Douglas representation requires that $\delta = 1$; i.e., *complete* depreciation of capital within a single period.

Substituting these special functional forms into (6.6) to (6.9), and assuming $\delta = 1$, we get

$$c_t + k_{t+1} = z_t n_t^\alpha k_t^{1-\alpha} \tag{6.6a}$$

$$\theta/c_t = \lambda_t \tag{6.7a}$$

$$(1 - \theta)/(1 - n_t) = \lambda_t \alpha z_t n_t^{\alpha-1} k_t^{1-\alpha} \tag{6.8a}$$

$$\lambda_t = (1 - \alpha)\beta E_t \lambda_{t+1}[z_{t+1} n_{t+1}^{\alpha} k_{t+1}^{-\alpha}] \tag{6.9a}$$

Now we must seek solution equations analogous to equations (6.10) to (6.13) for this special Cobb-Douglas case.

In the Cobb-Douglas case, it can be shown that employment n is a constant, determined entirely by the parameters α, θ, and β (see appendix 6A for derivations). It can be shown too that consumption and capital per household fluctuate over time according to

$$c_t = [1 - (1 - \alpha)\beta]n^{\alpha} z_t k_t^{1-\alpha} \tag{6.16}$$

$$k_{t+1} = (1 - \alpha)\beta n^{\alpha} z_t k_t^{1-\alpha} \tag{6.17}$$

As shown in Appendix 6A, employment does *not* fluctuate and is constant:

$$n = \frac{\alpha\theta}{[1 - (1 - \alpha)\beta](1 - \theta) + \alpha\theta} \tag{6.18}$$

This is indeed a strange business cycle in which output fluctuates due to the shocks z_t but employment remains *constant*! Furthermore, since the same shock hits both consumption and capital during the next period, the ratio c_t/k_{t+1} is a constant equal to $\alpha/(1 - \alpha)$. Indeed, since households have rational expectations, knowing c_t, they can work out k_{t+1} by the strict proportionality. So far, what has been described is an intertemporal Walrasian general equilibrium of pure exchange. The special example used by Long and Plosser expresses this equilibrium with both the utility and production functions taken to be of the Cobb-Douglas type. In this description of an intertemporal general equilibrium with agents holding rational expectations, there is no cyclical fluctuation of any magnitude. Even with a random shock z_t, the rational expectations equilibrium is the general equilibrium with actual output fluctuating randomly around the general equilibrium due to the random error. This is *not* a business cycle by any of the accepted definitions, since there is no comovement of any macro variables, nor is there persistent autocorrelation of output. In order to give the model some business cycle characteristics, important *additional* assumptions about the shock z_t have to be made. It is essential to note that without the additional assumption, there is no business cycle.

The standard features of business cycles are introduced by assuming that the shock z_t is of the first-order autoregressive form – i.e., AR(1):

$$\log z_t = \rho \log z_{t-1} + \varepsilon_t \qquad (6.19)$$

where ε_t is white noise.

Remembering that n is a constant (equation 6.18), and taking logs of both sides of equation (6.17), we get

$$\log k_{t+1} = \phi_0 + (1 - \alpha) \log k_t + \log z_t \qquad (6.20)$$

Substitute (6.19) into (6.20) to get,

$$\log k_{t+1} = \phi_0 + (1 - \alpha) \log k_t + \rho \log z_{t-1} + \varepsilon_t \qquad (6.21)$$

First rewrite (6.20) as:

$$\log k_t = \phi_0 + (1 - \alpha) \log k_{t-1} + \log z_{t-1}$$

$$\therefore \log z_{t-1} = \log k_t - \phi_0 - (1 - \alpha) \log k_{t-1}$$

Substitute this latter expression into equation (6.21) to get:

$$\log k_{t+1} = \phi_0(1 - \rho) + (1 - \alpha + \rho) \log k_t$$
$$- \rho(1 - \alpha) \log k_{t-1} + \varepsilon_t \qquad (6.22)$$

That is, equation (6.22) expresses k_{t+1} as an AR(2) process. Similarly consumption can be expressed as an AR(2) process:

$$\log c_t = (1 - \alpha + \rho) \log c_{t-1} - (1-\alpha) \rho \log c_{t-2}$$
$$+ \alpha(1 - \rho)\phi_1 + (1 - \alpha)(1 - \rho)\phi_0 + \varepsilon_t \qquad (6.23)$$

The log of output can also be expressed as an AR(2) process. The reason for doing this is simply that a number of detrended quarterly U.S. aggregate data series appear to be well described by AR(2) models.

To sum up the logic: if the exogenous random shock were AR(1), then a number of macroeconomic series can be represented as AR(2) processes, which display persistence. Thus equations (6.16) and (6.17) are made "cyclical" *post factum* by specifying that z_t in these two equations be AR(1) arbitrarily and without any theoretical justification.

Finally, we can show that the RBC model with Cobb-Douglas specification has a close affinity to the Lucas model, except that now the cyclical component is nothing but an infinite sum of past exogenous "technology" shocks, *without* any influence of demand.

Begin with equation (6.6a):

$$y_t = z_t n^\alpha k_t^{1-\alpha} \quad \text{or}$$

$$\log y_t = \alpha \log n + (1 - \alpha) \log k_t + \log z_t$$

but as shown in Appendix 6A, n is a constant. Therefore let $\alpha \log n \equiv A$; that is $y_t = A + (1 - \alpha) \log k_t + \log z_t$. Let $A \equiv y^p$ and let $y_t = y_t^p + y_t^c$; then

$$y_t^c = (1 - \alpha) \log k_t + \log z_t \tag{6.24}$$

Suppose that, as suggested by McCallum (1989),

$$\log k_t = (1 - \alpha) \log k_{t-1} + \xi_t, \quad \xi_t \sim N(0, \sigma_\xi^2)$$

and

$$\log z_t = \rho \log z_{t-1} + \gamma_t, \quad \gamma_t \sim N(0, \sigma_\gamma^2) \tag{6.25}$$

then

$$\log k_t = \frac{1}{1 - (1 - \alpha)L} \xi_t = \sum_{j=0}^{\infty} (1 - \alpha)^j \xi_{t-j}$$

$$\log z_t = \frac{1}{1 - \rho L} \gamma_t = \sum_{j=0}^{\infty} \rho^j \gamma_{t-j}$$

(where L is the backshift operator).

Substituting the above two expressions into equation (6.24), we get

$$y_t^c = \sum_{j=0}^{\infty} [(1 - \alpha)^j \xi_{t-j} + \rho^j \gamma_{t-j}] \tag{6.26}$$

Hence the cyclical component of output is nothing but an infinite sum of past random shocks. The cyclical component exists only because of the assumed lag structure of capital and of the technology shocks.

6.3 THE RBC MODEL WITH MONEY

The RBC model is an attempt to provide a competitive general equilibrium account of business cycles, but without monetary misperceptions. In fact, money does not enter into it. But the comovement of money and output can also be mimicked by incorporating a financial industry sector, as done by King and Plosser (1984). They achieve this by including financial transactions services in their production function, with *two* shocks $z_t^{(1)}$, and $z_{t+1}^{(2)}$:

$$y_{t+1} = z_t^{(1)} \cdot z_{t+1}^{(2)} f(n_t, k_t, d_t)$$

where d_t is itself determined by its own production function and yet another shock, $z_t^{(3)}$:

$$d_t = z_t^{(3)} \cdot h(n_t, k_t)$$

The financial industry provides 'accounting services that facilitate the exchange of goods by reducing the amount of time and other resources that otherwise would be devoted to market transactions' (King and Plosser, (1984), p. 365).

The two shocks $z^{(1)}$ and $z^{(2)}$ are mutually and serially independent, each with expectation 1. The first shock alters expected output next period. The second shock $z^{(2)}$ represents pure uncertainty and it alters y in an unexpected manner. Since both shocks are unrestricted in sign and are random, they can be mutually cancelling or mutually reinforcing in either direction. Thus only a special confluence of unexplained random events will produce peaks and troughs.

The third shock $z^{(3)}$, which affects the financial industry only, is interpreted as technological innovation, and consequently it is strictly positive, with expectation 1. King and Plosser sum three shocks, perhaps because three shocks were enough to produce the correlation between output and different measures of money; their main empirical finding-again using the Cobb-Douglas special case for both $f(.)$ and $h(.)$ – is that real activity is highly correlated with inside money, which supports their view that the financial industry simply supplies intermediate services, the demand for which rises or falls over the business cycle.

Apart from the comovement of real output and transaction services, the real rates of return move in a countercyclical direction as agents' opportunities to spread wealth over time are subject to diminishing returns – because, the authors claim, that "total time is fixed in supply"!

While the timing pattern of variables depends on the shocks, the model can generate *any* desired pattern; money variables can lag as in Burns and Mitchell (1946), or they can lead, as in Sims (1972) and in Friedman and Schwartz (1963). This applies to the price level too; it can be made countercyclical, procyclical, or even both – that is, it can be made ambiguous. Furthermore, King and Plosser claim that the model is so flexible that it can accommodate any number of other features without affecting comovement; one can introduce a fiat currency, unregulated banking, regulated banking, as well as alternative central banking policies.

To sum up: the empirical (Cobb-Douglas forms) calibrations and simulations with exogenous shocks reproduce six main empirical regularities of business cycles:

1 Quantities of all goods move roughly together;
2 Output variations persist for many periods, where persistence and sustained cycles are assumed to be synonymous with the degree of autocorrelation being greater than 1;
3 Real wages move procyclically as observed in reality even though the analytical aggregate production function shows that the real wage is anticyclical;
4 Nominal variables such as GNP are more highly autocorrelated than their corresponding real variables;
5 Nominal and real output are significantly correlated with nominal and real measures of inside and outside money respectively;
6 Inflation results "principally" from changes in the stock of outside money and variations in real output.

6.4 CRITIQUE OF THE RBC MODEL

As stated earlier the RBC model was an attempt to produce a business cycle theory that was compatible with a Walrasian competitive intertemporal general equilibrium, but *without* the assumption of asymmetric information or misperceptions, an approach that was a contradiction of rational expectations and the existence of complete contingent Arrow-Debreu markets. It also took the lessons of the Lucas critique (1976) as its point of departure. The essential elements of the RBC model are as follows:

1 Optimizing behavior on the part of the representative consumer and producer/seller; in particular, as all agents are intertemporally rational, they substitute consumption and labor intertemporally in response to technology shocks;
2 Exogenous random shock parameter(s) in the aggregate as well as other inter-industry production functions, that generate data that *looks* like actual business cycle data;
3 The assumption of extensive contingent markets and complete market clearance at every time period; and
4 The assumption of rational expectations.

In view of (3) and (4) above, all nonconvexities such as market failures or imperfections are ruled out. Therefore, the model being "too good to be true" (Tobin), the only way that fluctuations can be introduced in such a model is by way of exogenous, unexplained shocks. Tobin had offered the unexplained shock route as a *reductio ad absurdum*, which, to everyone's surprise, suddenly became "the theory," the theory of real business cycles.

In the process of presenting this theory, a number of compromises were made, such as the requirement that the depreciation rate of capital be 100 percent in each period, effectively meaning that there is no *capital* in the usual sense of the word, although a symbol k_{t+1} appears prominently throughout the theory. Then, throughout the cyclical fluctuation of output, employment remains constant, so that employment is not procyclical. Consumption fluctuates due to the shocks, but capital fluctuates exactly to the same extent; in fact, the ratio of consumption to capital is constant throughout the "cycle". Finally, it was shown that it is possible to decompose output in the

RBC model into a permanent and a cyclical component, where the latter is nothing but an infinite sum of past random errors.

The exposition in section 6.2 concentrates on the special Cobb-Douglas form of the utility and production functions because that has been prominent in the literature. As McCallum (1989, p. 21) states, there are very few functional forms[2] of $u(.)$ and $f(.)$ that permit the derivation of explicit closed form solutions of k_{t+1}, c_t, and n_t as required in equations (6.16) to (6.18). The requirement of special functional forms detracts from the generality of general equilibrium, which does not depend on any specific functional form. To that extent the RBC model is not a general equilibrium account of business cycles but only a limited special case, with all the attendant disadvantages (n constant, $\delta = 1$).

While the RBC approach is faithful to an equilibrium account, it has also accepted a Lucas definition of a business cycle, given in Chapter 5 (page 60). In this definition the business cycle is no more than a number of comovements, which is why Prescott (1986) prefers to call it business cycle *phenomena*, rather than an integral relationship between output, inflation, and unemployment. The second most important feature in RBC also comes from Lucas – namely, the strictures of the Lucas critique. The Lucas critique requires that economic modeling must not assume that parameters of demand and supply will remain invariant when policy regimes in which these parameters were estimated, undergo a change. This is because agents are assumed to hold rational expectations. Hence due to the Lucas critique, RBC models eschew demand and supply and seek to go "behind" demand and supply responses – to the primitive parameters of tastes and technology. The Lucas critique then becomes a justification for using the representative agent approach, with only tastes and technology taken as given.

The use of a representative consumer and a representative firm is valid if and only if both preferences and production are quasi-homothetic (see Blackorby and Schworm, 1988). Intuitively, this means that the Engel curve (and the expansion path) must be a straight line, but it need not pass through the origin. In their applied work, the real business cycle theorists use Cobb-Douglas utility and production functions. The use of Cobb-Douglas is sufficient (but not necessary) for aggregation. Geweke (1985) has argued persuasively that in avoiding the Lucas critique but using models with aggregate data, it is implicitly assumed that the aggregator function is structural with respect to policy intervention, whereas aggregator functions are "no

more structural than are within regime, reduced form relations"
(p. 206). Geweke also gives examples that show it matters a great deal
which representative agent is used, even when aggregation is exact, and
that aggregators are not the same for production, factor demand, and
supply – i.e., the familiar cross-equation restrictions of neoclassical
production fail. Geweke's numerical examples show that the aggregation errors are of the same order of magnitude as those that arise from
ignoring expectations, emphasized in the Lucas critique.

It is true that the RBC approach is strictly speaking not confined to
the Cobb-Douglas case, so that in principle it may be possible to show
variable employment, as in Hercowitz and Sampson[3] (1986). However
this variation in employment can only be explained as voluntary – i.e.,
consumers are choosing that level of employment in their attempts to
smooth out intertemporal consumption; after all, with the assumed
perfectly competitive capital markets, they can borrow as much as they
like against future income.

But employment variations can come about if either the demand for
labor, or the supply of labor changes. The demand for labor would
change only if the marginal product of labor changed. Now the
technology shocks need not necessarily change the demand for labor;
as the shocks are Hicks-neutral, a radial downward shift of the
aggregate production function will leave the marginal product of labor
unchanged. It follows that the level of employment will fluctuate,
mainly due to shifts in the labor supply function. There follow two
implications. First, in a recession (when employment is low) the real
wage would rise, or with an unchanged real wage, labor would be *off*
its supply curve – a disequilibrium phenomenon that is anathema to
the New Classical approach. Second, in the labor-leisure choice of
workers, lower levels of labor are associated with an income effect that
is greater than the substitution effect. But such a backward bending
labor-supply curve suggests that there must be at least two levels of the
real wage at which employment is the same. Why would entrepreneurs, with rational expectations, ever pay the higher real wage?

Although there is no disequilibrium phenomenon entertained by
RBC theory, an *ad hoc* explanation that is contrary to the spirit of real
business cycle theory is offered by Rogerson [1988] and Hansen (1985)
by making labor indivisible. The essence of the argument is to let
employment in the real business cycle model be determined by chance.
If productivity conditions dictate that everyone would work part-time
if labor were divisible, a Pareto optimal allocation may involve *some*
working full-time, and others not working, even when all workers are

identical *ex ante*. But who works and who does not is determined randomly by an exogenous lottery.

If the above explanation of unemployment is unconvincing, then the only remaining explanation of employment fluctuations is a *deus ex machina*: there is an exogenous shift in workers' tastes that produces a "new" labor-leisure indifference map. Since the Lucas critique requires a return to the primitive parameters of tastes and technology, macroeconometrics (of the representative consumer) would then have to detect, in the aggregate data, a structural shift in the taste parameter. Thus an increase in unemployment observed in the aggregate data can be interpreted only as an "optimal response" of the representative consumer in rearranging his or her lifetime consumption and work decisions. As this is an optimal response, it would be unnecessary to undertake any policy action to reduce unemployment.

An important feature of actual GNP time series is cyclical growth; growth and cycle are inextricably intertwined. As pointed out in Chapter 5, there can be no growth without cycles and no cycles without growth.

This discussion has resurfaced recently as some econometric work has found that output fluctuations are dominated by trend, as opposed to cyclical fluctuations (Nelson and Plosser, 1982). This empirical finding has troubled researchers both in the New Keynesian and the New Classical traditions, as the work of Campbell and Mankiw (1987), Clark (1987), Cochrane (1986), Stock and Watson (1986), Watson (1986), and King, Plosser and Rebelo (1988) show. It would be true to say that disentangling the nonstationary (or growth) component of real GNP and the stationary (or the short-term fluctuation) component has proved to be elusive: measures of the relative sizes of the stationary and nonstationary components depend very much on the methods used. Without invariant measures, this approach may not be theoretically fruitful; it might be best, as suggested above, to view cycles in the Keynes-Harrod manner and regard the cycle as a necessary condition for growth.

Nevertheless the problem of the nonstationary and stationary component has taken two distinct directions, which are described briefly.

One direction, taken by Nelson and Plosser, is to turn to the "source" of growth, the technology shock z_t, which has the time series representation

$$z_t = z_{t-1}^\rho \exp(\varepsilon_t) \qquad (6.25a)$$

which in log terms yields equation (6.25). If the estimate of ρ is 1 (i.e., unit root), then growth is trend dominated. If however ρ is less than 1, then some form of filtering technique (e.g. first differencing) may still be appropriate to decompose the growth and cyclical components (McCallum, 1986).

The other direction is to view z_t in the aggregate production function such as equation (6.2) as "disembodied technical progress", or simply view z_t as the "Solow residual," or "total factor productivity" in a growth accounting framework. For instance, Eichenbaum (1990) finds that there is almost complete uncertainty about the estimate of both ρ and ε, and that the standard error of ρ is very large, so that the claim that technology shocks explain a large part of the variability of postwar U.S. output is based on very flimsy evidence. Nelson and Plosser also argue that the estimates of technology shocks are highly sensitive to small perturbations in the theory, to small changes in the statistical methods used, and to small changes in the sample period. Furthermore, the fragility of the evidence is fundamentally affected once one abandons the convenient fiction that the structural parameters of the standard RBC model are actually known. This research on the Solow residual is worth mentioning, as it is a return to the controversies about growth accounting[4] (see Cornwall [1987] in the *New Palgrave*).

We conclude that decomposing a nonstationary time series such as GNP(GDP) (which grows over time) into a trend component and a cyclical component is arbitrary and unjustified. As this is an important issue, it is discussed further in appendix 6.B.

Finally, the most recent work, both empirical and theoretical, casts considerable doubt on the RBC attempt to account for cycles through exogenous technology shocks. As seems evident from essays collected by Barro (1989), the RBC approach is likely to lose favor even within the New Classical tradition, with growing attention being given to *endogenous* growth (Romer, 1989). It remains to be seen whether this new interest in growth will integrate cycles into it. This is the subject of chapters 9 to 12, where it is shown that such models already exist but have not received adequate attention, especially in North America.

CONCLUSION

RBC theory was an attempt to remedy the defects of the New Classical business cycle theory of Lucas and Barro, which relied on misperceptions or informational asymmetries that were incompatible with rational expectations. The Lucas and Barro models were not in fact "equilibrium" accounts of the business cycle. In contrast, RBC is indeed an equilibrium account, provided output can be decomposed into a permanent and a cyclical component. The cyclical component is then expressed as a sum of exogenous random shocks, which can be done only by arbitrarily imposing a particular lag structure on the exogenous technology shock parameter. The particular lag structure is not determined endogenously in the model. In effect the cyclical component differs hardly at all from that of the Lucas model.

The model is presented as a cyclical model by, simulations and calibrations which generate a series that looks like a GNP time series, although fluctuations in employment are largely ignored. Money is incorporated into the model by admitting more arbitrary shock parameters in order to produce some comovements. The integral relationship between output, employment, and inflation cannot be explained by an RBC model. Thus it fails to reflect the stylized facts of chapter 2, and in terms of the criteria of chapter 3, it contains redundant mathematics to generate the cycle.

APPENDIX 6A

In this appendix, the derivations of equations (6.16), (6.17) and (6.18) are given. Following McCallum, suppose we conjecture that c_t and k_{t+1} are proportional to the product $z_t k_t^{1-\alpha}$:

$$c_t = \pi_{10} z_t k_t^{1-\alpha} \tag{A6.1}$$

$$k_{t+1} = \pi_{20} z_t k_t^{1-\alpha} \tag{A6.2}$$

First substitute (6.7a) into (6.8a) in order to eliminate λ_t:

$$\frac{1-\theta}{1-n_t} = \alpha \frac{\theta}{c_t} . z_t n^{\alpha-1} k^{1-\alpha}$$

$$\frac{1-\theta}{1-n_t} = \frac{\alpha\theta z_t n^{\alpha-1} k^{1-\alpha}}{\pi_{10} z_t k^{1-\alpha}} = \frac{\alpha\theta n^{\alpha-1}}{\pi_{10}} \tag{A6.3}$$

Next substitute (A6.1) and (A6.2) into (6.6a):

$$\pi_{10} z_t k_t^{1-\alpha} + \pi_{20} z_t k^{1-\alpha} = z_t n_t^{\alpha} k_t^{1-\alpha} \qquad \text{or}$$

$$\pi_{10} + \pi_{20} = n^{\alpha} \qquad (A6.4)$$

Now substitute (A6.1) and (A6.2) into equation (6.9a):

$$\frac{\theta}{\pi_{10} z_t k_t^{1-\alpha}} = (1 - \alpha)\,\beta \left[\frac{\theta}{\pi_{10} z_{t+1} k_{t+1}^{1-\alpha}} \right] z_{t+1} n_{t+1}^{\alpha} k_{t+1}^{-\alpha}$$

$$\frac{\theta}{\pi_{10} z_t k_t^{1-\alpha}} = \frac{(1 - \alpha)\beta\theta n_{t+1}^{\alpha}}{\pi_{10} k_{t+1}}$$

$$\frac{\theta}{\pi_{10} z_t k_t^{1-\alpha}} = \frac{(1 - \alpha)\beta n^{\alpha}\theta}{\pi_{10}\pi_{20} z_t k_t^{1-\alpha}} \qquad \text{or}$$

$$\pi_{20} = (1 - \alpha)\beta n^{\alpha} \qquad (A6.5)$$

Substitute (A6.5) into (A6.4):

$$\pi_{10} + (1 - \alpha)\beta n^{\alpha} = n^{\alpha}$$

$$\therefore \pi_{10} = n^{\alpha}[1 - (1 - \alpha)\beta] \qquad (A6.6)$$

Substitute (A6.6) into (A6.3):

$$\frac{1 - \theta}{1 - n_t} = \frac{\alpha\theta n_t^{\alpha-1}}{n_t^{\alpha}[1 - (1 - \alpha)\beta]}$$

$$\frac{1 - \theta}{1 - n_t} = \frac{\alpha\theta}{n_t[1 - (1 - \alpha)\beta]} \qquad \text{or}$$

$$n_t[1 - (1 - \alpha)\beta](1 - \theta) = \alpha\theta - \alpha\theta n_t$$

Therefore

$$n = \frac{\alpha\theta}{[1 - (1 - \alpha)\beta](1 - \theta) + \alpha\theta} \qquad (A6.7)$$

Equation (A6.7) is the same as equation 6.18 in the text. (We can drop the subscript t for n, when n is shown to be a constant, determined solely by the constant parameters α, θ, and β). Hence employment n is always constant and does not vary over the "cycle."

Finally substitute (A6.6) and (A6.5) into (A6.1) and (A6.2) respectively to obtain equations (6.16) and (6.17).

APPENDIX 6B

It has been argued that the RBC model rests *entirely* on the assumed structure of z_t; without this assumed structure of z_t, there is no business cycle. While RBC imposes an autoregressive structure on z_t to get the cyclical behavior, it might be entirely legitimate to inquire exactly what this structure of z_t ought to be.

Recall that z_t is nothing but the disembodied technical change in the neoclassical growth model, or the "Solow residual." Is it legitimate to *decompose* a growing output y_t into a "trend" component and a "cyclical" component, y_t^c? In other words, the question is whether it is correct to write y_t as follows:

$$y_t = y_t^p + y_t^c \qquad (B6.1)$$

As shown above, this decomposition is implicit both in the Lucas model and in the RBC model.

How is y_t^p to be modeled? A casual look at most GNP(GDP) series suggests that the "trend" rate depends on the time period chosen. Is it possible that the trend itself is variable, that there is an average trend plus some unexplainable term called "innovation"? If this were true, we would write y_t^p (in log terms) as:

$$y_t^p = \mu + y_{t-1}^p + e_t \qquad (B6.2)$$

where μ is the average (quarterly) growth of real GNP (over its previous value y_{t-1}), and e_t is the innovation. If e_t has zero mean and a constant variance σ_e^2, and e_t is serially uncorrelated (i.e., $cov(e_t, e_s) = 0$ *for* $t \neq s$), then equation (B6.2) is said to be a *random walk with drift*, where the drift is μ. Then y_t^c must be *without* any trend, that is, it must be the *stationary* component of real output. If that is the case, then y_t is said to have a stochastic trend.

If, on the other hand, the innovation e_t is serially correlated, then y^p is said to be **integrated of order one**, if first differencing yields a constant plus a stationary component:

$$y_t^p - y_{t-1}^p = \mu + e_t \qquad (B6.3)$$

(Generally, the order refers to how many times a series is "differenced" in order to obtain a constant and a stationary term.) Equation (B6.3) is also called an **integrated process**, and even a 'variable with a unit root," meaning the coefficient of the lagged variable is 1.

Now substitute (B6.3) into (B6.1), and recall that the cyclical component y_t^c is nothing but a sum of past random shocks, which are serially uncorrelated. In any econometric estimation, how is e_t to be distinguished from these shocks, which are in fact transitory "innovations"? In terms of econometrics, the innovations cannot be separately identified from a single GNP(GDP) time series.

One way out is to treat the trend and stationary innovations as one, following Beveridge and Nelson (1981) and proceed with the econometric estimations. This implies assuming that the innovations arise from the same source and are perfectly correlated.

The alternative is to treat GNP(GDP) as being explicitly represented as a sum of its permanent component, modeled as a random walk with drift, and its transitory component y_t^c modeled as a stationary process so that the two innovations are *assumed* to be uncorrelated.

In their survey, Stock and Watson (1988) show that the numerical results depend heavily on which of the two alternative approaches is taken, where the estimates vary by a factor of two. Not surprisingly Nelson and Plosser (1982) questioned the validity of decomposing a GNP(GDP) time series into permanent and cyclical components, as done by Lucas and by advocates of RBC models.

In general, we know that in the *special* case of a linear dynamical system that is made up of say a trend and two cyclical components, in which each motion is independent of the other, we can get the total response of the system by simply adding the separate components. Conversely, we can decompose the observed behavior of such a system into distinct parts and observe the separate influences. However in a nonlinear system, such decomposition is not possible, or any attempted decomposition will be arbitrary.

Our knowledge of linear and nonlinear dynamic systems suggests that perhaps economic time series are strongly nonlinear, a conclusion that Goodwin (1953) came to early in his studies in business cycle theory. To quote Goodwin (1953, 1982, p. 117):

There is no such thing as a trend factor that continues to rise right through the depression. Conversely, the cycle would be quite different were it not for these special relations which give rise to the trend. Therefore we cannot separate out trend and cycle and discuss each independently.

NOTES

1 In order to derive the necessary conditions in (6.4), write the Lagrangian as follows:

$$\mathcal{L} = E_t \Bigg\{ \sum_{j=0}^{\infty} \beta^j u(c_{t+j}, \ell_{t+j}) + \lambda_{t+j} [c_t + k_{t+1} - z_t f(n_t^d, k_t^d)$$
$$- (1 - \delta) k_t + w_t (n_t - n_t^d) + r_t (k_t - k_t^d)]$$
$$+ \lambda_{t+j+1}[c_{t+j+1} + k_{t+j+1} - z_{t+j+1} f(n_{t+j+1}^d, k_{t+j+1}^d)$$
$$- (1 - \delta) k_{t+j+1} + w_{t+j+1} (n_{t+j+1} - n_{t+j+1}^d)$$
$$+ r (k_{t+j+1} - k_{t+j+1}^d)] \Bigg\}$$

Then differentiating with respect to the first argument of $u(.)$ gives (6.4a) and so on.
2 Hercowitz and Sampson (1986) have shown explicit closed form solutions using a different special case that (1) does not require 100 percent depreciation and (2) does not make employment a constant. They use a utility function, $u(c_t, 1 - n_t) = \log (c_t - an_t^\sigma)$, with $a > 0$, $\sigma > 1$, which has the disadvantage of making the marginal rate of substitution between consumption and leisure independent of c_t. There is also no possible justification for this bizarre utility function that violates dimensionality.
3 See preceding endnote.
4 To those familiar with the controversies on growth accounting, the Eichenbaum (1990) results are hardly surprising.

7

New Keynesian Business Cycle Theory

INTRODUCTION

Keynes (1936, p. 313) begins his chapter on business cycles (also called "trade cycles" in Great Britain) by claiming that as his *General Theory* shows what determines the volume of output and employment at any *given* time, his theory must be capable of explaining the phenomena of the trade cycle. He identifies the main cause of the cycle as the *cyclical* and sudden (or nonlinear) collapse of the schedule of the marginal efficiency of capital, though complicated and aggravated by fluctuations in all other Keynesian variables, particularly the propensity to consume and the state of liquidity preference.

Being familiar with the long history of business cycles under capitalism, Keynes did not expect private capitalism to overcome the cycle unaided (*ibid.*, p. 320):

In conditions of *laissez-faire* the avoidance of wide fluctuations in employment may, therefore, prove impossible without a far-reaching change in the psychology of investment markets such as there is no reason to expect. I conclude that the duty of ordering the current volume of investment cannot safely be left in private hands.

In other words Keynes had fully anticipated the results of welfare economists who later analyzed the welfare consequences of suboptimal investment as leading to the intertemporal redistribution of income, or what Graaff (1957) called the *political nature of investment* (see also, Dore [1989] p. 159).

Although there was no wholesale adoption of the above-mentioned Keynesian proposition, the maintenance of full employment became an explicit public responsibility in the United States and elsewhere after World War II. The burgeoning growth of the state sector and the growth of fiscal policy in the maintenance of full employment served not only to alter the composition of GNP(GDP) but also to affect the nature of the business cycle itself (see Gordon, 1986).

In New Classical models the large share of state expenditure in the total composition of GNP is ignored. Indeed, the state itself is viewed either as a major source of macro disturbances (Friedman) or at least as being irrelevant and ineffective. The ineffectiveness of the state is formalized in an array of ineffectiveness and neutrality propositions (Sargent, 1987). In addition, New Classical theory revived the classical proposition that a *laissez-faire* economy would settle at the "natural" or full-employment level of output, unaided – i.e. that the market mechanism was self-equilibrating. This is the exact opposite of the central result of the *General Theory* of Keynes, which demonstrated that the "natural" level of output in modern capitalism was an underemployment equilibrium, and that full employment is a *special case*. Thus Keynesian macroeconomics argues that the slump is the general case, and that since World War II prosperity has been achieved by growth in aggregate effective demand *usually*, but not exclusively, stimulated directly or indirectly through an activist monetary and fiscal policy.

It is this last-mentioned Keynesian proposition that has been formalized by the New Keynesian business cycle theory. The proposition bears repeating: The normal and general condition for capitalism is an underemployment equilibrium, a slump![1] An expansion requires intervention!

This Keynesian proposition suggests a particular *view* of the business cycle. First, it is the Keynes-Harrod-Goodwin view that every downturn irrevocably alters the entire future trajectory of the economy with the enormous welfare costs of forgone output and forgone *growth* of output. (There is some renewed interest in this "path dependence" problem; see, for example, Durlauf [1991a, b, c]; David [1988]; on which more below). Second, explaining the downturn and persistent underemployment equilibrium as a logical consequence of the actions of rational agents becomes the core of new Keynesian business cycle theory. Third, upturn or expansion is a special case, and as argued above, the result of either autonomous increases in aggregate effective demand or increases that are injected by state action, through expansionary monetary and fiscal policy. Fourth, expansionary policies are necessary and desirable following a downturn: it is the course of responsible social action, and governments fall from office if they refuse this path, or are foolish enough to call an election without reflating the economy.

It was mentioned that Keynes identified the sudden collapse of the schedule of the marginal efficiency of capital (MEC) as the main cause of the business cycle. The MEC is at first shifting to the right, calling forth more investment. But when it reverses direction and begins to shift to the left, this reversal is a *nonlinearity*. Although this is an early and crude form of nonlinearity, which is exogenously imposed, with its "ultimate" explanation relegated to the psychology of entrepreneurs, in the New Keynesian school nonlinearities in the form of wage and price rigidities arise *endogenously* as a consequence of either strict optimizing behavior, or near-optimal behavior, *given* the structural characteristics of the economy.

In the New Classical models, the particular structural characteristics of an economy are ignored. In a first approximation, this technique is always legitimate, but bringing theory closer to reality requires a reduction in the level of abstraction, just as the physics of Einstein reduced the level of abstraction implicit in the physics of Newton. New Keynesians, using the same techniques as the New Classical economists, reduce the level of abstraction by taking account of particular characteristics of modern economies. In this sense the New Keynesian theory is a *better* approximation than the New Classical approach. It goes without saying that "better" does not mean that the theory cannot be improved further.

In section 7.1 these particular characteristics of the economy, where the U.S. economy is the representative economy, are first presented as analyzed by New Keynesian economists. In section 7.2 the theory of business cycles that takes these particular characteristics into account is reviewed. A brief critique is offered in section 7.3, where the assumption of a representative agent turns out to be crucial: it leads to fallacies of composition. An alternative strand in the New Keynesian approach that is *not* subject to this criticism is the modeling of coordination failures in a multiagent economy, which is the subject of section 7.4.

7.1 THE MARKET STRUCTURE OF THE U.S. ECONOMY

As a result of the debate on the micro foundations of macroeconomics that took place during the 1960s (a debate that is outside the scope of this book; see Weintraub, 1979), both New Classical and New Keynesian economics have accepted the desirability of seeking macroeconomic explanations from microeconomics. Typically, this has meant beginning with a representative consumer and a representative firm. To obtain determinate results, this has required the use of specific functional forms of both the utility and the production functions. Although this is called a "general equilibrium approach," general conclusions are drawn for the specific examples, which is a reversal of ordinary logic. In the New Classical approach, the Keynesian aggregate expenditure categories are completely abandoned, and aggregate consumption is treated as if it were an analysis of the consumption of a single individual, who sometimes lives forever. Similarly, the labor market is treated as a single worker, and economy-wide "income" and "substitution" effects are estimated. While some are aware of the aggregation problems, all New Classical economists and perhaps many New Keynesians commit this fallacy of composition, a classic example of a false argument that any student who has taken a first course in logic would recognize. If a model does not begin by assuming optimizing behavior on the part of the representative agent (this is called a "choice-theoretic foundation"), then the model is dubbed *ad hoc*. But it is clear that the advocates of the choice-theoretic or neoclassical approach are willing to accept this fallacy of composition. [2] Nevertheless, the choice-theoretic approach has been embraced by a number of New Keynesians, who seek to generate "Keynesian" results from such an approach.

The New Keynesian approach arose in an effort to counter the growth and influence of the New Classical school with its emphasis on "free" markets and an attempt to reverse the secular disinvestment and decay of social infrastructure in the 1970s in the United States and the English-speaking countries. Perhaps the central objective of the New Keynesians was to rehabilitate the role of stabilization policy, which could best be done by adopting the microeconomic methods of the New Classical school, which were supposedly not *ad hoc*. However, the New Keynesians did reject the notion of continuous market clearance in a fully competitive economy. The challenge to the assumption of competition in New Classical models took the form of a wide-ranging theoretical and empirical analysis of the U.S. economy. They asked:

1 What is the nature of markets and what does market clearance mean?
2 What are the characteristics of the product market in the United states?
3 How are prices set, and how often do they change to reflect changing supply and demand conditions?
4 Do labor markets function like Walrasian auction markets, and is it reasonable to expect the wage to reflect the marginal product of labor?
5 Are financial markets efficient and is the interest rate determined by competition?

Finally, what sort of overall picture do the answers to the above five questions present of the nature of the U.S. economy? Before these questions are considered, it is essential to note that in a competitive model there would be no cycles, as any exogenous fall in demand for goods would lead to a fall in their prices and a lower demand for labor would lead to a fall in real wages so that both the goods and labor markets would be in equilibrium, with demand equal to supply in both markets and no involuntary unemployment. With full wage and price flexibility, there would be full utilization of capacity and any exogenous demand or supply shocks would be accommodated by the price mechanism. Any observed business cycles due to the shocks would have no welfare losses associated with them, as there would be no involuntary unemployment and no excess capacity. On the other hand, if full wage and price flexibility did not hold, then changes in demand would not lead to adjustments in supply: the price mechanism may fail to coordinate the macroeconomy with the result that cycles with involuntary unemployment and excess capacity may occur. The five questions posed above may shed light on the nature of the modern (U.S.) economy. New Keynesians have attempted at least a partial answer to these questions, as shown next.

7.1.1   The nature of markets and market clearance

New Classical business cycle theory assumes market-clearance to be fundamental to its "equilibrium" approach. But just what is market-clearance and how is it achieved? If there were well organized auction markets for all goods, why would firms devote large budgets to marketing? In practice, is the price system the only rationing device when capacity is limited?

The standard competitive model is based on the following assumptions:

1 All buying and selling decisions are static and independent of time.
2 There is full and symmetric information among buyers and sellers about the price *and* quality of the goods in question,
3 The transactions costs are zero, so that no one has to *make* markets for the buying and selling of goods,
4 Goods are allocated to the highest bidders, through fully flexible prices, that instantaneously reflect changes in supply or demand,
5 The *ceteris paribus* separation of the demand schedule and the supply schedule as conceptually distinct entities is valid.

Each of the above assumptions merits a brief discussion. Consider each in turn. The first assumption completely ignores intertemporal substitution possibilities in demand and in supply in pure competition, oligopoly, and monopoly models. The possibility of intertemporal substitution means that demand/supply changes need not have their full impact on price alone. If a consumer can wait and buy tomorrow, or a supplier can substitute production today for production tomorrow through inventories, the variance of price must necessarily fall. If demand is time shiftable, as is usually the case, then the adjustment might occur through quantity changes without large changes in price. This may simply be reflected in large swings in delivery lags. Carlton (1983, Table 1) shows that for textile mill products, paper, steel, metals and machinery, the standard deviation of the log of deliveries is two to six times that of the log of price. Thus delivery lags may be just as important as price in the equilibration of demand and supply (see also Zarnowitz, 1962, 1973).

Intertemporal substitution is indeed a rational response and the introduction of time into the simple competitive model would result in large quantity fluctuations, as consumers and producers take advantage of intertemporal substitution.

Second, the assumption of symmetric information in competitive and noncompetitive models often fails to hold. Asymmetric information, as in Akerlof's (1970) model could in fact lead to the vanishing of the entire market so that there is nothing left to clear. The principle-agent problem, identified in the Akerlof model, has been extended to the analysis of both labor and credit markets, a subject that will be discussed below.

As quality is one of the vectors of characteristics of goods (Rosen, 1974), demand/supply shocks can be partly accommodated by changes in quality so as not to affect total sales. In some cases, if this is temporary, it can even be done with the support of the customers.

Third, the zero transactions costs assumption is patently false. The making of markets takes up real resources. Organized spot and futures markets exist only for a handful of commodities. As there are definite social benefits to the creation of markets and at least some of the benefits can be privately appropriated, the lack of large numbers of such markets is indicative of their costly nature. In the absence of such organized markets, buyers typically use long-term supply agreements or enter into some form of association with sellers in such a way that their anonymity (typical in an auction market) is lost.

Indeed, the lack of this anonymity may in fact be mutually advantageous, which is relevant to the fourth assumption. The empirical evidence does not support the assumption that goods are allocated to the highest bidder; on the contrary, the evidence that correlation of price movement *across* buyers of the same product is low implies that some buyers are in a more favorable position. Steady customers obtain delivery when supplies are tight and new customers have to wait for delivery. It is indeed rational to build trusting and long-lasting relationships in business. Even dominant oligopolists prefer a price lower than one that the market would sustain for fear of inducing substitution away from the product in the long run. Saudi Arabia's moderating influence in OPEC stems from a very real concern for longterm demand. Dynamic optimization is obviously a rational response that in the short run may require informal rationing of stochastic demand in favor of regular customers even if in the short run the market-clearing price would be a higher price than that charged to regular customers.

Fourth, the information flows of 'changed' market conditions are slow for most traded goods, except for those that are traded on organized exchanges (foreign currency, metals, and other commodities such as coffee, wheat, and meat). Even for commodities traded on the exchanges, the steady buyers buy at 'producer prices' for long-term contracts, whereas occasional buyers pay the higher spot prices (Charles River Associates, 1986). For goods not traded on exchanges, which are all manufactured goods, information flows on changed demand or supply conditions do not become apparent until a time after inventory buildup or depletion in the *entire* industry becomes known.

Finally, one of the most interesting developments in some models (e.g., DeVany and Saving [1977]; Gould [1978]), is that buyers prefer to buy from a particular firm not because of its pricing policy but because of its inventory policy. If firms stock inventory to satisfy customers, then the variability of consumers' demand for a product will affect the firm's costs. Therefore the cost function of the firm now depends on the **demand characteristics** of customers. Hence in these models the conceptual separation of demand and supply functions is lost: supply now in part depends on demand. Market-clearance now lacks the simplicity of the equilibrium of a competitive model; the auction market for most goods is simply irrelevant.

7.1.2 Characteristics of the product market

Although market structure is usually studied by experts in industrial organization, Hall (1986) investigated market structure through time series variation in individual industries associated with the aggregate business cycle. Specifically, he investigated whether there was evidence of market power, indicating departures from the competitive model. For with market power, there is no longer a presumption of full and efficient utilization of resources.

In order to determine the nature and extent of market power, Hall focuses on two issues crucial to market structure: the divergence (over the cycle) between price and marginal cost in some fifty U.S. industries, and whether the market power translates into excess profits. But actual data do not show excess profits, only normal rates of return. Could it be that excess profits are somehow dissipated? If so, how are they dissipated? Hall proposes some hypotheses, which will be considered in some detail next.

Divergence between price and marginal cost

A natural definition of marginal cost arises over the business cycle. In the expansion phase, firms increase output, but this increase in output is obtained by incurring extra costs of production. The ratio of the cost increase to the output increase is marginal cost (MC). Alternatively, if $C(Q)$ is the cost function, then

$$MC = \frac{\partial C(Q)}{\partial Q}$$

which means holding the capital stock constant. In practice, some of the change in output will be due to technological change, and an adjustment for that must be made in order not to underestimate marginal cost. Then in discrete terms marginal cost MC can be estimated as follows:

$$MC = w\,\frac{\Delta N}{\Delta Q - \theta Q} \tag{7.1}$$

where w is the hourly wage, N is hours of work, Q is the quantity of output and θ is the rate of technical progress. Hence θQ is the adjustment. Suppose that technical progress can be modeled as

$$\theta_t = \theta + u_t \tag{7.2}$$

where u_t is a random variable uncorrelated with the business cycle. This differs from the real business cycle school in that Hall does not assume that technical progress or productivity shocks themselves cause the business cycle.

Next define the ratio of price to marginal cost as μ:

$$\mu \equiv \frac{P}{MC} \tag{7.3}$$

It is clear that μ is markup; in a competitive industry $\mu = 1$. Substituting (7.2) into (7.1) and then using that expression in (7.3) we have:

$$MC = \frac{P}{\mu} = \frac{w\Delta N}{\Delta Q - (\theta + u)Q}$$

Solve for ΔQ:

$$\Delta Q = \mu\,\frac{w}{P}\Delta N + (\theta + u)Q$$

In rates of change this becomes

$$\frac{\Delta Q}{Q} = \mu \frac{wN}{PQ} \cdot \frac{\Delta N}{N} + \theta + u$$

Let Δq and Δn be the rates of change, and let α be the revenue share of labor wN/PQ, and the above expression can be written as

$$\Delta q = \mu\alpha\Delta n + \theta + u \tag{7.4}$$

Under perfect competition, $\mu = 1$ and α is the elasticity of the production function with respect to labor input. Note too that Solow's method of measuring productivity growth was to assume competition ($\mu = 1$) and estimate θ as $\Delta q - \alpha\Delta n$, which is the "Solow residual," or the part of output growth not explained by growth in labor input.

Hall estimates equation (7.4) by using U.S. data for the period 1949 to 1978. He finds that the value of $\mu = 1$ (competition) is decisively rejected in favor of market power, and the value of μ ranges from 1.5 to 3.

Second, Hall finds the Solow residual θ to be procyclical, which is also incompatible with competition. In pure competition, if workers are idle, then marginal cost is very low, as additional labor hours are available at near-zero cost, so that price should fall to this low marginal cost, and the low price should stimulate demand to the extent that workers will no longer be idle. On the other hand a decline in productivity in a downturn (i.e., a low θ when output is low) suggests labor hoarding, when firms hang on to labor in anticipation of a future upturn, without changing prices now. We can conclude that procyclical productivity is compatible only with noncompetitive behavior.

Excess profits

The evidence on market power suggests the possibility that U.S. industry must make excess or pure profits, although *actual* and reported business profits represent no more than a reasonable return on capital. Hall indeed finds evidence of pure profits – typically of the order of 20 percent per dollar of sales. The pure profit should in theory encourage entry that would drive prices down and eliminate pure profits. But entry does not take place mainly because minimum threshold scales of plants are large and the existing firms in the industries have excess capacity, implying that firms are operating on the decreasing portion of their average cost curves. The excess capacity implies that firms have a significant amount of fixed costs. Potential entrants into the industry foresee that they cannot cover the fixed costs at a price that would result from competition between the existing firms in the industry and the new entrants. The pure profits of the existing firms are dissipated in the large fixed costs and in advertising costs that are necessary to maintain product differentiation. Thus market power does not lead to entry as fixed costs serve as barriers to entry, and the fixed costs themselves absorb a good part of latent monopoly profit. The result is that *actual* profits are not very high.[3]

Finally, what lessons can be drawn for macroeconomics from the above analysis? First, productivity is procyclical, which suggests there must be a significant amount of labor hoarding, as small fluctuations in employment produce large fluctuations in output. A competitive firm is unlikely to let its work force remain idle; it can sell additional output without depressing the price. Unless the price is so low that it cannot cover the cost of materials, the firm can make added profit by putting all of its workers to work. But a firm with market power may well hoard labor and not expand output in a temporary downturn, because the additional output may not increase profit at all as the decline in price may fully offset the increase in sales volume.

Second, Hall's finding of excess capacity suggests that it is physically possible for aggregate supply to be highly elastic. Thus firms are capable of increasing their output above their *normal* level by hiring only a little additional new labor. And since price far exceeds marginal cost, the increment to GNP(GDP) from the added output will be worth more than the added cost. Thus output in such an economy is constrained by demand; a major war, or a prolonged monetary stimulus can draw forth huge increases in GNP(GDP). But a prolonged monetary or fiscal stimulus will also lead to even more capacity being added. This is because high demand that is expected to be long-lasting raises expected profits in the existing market niches, and also makes new niches sufficiently profitable for exploitation. In the long run the expected pure profit will be zero, but with a higher total capacity.

Third, industries with excess capacity and market power have no incentive to expand output to full employment; such firms will set prices to maximize profit, but they will pick a price where profit is locally unaffected by small changes in price. That is, the curve showing profit as a function of price is flat at its maximum. Consequently, within some region the firm cannot improve its profit by a significant amount even if the cost of changing the price and moving to a higher output is small. Thus the firm keeps its price at the previous level even though new conditions justify a different level of output. This important idea is formalized in the theoretical section (7.2) below.

Fourth, in a competitive model, marginal cost rises with output. In such a model a profit maximizing level of output is well defined. But when an equilibrium of output is along a flat portion of the marginal cost curve, then we may either view it as multiple equilibria or think of it as indeterminate. With indeterminacy, the firm perceives itself as capturing a fixed amount of profit no matter what its price and output are. Thus with flat marginal costs, adjusting price and output decisions are not a matter of priority for management. Other areas of management, such as better products, more effective advertising, and reductions in overhead and production costs receive higher priority.

Hall's analysis is free of transcendental and nonverifiable expressions; its elegance lies in the sparse theoretical structure with which he is able to show empirically that the product market in the United States is far from the competitive ideal; it is in fact characterized by monopolistic competition, a finding that must influence the formulation of New Keynesian business cycle theory.

7.1.3 The nature of prices

How are prices set, and how often do they change to equilibrate demand and supply? There is a large literature in industrial organization on administered prices that fail to respond to changes in supply and demand. Earlier studies of price rigidity have relied exclusively on price indices collected by the U.S. Bureau of Labor Statistics. The use of BLS data has been criticized on the grounds that they are inaccurate measures of transaction prices. Stigler and Kindahl (1970) sought to remedy this deficiency by collecting price data on actual transactions. Their price indices of average transaction prices are more flexible than BLS price indices. Because the use of indices can hide the behavior of individual transaction prices, Carlton (1986) utilized the Stigler-Kindahl data on manufacturing.

Although Carlton found significant price rigidity in many industries, the degree of price rigidity varies enormously across product groups. For instance, steel, chemicals, and cement have average rigidities that exceed one year, while household appliances, plywood, and nonferrous metals have average price rigidities of less than five months.

Second, even for homogeneous commodities the correlation of price changes across buyers is low. This suggests that allocative mechanisms other than price may be at work. Nonprice rationing may be an efficient response to economic uncertainty.

Third, there is a positive correlation between price rigidity and length of buyer-seller association, but there is also a negative correlation between the length of buyer-seller association and average absolute price change. This suggests that the longer a buyer and seller deal with each other, the smaller is the average price change when prices do change.

Finally, the level of industry concentration is strongly correlated with rigid prices: the more concentrated the industry, the longer is the average spell of price rigidity.

One of Carlton's main conclusions is that allocation of goods does not occur through price alone, and there is good reason to search for new theories that consider non-market-clearing behavior.

Although Carlton could not find evidence of downward price rigidity, Domowitz, Hubbard and Peterson (1986a, b, c) found that price-cost margins in concentrated industries are procyclical. But if margins are never negative then there is a *prima facie* case for downward price rigidity that could be investigated further.

Although the U.S. economy is the prototype for this section, there is evidence of price rigidity from countries other than the United States (Gordon, 1983; Encaoua and Geroski, 1984).

7.1.4 The nature of the labor market

In the competitive model, labor is treated like any other input such as electricity or raw material. The price of labor is nothing but its marginal productivity. If labor were "sold" in a competitive auction market, then its demand and supply would determine its price, and in equilibrium, the real wage would equal the marginal product of labor. This occurs because the demand curve for labor is nothing but the marginal physical product of labor. Consequently, the point that is chosen on the demand curve depends on the supply curve of labor. By definition, in equilibrium demand and supply of labor are equal. In such a model there can be no involuntary unemployment because the amount supplied is chosen by workers.

Unfortunately, labor is *not* like any other input; suppliers of labor cannot "leave" their supplies with firms. Workers typically undertake to work for a given period, or the length of period of work is left unspecified in an implicit contract. Why have real wages risen even when there is no scarcity of labor? If it is argued that the increase in the real wage is due to an increase in the marginal productivity of labor, why do firms make investments that increase the real wage that they will have to pay? When there is unemployment, why does the wage not fall to clear the market?

In a competitive model, *all* workers receive the market-clearing real wage. The worker who shirks (Shapiro and Stiglitz, 1984) could be fired, but in the competitive model such a worker is immediately hired, as there can be no unemployment. To induce workers not to shirk, the firm pays a wage greater than the market-clearing wage. But if it pays one firm to raise wages, then it must pay all firms to raise wages, in which case the incentive not to shirk disappears again. However, when firms raise wages, their demand for labor falls, which creates unemployment. With the prospect of unemployment, the worker again has an incentive to work diligently, and the firm is willing to reward such effort on the part of the worker. That is the basic idea behind the efficiency wage hypothesis (Yellen, 1984), considered next.

Suppose that production is determined by the following function:

$$Y = af(L), f' > 0, f'' < 0 \tag{7.5}$$

where Y is output, L is labor services, and a is an exogenous technology parameter.

However, instead of L representing labor-hours, treat L as the number of efficiency units of labor, where an efficiency unit of labor is the size of the labor force N multiplied by the level of *effort*, e, per worker. Suppose that e is an increasing function of the real wage w. Then $L = e(w)N$. Now real profits of the firm, denoted by Π/P are given by

$$\Pi/P = af[e(w)N] - wN \tag{7.6}$$

The representative firm will maximize profits by setting both the real wage w and the number of workers N. That is,

$$\max_{w,N} \left\{ \Pi/P = af[e(w)N] - wN \right\} \tag{7.7}$$

The first-order conditions for a maximum are given by

$$\frac{\partial(\Pi/P)}{\partial N} = af'e - w = 0 \tag{7.8}$$

$$\frac{\partial(\Pi/P)}{\partial w} = af'e' - 1)N = 0 \tag{7.9}$$

Substitute (7.8) into (7.9) and divide both sides by N:

$$\left(\frac{w}{e}e' - 1 \right) = 0$$

or

$$\frac{w}{e} \cdot \frac{\partial e}{\partial w} = 1 \tag{7.10}$$

Equation (7.10) states that the profit-maximizing wage rate (the *efficiency wage*) requires that the elasticity of effort to that wage be equal to unity. If the efficiency wage is greater than the market-clearing wage, then involuntary unemployment will exist in equilibrium. It will equal the market-clearing wage only by fluke; it cannot be lower than the marketclearing wage. Therefore it must be higher, for otherwise there is an incentive to shirk.

The efficiency wage hypothesis is incentive compatible; it avoids adverse selection (Weiss, 1980) and the firm pays a premium (efficiency wage minus market-clearing wage), for premium effort, although Akerlof (1984) has modeled it as a gift exchange. Incentive-compatibility should also reduce labor turnover (Salop, 1979), which is wasteful and disrupts production, because the higher the turnover, the more time must be spent on retraining.

The efficiency wage hypothesis is an alternative to the competitive theory of the labor market, for in the latter workers receive wages equal to their opportunity cost, and job attributes that do not affect the utility of workers should have no effect on the level of wages. Therefore, for equally skilled workers the real wage should be the same irrespective of the worker's industry affiliation. This is indeed the hypothesis that Krueger and Summers (1988) consider in their empirical work. Their main conclusion is that the existence of significant wage differentials for equally skilled workers does not support the competitive model. This evidence is worth considering briefly.

The authors estimate the impact of industry affiliation in explaining wage differentials in the United States, after controlling for human-capital, race and gender, working conditions, and other factors. They find substantial interindustry wage differentials that persist over time as well. The stability of the wage structure is such that other explanations of wage differentials, such as the short-run immobility of labor or transitory labor-demand shocks, are not plausible.

To appreciate the flavor of the results, consider one or two examples. The estimations show that in 1984 the average employee in the mining industry earned wages 24 percent higher than the average employee in all industries, after controlling for human capital and demographic background; in 1984 the industry differentials ranged from a high of 37 percent above the mean in the petroleum industry to 37 percent below the mean in private-household services.

Overall the results show that durable manufacturing products and chemical industries tend to be high wage industries, while wholesale, retail, and service industries tend to be low wage industries. The overall variability in industry wages is measured by the standard deviation of the industry wage differentials. The results show that industry variations in wages are substantial. In 1984 the standard deviation of industry wage differentials was 14 percent; in 1979 it was 11 percent, and in 1973 it was 13 percent.

The demonstration of important interindustry wage differentials creates a *prima facie* case for involuntary unemployment; the wage differentials provide a motivation for 'wait' unemployment: workers wait to get into a high-paying job rather than be locked in a low-paying one (Hall, 1975; Bulow and Summers, 1986). This suggests that the natural rate of unemployment is likely to be inefficiently high. Consequently, Pareto improvements are possible. In fact, Shapiro and Stiglitz (1984) go on to show that there is scope for government intervention both with respect to unemployment benefits and subsidies to increase employment.

7.1.5   The nature of financial markets

There are two dimensions of the financial markets: their nature, as well as the problem of incorporating the financial markets into a complete macro model. Both issues are worth considering.

Regarding the nature of financial markets, an obvious question to ask is whether financial markets are *efficient*, in the full sense of the competitive model. But as Tobin (1984) notes, there are at least *four* meanings of efficiency that can be applied to the financial markets.

The first, Tobin called **information arbitrage efficiency**. For example, in a well-organized and well-informed market for foreign exchange, it should not be possible to gain by exploiting differences in cross rates; an efficient market would eliminate such anomalies quickly. The securities markets are also efficient in this sense: a randomly chosen portfolio of stocks should do just as well as a professionally managed portfolio.

The second sense of efficiency is that prices of financial assets should reflect the future expected stream of earnings. This Tobin calls **fundamental valuation efficiency**. But the extreme volatility of both stocks (Shiller, 1981) and bonds (Golub, 1983) suggests that even the mean price, computed over a period, is unlikely to reflect the real underlying value of a share. Systematic undervaluation often leads to takeovers, and although the takeover is a market phenomenon, it reflects the periodic existence of unexploited opportunities for gain – which casts doubt on information arbitrage efficiency of equities. Such opportunities arising discontinuously does say something about the efficiency of the stock market.

Third, a system of financial markets is efficient if there are **insurance markets** for *all* contingencies in the Arrow-Debreu sense. Only a handful of such insurance markets exist, partly because *making* markets costs resources, and if they are established, very few succeed because such markets are too thin to operate (Carlton, 1989). Even the existing futures markets would not survive if they depended entirely on true hedgers, as most trades (perhaps as much as 90 per cent) on futures exchanges are of a purely speculative nature.

Lastly, the financial markets have an economic function directly useful to both producers and consumers (**functional efficiency**): the pooling of risks, the provision of a means of payments through a network of banks and other intermediaries, and the mobilization of savings for investment. When we consider the size of the financial markets by some index, a very small fraction of their total transactions is geared toward financing real investment in any direct way, or to financing international trade. The thousands of trillions of dollars transacted *daily* – check clearings, transfers, bills of exchange, etc.– are mainly of a speculative nature. This is made possible by a vast amount of resources tied up in the financial sector: employment, computers, and real estate.

In the provision of such services, whether they be new investment or speculative positions, the financial sector does not compete in the sense of the purely competitive model; rather it engages in product differentiation through advertising, personal attention, or other gimmicks. Therefore this sector, made up of banks, commodity exchanges, insurance companies, trusts, and brokerage houses, is an oligopolistic structure. Most of its transactions are akin to gambling (see Susan Strange's [1986] *Casino Capitalism*).

Unfortunately, although most of the financial activity is speculative, the financial sector nevertheless affects real activity, as stock market valuations surround the real assets of corporations in a shroud of uncertainty, which is partly positive and partly negative. It is positive because no past investment is always a "sure thing"; the markets continue to pass judgments on the investment actions of companies. This makes companies sensitive to current market conditions, so that they evaluate new investments cautiously; it makes corporations continuously evaluate both optimal capacity and its location. It is negative because financial markets may aggravate business cycles, as they did in the Great Depression (Bernanke, 1983).

Incorporating such a financial sector into a macromodel of business cycles is by no means an easy task. If it is granted that the very large speculative activity does not affect the real economy, there still remains the rather obvious fact that it is finance which is the means of carrying out investment and conducting daily business. The earlier static macro model, the *IS-LM* model, acknowledged this by incorporating outside money and the rate of interest. But outside money is now typically a small fraction of the means of payment utilized by a modern economy.

Even if the central bank can control the narrowly defined stock of outside money, the availability of close money substitutes may fully adjust to offset changes in the demand or supply of outside money (Gurley and Shaw, 1955; Godley, 1984). If this is true, then the existence of money substitutes makes money as a means of payment essentially endogenous (Wray, 1990): any desired volume of credit can be created by the intermediaries to meet the requirements of transactions. Even reserve requirements do not pose a constraint in a capital market that is in effect international in scope.

So why does a business cycle downturn occur? Not because of the lack of available credit; there must be real factors that account for the downturn. Nevertheless every recession in the United States since the mid–1950s was preceded and triggered by a credit crunch (Eckstein and Sinai, 1986). Late in the expansion phase, the demand for credit accelerates, but an *accompanying* accelerating inflation in the first place increases the demand for credit still further; in the second place the central bank becomes alarmed by the accelerating inflation and initiates a credit crunch through tight monetary policy. As interest rates rise, there is credit rationing, and firms place a premium on liquidity, and reduce total spending. They also reduce new hiring, and a downturn is well underway. In this way, real and financial aspects of the cycle are integrated.

According to Eckstein and Sinai (1986, p. 53), "(t)he crunch is at the heart of the business cycle mechanism, particularly the upper turning point." The trick is to produce a model that reflects the integration of the real and financial aspects of the cycle. It is unlikely that credit market conditions are the dominant factor in explaining cycles, but they may indeed aggravate the cycle. This is the approach taken by Scheinkman and Weiss (1986), who show that borrowing constraints can increase the variability of consumption, output, and employment. Consider a negative productivity shock. In a frictionless competitive environment with perfect capital markets, consumers can insure against the risks involved when the negative productivity shock occurs by borrowing on the capital markets, which thus smooths out consumption. However, in the absence of perfect capital and insurance markets, consumers must self-insure by adjusting consumption, saving, and labor supply. Blinder (1987) has also shown that borrowing constraints may increase the variability of output in an *IS-LM* model. But the integration of the real and financial aspects of the cycle is far from complete.

In summary, the answer to the five questions about the nature of the U.S. economy is that it is characterized by imperfect competition in the goods, labor, and financial markets. The market structure is the single most important fact for business cycle theory for New Keynesians. Such an economy is characterized by price rigidities, wages above market-clearing levels, credit rationing, and profits that should be high but are dissipated through socially undesirable expenditures in advertising, product differentiation, and conspicuous consumption by large corporations and their officials.

7.2 THE NEW KEYNESIAN BUSINESS CYCLE THEORY

Not all the real features of the U.S. economy outlined above can be reflected in a single model of cycles. But the single most important feature of monopolistic competition is captured well in the "menu cost" model of cycles. It also has the advantage that in such a model price rigidity is derived as a consequence of optimizing behavior.

It should be emphasized that New Keynesians agree with the New Classical school on two crucial assumptions. One is the representative agent approach, which involves assuming utility maximization as the fundamental starting point. If the representative agent also owns the firm then utility cannot be maximized unless profits are also maximized.

The second crucial assumption that both schools share is the quantity theory of money. The only difference here is that the New Classical position holds that money can have real effects only if it is an unanticipated surprise; the New Keynesian position is that money has real short-term effects because of nominal price rigidities or because of 'near-rational' (suboptimal) behavior, where the marginal cost of suboptimal behavior is negligible or 'second order' to the agent. But both the New Classical and the New Keynesian schools accept the *long-run neutrality of money.* Thus both schools are committed to the microeconomics research program – that is, explaining business cycles from the fundamentals of microeconomic behavior.

In this section, it is shown that price rigidity is an optimizing response on the part of the agent. The consequence is both the short-run nonneutrality of money *and* a slump that is long lasting. This is followed by a brief consideration of near-rationality.

7.2.1 The menu cost model

The inspiration for the sticky price-menu cost model comes from Keynes himself, who presented three cases that violated the automatic tendency for the restoration of a full employment equilibrium. One of these cases was that of the existence of a nominal wage floor. Mankiw (1985) generalizes this idea but in a microeconomic framework.

Consider a monopoly firm facing a constant cost function (7.11) and an inverse demand function (7.12):

$$C = kqN \qquad (7.11)$$

$$P = f(q)N \qquad (7.12)$$

where C is the total nominal cost of producing q, k is a constant, and P is the nominal price received by the firm if it sells the output q. N is a nominal scale variable representing aggregate-demand, which increases costs C and price level P proportionately. An increase in the nominal scale variable shifts cost and demand functions proportionately, which would increase the price P_m (see figure 7.1). A proportional increase in price would leave the quantity supplied, q_m, unchanged, as the monopolist must equate marginal revenue and marginal cost, which have both risen by the same factor. Next, let $c = C/N$ and $p = P/N$, so that equations (7.11) and (7.12) become:

$$c = kq \tag{7.11a}$$

$$p = f(q) \tag{7.12b}$$

Written in this form, the firm maximizes profits $\Pi = f(q)q - kq$, which gives

$$q_m = \frac{k - f(q_m)}{f'(q_m)}$$

where $f'(q_m) < 0$ *and* $p_m = f(q_m)$ (see figure 7.2). Total surplus is the sum of consumer surplus plus monopoly profits, as shown in figure 7.2. The firm's nominal price is $p_m N$.

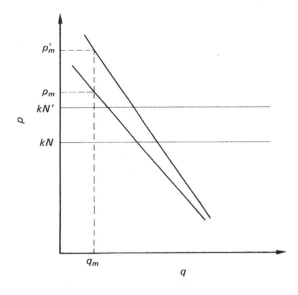

Figure 7.1　A Monopoly Firm with Constant Marginal Cost

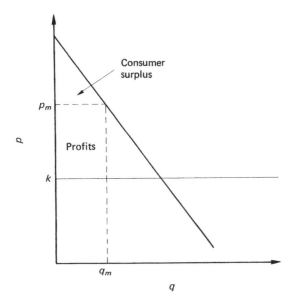

Figure 7.2   Consumer Surplus Under Monopoly

Suppose now that the firm must set the price one period ahead based on expected aggregate demand N^e. Thus nominal price is $p_m N^e$. If it turns out to be incorrect, then the observed price is $p_0 = p_m(N^e/N)$. If $N < N^e$, p_0 is higher than p_m (see figure 7.3). Then the firm's profits are lower by the area $B - A$. It should be obvious that as the profit-maximizing price is p_m, a higher price must mean lower profits. Hence $B - A$ is positive, or $B > A$. Consequently, total surplus is reduced by the area $B + C$. But $B + C > B - A$ because $B > A$. This means that the reduction in welfare due to a contraction in aggregate demand is greater than the reduction in the firm's profits.

First, if the firm could correctly anticipate its loss of profit, and it faced a menu cost z to change prices, then it would do so if $B - A > z$. But from the social point of view, the price should be lowered *at least* to p_m in order to regain $B + C$ that would otherwise be lost.[4]

Second, if there is a contraction in demand, and $B + C > z$ but $z > B - A$, then the firm will not cut the price to p_m, even though doing so would be socially optimal. The inefficiency arises because there is an external social benefit (i.e., an externality) equal to $C + A$ that does not enter into the private calculation of the monopolist.

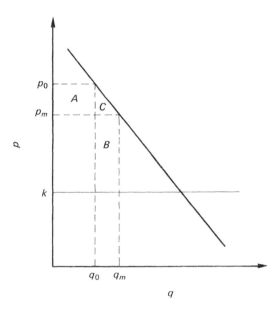

Figure 7.3   Reduction in Total Surplus $B + C$

One measure of this externality is the ratio of the social benefit $B + C$ to the private benefit $B - A$. Since the firm would adjust the price to a profit maximizing p_m but not to the socially optimal price k, the ratio will approach infinity as the demand change approaches zero. Alternatively, we may say that the increment to profit $B - A$ is of second order but the social benefit $B + C$ is of first order.

One more example is worth considering. Suppose there were an expansion of aggregate demand. The observed price p_0 will now be below p_m, and output q_0 above q_m. Now price is lower and output is above the monopoly level, so profits are reduced by $D - F$, as shown in Figure 7.4. Again $D - F > 0$ because the profit-maximizing output is q_m. Total surplus is increased by $E + F$. Here too the firm will raise its price to p_m only if $D - F > z$.

We may conclude that an expansion in aggregate demand may reduce welfare by no more than the menu cost, and may even increase welfare. A contraction in aggregate demand unambiguously reduces welfare, possibly by much more than the menu cost.

The model displays an asymmetry between contractions and expansions, as the natural rate of output is below the social optimum. Profit-maximizing price adjustment following an expansion is likely to be higher than in a contraction. Thus from a social point of view the

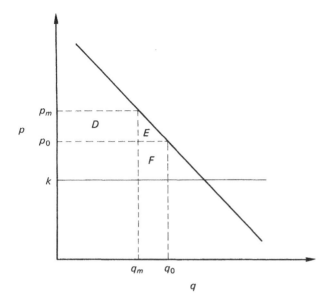

Figure 7.4   An Expansion Increases Total Surplus by $E + F$

nominal price level may get stuck at too high a level, so that markets fail to clear. Thus the model predicts downward rigidity of prices but not upward rigidity. In particular, if costs go up during an expansion, prices go up, too. But in a contraction, most fixed costs do not go down, particularly if labor is hoarded in anticipation of a future expansion. In a contraction the monopolist tolerates excess capacity, but profit maximization *entails* excess capacity anyway; a bit more excess capacity does not make much difference, a point we turn to in the next subsection.

The small menu cost (of changing prices) turns out to impart price rigidity to optimizing behavior in a very simple model with no interindustry purchases. If interfirm and interindustry transactions were included, then the failure of one firm to reduce price following a contraction would mean that the costs of other firms that buy from it would exhibit rigidity. Consequently, the buying firms would have no incentive to cut prices when their costs have remained unchanged. In an interindustry structure, price rigidity is likely to increase. Thus when there is no Walrasian auctioneer who costlessly adjusts prices, the rigidity of prices means changes in money supply will be non-neutral in general.

Suppose that the demand for product i depends on aggregate spending and on the firm's relative price:

$$y_i^D = (P_i/P)^{-\eta}Y \qquad (7.13)$$

Let aggregate demand be given by a simple quantity theory equation:

$$Y = M/P \qquad (7.14)$$

Substituting (7.14) into (7.13) yields:

$$Y_i^D = (P_i/P)^{-\eta}(M/P) \qquad (7.15)$$

According to equation (7.15), firm i's demand depends on its relative price and on real money, which represents aggregate demand. Changes in real money shift the demand curve facing firm i, and the firm's price determines its *position* on the demand curve.

Now consider a fall in nominal money M, say by a factor λ, where $\lambda < 1$. If firm i does not reduce its price to λP_i, then the nominal rigidity contributes to aggregate price rigidity. But if *all* firms reduced their prices by the fall in the money supply, then the aggregate price level would be λP, so that the demand curve would be

$$Y_i^D = (\lambda P_i/\lambda P)^{-\eta}(\lambda M/\lambda P)$$

which is the same as equation (7.15). Hence it is nominal rigidity that yields **nonneutrality of money**. The fall in nominal money is an externality, which if all firms acted together they could neutralize.

The importance of the externality becomes clear if one considers a recession caused by contractionary monetary policy. This causes the aggregate demand curve to shift inward, which leads to a first-order loss in profits. But a firm in monopolistic competition faces only a second-order gain by lowering its price, because a lower price leads to increased volume of sales but a lower per unit revenue. Hence total profits may not be changed very much.

The conclusion is that no single firm can end the contraction by its own action. In other words, the externality invites collective action, or "coordination." The presence of a macroeconomic externality can also be analyzed as a **coordination failure**, as done by Cooper and John (1988), Diamond (1982), Howitt and McAffee (1988), and others.

Coordination failures generally require more than one agent; such failures are discussed further in section 7.4.

7.2.2 Near-rationality

In the above subsection it was argued that when the consequences of actions are of second-order importance, the adjustment may not be carried out. This idea has an important dimension that can be established independently of small-menu costs. It again entails taking into account the market structure of the economy, namely monopolistic competition in the goods market.

Even if there are no menu costs, inertial wage and price behavior may be explained as **near-rational** if the losses expected due to suboptimal action are small. Near-rational behavior may nonetheless impose first-order changes in aggregate real activity. That is, a small amount of nonmaximizing behavior can cause a significant business cycle in response to money supply shocks that would be neutral in the absence of such inertial behavior.

Consider a shock that perturbs an equilibrium in which all agents are maximizing. Then wages and prices that do not change in response to the shock may be described as near-rational for any agent whose objective function is *differentiable* as a function of her/his own wages and prices. This differentiability does not hold in a competitive model, as explained below.

In the competitive model a firm that pays a wage lower than the market wage w^* can hire no labor. At the wage w^*, labor availability jumps discontinuously and so do profits. If the firm pays a wage higher than w^*, its profits fall below the market rates of return and it will be forced to lower the wage to w^* or terminate operations. Therefore in the competitive model, profit as a function of the firm's wage is not differentiable at the optimum wage w^*.

The same applies to prices. At the market-clearing price p^*, the firm in the competitive model can sell all it wants. But at $p > p^*$, its sales are zero. At a price $p < p^*$, its sales are infinite but its profits are below normal. Therefore in a competitive model, $p < p^*$ and $w > w^*$ confer no benefits to the firm.

In contrast, in a monopolistic competition model with differentiated products, a firm's profits vary differentiably with its own price, as sales do not go to zero when prices depart marginally from prices charged by others. The same argument holds for wages – that is, the firm's profit function is differentiable in wages: when firms offer a wage $w > w^*$, part of the higher cost is offset by increased productivity (efficiency wages).

To illustrate near-rationality, consider a firm that initially sets its price at the profit-maximizing level, but does not adjust the price after a fall in nominal money supply. Let P be the price before the change in money supply, and P^* the new profit-maximizing price that the firm would have set had it adjusted in response to the fall in money supply. Let $\Pi(.)$ denote profit as a function of its price. Using a Taylor expansion (Ball, Mankiw and Romer, 1988), we can approximate the firm's profit loss from not adjusting as:

$$\Pi(P^*) - \Pi(P) \simeq \Pi'(P^*)(P^* - P) - \tfrac{1}{2}\Pi''(P^*)(P^* - P)^2$$

However, as P^* maximizes profits, $\Pi'(P^*)$ is zero. Thus the profit loss from not adjusting is proportional to the square of $(P^* - P)$, which is of second-order importance as long as P is close to P^*. In other words, the cost of price rigidity to the firm is small. However the rigidity will have first-order macroeconomic effects. For example, with the simple aggregate supply curve in equation (7.15), price rigidity implies a change in aggregate output proportional to the change in money supply.

The effect on social welfare is large, as shown by areas $B + C$ in figure 7.3 and $E + F$ in figure 7.4. Under imperfect competition, the profit-maximizing price is socially suboptimal. The price is too high and output is too low. Thus at P^* the first derivative of welfare with respect to the firm's price is negative – that is, welfare would rise if the price fell below P^* (to the point where $P^* = k$ in figure 7.1). Nonadjustment to a fall in money supply implies that $P > P^*$. Since the first derivative of welfare is negative, the welfare loss is first order. But the cost of the rigidity to the firm is only second order. Near-rationality does not impose a large cost to the firm, but the rigidity can be seen to explain the nonneutrality of money as well as large business cycles.

7.3 NEW KEYNESIAN BUSINESS CYCLE THEORY: AN ASSESSMENT

New Keynesian business cycle theory explains the nonneutrality of money through nominal rigidities, where the rigidities are derived from optimizing or near-rational behavior. The theory is based on sound theoretical and empirical work on the goods market, the labor market, and the financial market. The empirical work supports a framework of imperfect competition and market power. Hence prices are endogenously set without resorting to some mythical Walrasian auctioneer who arrives at equilibrium prices in a costless manner.

The theory relies on demonstrating the existence of price rigidity at the *micro* level, asserting implicitly that it is sufficient for aggregate *macro* level price rigidity. Is this warranted? Is a micro description adequate for explaining the business cycle, which is an aggregate phenomenon? The rest of this section attempts to answer these questions.

While it is tempting to consider the entire question of the relationship between microeconomics and macroeconomics, such an undertaking is beyond the scope of this book. But it is not possible to evade the issue completely: reference has already been made to the adoption of the *representative agent* as an analytical starting point, which was designed to avoid the (aggregate) Keynesian expenditure categories, and the analysis that followed from it. Friedman did this largely to rehabilitate the classical quantity theory tradition, although the use of the representative agent or methodological individualism is alien to the classical tradition; it is specifically a *neo*classical invention in economics, though the influence of methodological individualism can be seen in other social sciences.

Yet it is commonly perceived that the outcome of the debate on the so-called "microfoundations of macroeconomics" was that macroeconomics can be done "properly" only by starting with the behavior of *micro* units, the household and the firm who are referred to as 'agents.' In the conclusion to his survey of microfoundations, Roy Weintraub (1979, p.161) states clearly that the question of what constitutes the appropriate foundations for macroeconomics is an open one. In logic, such a common consent fallacy is called a *consensus gentium* fallacy. It involves arguing that something is true on the basis that the majority of people (economists in this case) believe it, or that it is a universal truth held by all people at all times. New Keynesians like Peter Diamond and other Keynesians like Negishi have explicitly rejected the Walrasian auctioneer as the appropriate "foundation" of their macro analysis. Yet the representative agent persists in the analysis of many New Keynesians. But the proposition that characteristics of the aggregate merely reflect characteristics of individual units may in fact be a fallacy of composition. Such a fallacy is now beginning to be investigated, both in Europe and in North America (e.g., Garretsen and Janssen [1989]; Bertola and Caballero [1990]; Caballero [1991]).

Before turning to that, it might be useful to define a *fallacy of composition*. In *Dictionary of Philosophy*, Angeles (1981, p. 97) defines it as:

Arguing (a) that what is true of each part of a whole is also necessarily true of the whole, or (b) that what is true of some parts of a whole is also necessarily true of the whole itself. Example: 'Each member (or some members) of the team is married; therefore the team also has (must have) a wife.' Inferring that a collection has certain characteristics merely on the basis that its parts have them erroneously proceeds from regarding the collection distributively to regarding it collectively.

Consequently a whole host of propositions derived from the behavior of micro units (price rigidity or excess capacity at the level of the firm, near-optimal or suboptimal behavior) need have no significance for the analysis of the aggregate. Thus the existence of price rigidity due to menu cost at the level of the firm is quite consistent with complete aggregate price flexibility, as demonstrated by Caplin and Spulber (1987). It is clear from this work that the aggregate business cycle in New Keynesian literature results from aggregate price rigidity which in turn rests on the positive menu cost at the firm level. But it is the representative-agent framework that leads to the fallacy of composition: when one firm fails to adjust the price, all firms are assumed to fail to adjust the price. This is then the basis of aggregate rigidity, which then leads to the nonneutrality of money in Akerlof and Yellen [1985].[5] Once we depart from the representative agent, and consider *a distribution of firms*, the aggregate rigidity disappears.

Menu costs impose integer constraints in pricing; if the profit-maximizing price is S, and the menu cost is z, then $S - z = s$, where s is the trigger point at which firms raise their prices back to S. This is called an (S,s) pricing policy (Barro [1972]; Sheshinski and Weiss [1977, 1983]). In a model similar in conception to the (S,s) pricing model,[6] Caballero (1991) analyzes the sources of several fallacies of composition in representative agent models. These fallacies arise because direct microeconomic arguments do not take into account the strong restrictions that probability theory puts on the joint behavior of a large number of units whose actions are not fully synchronized.

Caballero (1991) uses the example of nonconvex adjustment costs – that is, with thresholds that prevent a firm from making smooth and continuous adjustments. These adjustment costs may be costs of changing prices (menu costs), or the cost of hiring and firing labor, or the costs of adjusting the capital stock to shocks that are particular to a given firm (called "idiosyncratic shocks") or shocks that are common to all firms.

To begin with, assume that all firms have the same adjustment costs, and their shocks are perfectly correlated. Then whatever the asymmetric microeconomic phenomenon (say firm level price rigidity), it carries over to the aggregate phenomena (aggregate price level rigidity). However, here everything is exactly the same for every firm at *all* times. In effect, there is only one firm.

Suppose next that the shocks are less than perfectly correlated across firms. Caballero shows that it is possible to construct examples in which any microeconomic asymmetry vanishes at the aggregate level. It is also possible to show that, provided there are idiosyncratic shocks, any microeconomic asymmetry does not carry over to aggregate data. Similarly, in the author's Monte Carlo experiments, microeconomic asymmetries do not carry over into aggregate level asymmetries, and even when they do, they are not necessarily the consequence of a microeconomic asymmetry.

Suppose firms adjust their factors of production, or prices, at different speeds in the upward and downward direction – this is the asymmetry. Then whichever is the slower speed will take a longer time to adjust. But the aggregate would exhibit substantially *less* asymmetry in its response to positive and negative shocks than individual firms would.

The conclusions of Caballero's paper are clear: asymmetric pricing policies at the firm level do not necessarily imply asymmetries at the aggregate level; and asymmetries at the aggregate price level need not come from asymmetries at the firm level. Similarly, asymmetric factor adjustment costs at the firm level need not imply asymmetric responses of the capital stock and the level of employment to positive and negative shocks. *To assert otherwise is to commit the fallacy of composition.*

To claim that both the New Classical and the New Keynesian are "general equilibrium approaches" is a misnomer. In Arrow-Debreu general equilibrium, no specific functional form of the utility function is required; that is the beauty and generality of the Arrow-Debreu model. It is compatible with all agents having different utility functions, as long as the basic assumptions (such as diminishing marginal utility, etc.) are satisfied. By optimizing with respect to the given prices of all goods and the given endowments, demand functions are derived, which are then expressed as excess demand functions by subtracting the given initial endowments (supplies).

In contrast, in the representative agent models, it is necessary to start with a *specific* functional form of a utility function; it may be Cobb-Douglas, as in New Classical models, or some variant (Rotemberg, 1987] that yields constant elasticity demand function for the representative consumer. This means that there is one consumer or that all consumers are alike. If they are all alike, why do they trade? In the Arrow-Debreu model consumers trade because they have different preferences and different endowments.

In the New Keynesian representative agent models the demand function is not of the Arrow-Debreu type, for in the latter, demand functions are homogeneous of degree zero, which leaves no role for money. But, as it is clear from equation (7.15), the representative agent's demand is a function of relative prices as well as the real supply of money. Hence the homogeneity property of Arrow-Debreu demand functions is lost. For these reasons it is not correct to describe the representative agent model as a "general equilibrium" approach.

We conclude that the representative agent framework is the most serious limitation of New Keynesian business cycle theory, despite some of its other merits. It rests on a fallacy of composition. Such micro-based models do not yield a satisfactory theory of business cycles.

7.4 Coordination Failure Through Multiplicity of Agents

It has been argued that the most important *single* weakness of New Keynesian economics is the adoption of the New Classical method of using the *representative agent* as the basis of analysis. This leads to a fallacy of composition; it also detracts from much that was novel in Keynes's *General Theory*. However, there is another strand in New Keynesian analysis that does not use the representative agent framework, and which could be potentially rewarding.

In their introduction, Mankiw and Romer (1991) define "New Keynesian economics" as directed toward two questions: the non-neutrality of money and market imperfections as being crucial to the understanding of the macroeconomy. With imperfect markets, there arises the possibility that not all potentially realizable gains will in fact occur. The failure to exploit mutually beneficial trades can be called *coordination failures*.

With one representative agent, there is nothing there to coordinate. Thus in a Robinson Crusoe economy, there is no coordination problem. But if there are at least two agents, with some degree of specialization, so that each agent consumes some of the output produced by the other, then in principle one has the foundations of a macroeconomy.

The minimum requirements for macroeconomic analysis are as follows:

1 At least two agents
2 Some positive trade between the two agents.

Indeed (2) implies (1), since trade with one agent is impossible. Both (1) and (2) are very weak requirements; they may even be necessary for any micro analysis that will involve a price, but we will not pursue that here.

With at least two agents, a natural way to begin the analysis is through game theory, an approach used by Cooper and John (1988). The requirement of more than one agent is also a necessary condition for *"thick-market" externalities* (Diamond, 1982), which lead to one kind of coordination failure. With two agents or more, actions of one agent may affect the *options* of the actions of the other. This will then give rise to spillovers and *strategic complementarities* (Bulow, Geana-koplos, and Klemperer [1985], Cooper and John [1988]), which admit the possibility of multiple equilibria. Typically, these equilibria are Pareto-rankable, and without some outside coordination the typical outcome will be Pareto-inferior (Dore, 1989, pp. 153–58).

The logic of more than one agent is to admit spillovers and complementarities, and once complementarities are admitted, a number of nonconvexities will intrude which will destroy optimality properties. We give just two examples.

In Dore (1989, Ch. 9), it is argued that although von Neumann's growth model is the first rigorous proof of the optimality of a competitive equilibrium [Koopmans, 1964], Von Neumann achieves this optimality by *stripping* his minimax theorem of all economic agents. Dore then investigates what happens to the growth model when agents who may have conflicting interests are in fact restored into the model. The dynamic game numerical example presented there shows strategic complementarities and multiple equilibria, and shows that the uncoordinated outcome will be a Nash equilibrium, which will be inferior to a number of other outcomes. Thus, restoring agents, where their number is at least two, leads to the loss of the optimality property of the Von Neumann growth model.

Durlauf (1991b) considers a model with a "countable set of industries *i*", where *i* must be greater than 1. The model has the added advantage of persistent output being **path dependent**, which means that any particular initial condition or shock leads to a path of the economy over time that is entirely different from any other path. Thus one shock will alter the entire history of the economy: the shock will have a permanent effect. This is what we have repeatedly called the Keynes-Harrod-Goodwin view of business cycles.

In Durlauf's model, the microeconomic specification of the economy is expressed as a set of conditional probability measures describing how individual agents behave, given the economy's history. An aggregate equilibrium exists when one can find a joint probability measure over all agents that is consistent with these conditional measures. When more than one such measure exists, then there is a multiplicity of aggregate equilibria. It is then possible to describe the time series properties of aggregate fluctuations along difference equilibrium paths.

Suppose that firms in each industry face a nonconvex production technology that displays technological complementarities: past high production decisions by each industry increase the current productivity of a number of other industries. Industries cannot coordinate production decisions because of incomplete markets. Suppose that firms experience industry-specific productivity shocks as well as aggregate-level productivity shocks. With such a model, Durlauf shows that with complementarities and incomplete markets, there will be multiple equilibria in aggregate activity where each of these equilibria have a different mean and variance of output. Second, the aggregate productivity shocks indefinitely affect output by shifting the economy across equilibria. Finally, the aggregate productivity shocks will shift the economy between high and low equilibria, thus displaying the characteristics of business cycles. Some numerical simulations then confirm the irregular shifts between high and low equilibria.

The shocks are reminiscent of real business cycle theory, treated in chapter 6, and are as unaccounted for here as they are in real business cycle theory. Although Durlauf does not have a credible business cycle theory, his use of a multiplicity of agents and the implied complementarities lead to coordination failures.

Much earlier, Leijonhufvud (1981) had emphasized the role of coordination, so that the idea is not new (see Howitt, 1984). But perhaps the New Keynesians who model coordination failures have vindicated the earlier work on "Keynesian reappraisal" associated with the work of Leijonhufvud, Clower, Howitt, Benassy, and others.

CONCLUSION

The New Keynesians attempt to obtain Keynesian results (e.g. an underemployment equilibrium) from microeconomic, representative agent models. These models are similar to those of the New Classical approach. But fundamental to New Keynesian analysis is the short-run nonneutrality of money, and imperfect competition in the goods, labor, and credit markets. Indeed the integration of imperfect market structures and macroeconomics is a prelude to New Keynesian business cycle theory. In fact, this "prelude" is a large part of the New Keynesian research agenda, a theme to which section 7.1 was devoted.

The particular characteristics of the U.S. economy show why the assumptions of perfect competition, complete contingent markets, and market clearance are not valid. Wide-ranging empirical work establishes that quite convincingly. Perhaps one of the objectives of the New Keynesian approach was to rehabilitate the role of monetary and fiscal policy in an economy subject to a number of rigidities, excess capacity, and uncompetitive practices.

New Keynesians accept Keynes's key message in the *General Theory*, that the normal condition for capitalism is an underemployment equilibrium, and that an expansion requires intervention. However, the underemployment equilibrium can be seen to be a logical consequence of the actions of rational agents.

The representative agent framework identifies micro level rigidities as being responsible for the failure of the economy to adjust to changing conditions. More recent work suggests that the representative agent framework leads to a fallacy of composition: asymmetric adjustment costs at the firm level do not imply asymmetric response at the aggregate level, and price rigidities due to menu costs or near-rational behavior at the firm level do not imply rigidities at the aggregate level. Thus micro level rigidities are neither necessary nor sufficient for aggregate level rigidities.

However, New Keynesians who emphasize coordination failures are much better able to generate Keynesian results. But apart from exemplifying the possibility of an underemployment equilibrium, and market failure, they do not appear to have a full theory of business cycles that accounts for lower and upper turning points. There appears to be no systematic attempt to account for the dynamic stylized facts stated in chapter 2. Nor does New Keynesian theory identify a governing mechanism for the cycle as a whole. For them, the most important aspect of the business cycle is the downturn or the recession, with which are associated huge welfare losses. For practical purposes, the downturn *is* the business cycle, for it is recurrent. Perhaps the New Keynesians see the observed rigidities as the stylized facts, but that misses an important time dimension, shown in figure 2.1 in Chapter 2 (page 20). What is important is the integral relationship between output, inflation, and unemployment over time. The logical extension of the New Keynesian analysis leads to the endogenous cycle models of part III.

NOTES

1 The proposition is a familiar result of intermediate-level macroeconomics: every act of saving is a withdrawal from the income flow, and every act of saving cannot automatically be offset by a corresponding act of investment of an equal amount. Thus nothing guarantees that *ex ante* aggregate saving will equal *ex ante* aggregate investment.

2 For a critique of this approach, called "methodological individualism," see Hodgson (1986).

3 It should be noted that Hall defines pure profits as "all earnings of the firms not paid out as compensation" (1986, p. 403). Thus pure profit is profit before deducting expenditures on human capital, research and development, and advertising. For details, the reader is encouraged to consult Hall's stimulating article.

4 There is an unstated assumption here that society must "live with" the monopoly. The socially optimal price is of course k.

5 Perhaps too much must not be made of the Caplin-Spulber result that menu costs at firm level are compatible with price flexibility at the aggregate level. After all, their result depends *inter alia* on rational expectations in which firms expect that the aggregate price inflation equals the growth rate of money supply. Nevertheless, the introduction of a *distribution* of firms that follow (s,S) pricing policies (i.e., raise the real price back to the original

level after the real price hits the lower threshold due to menu costs) has an important impact. Even when some firms are prevented from revising prices due to menu costs, and only a few firms revise their costs discontinuously, they do so by a large amount. The net result is that *aggregate* price rigidity due to menu costs (or near-rationality) is lost. In order to assert aggregate price rigidity, it may be necessary to go back once again to reliance on fixed-length contracts.

6 The (S,s) pricing model is really a problem of nonconvex adjustment costs, a problem that arises in engineering, operations research, and finance. The problem is akin to determining the optimal timing and scale of plants when there are thresholds, discrete plant sizes, and economies of scale in investment and operating costs (Dore, 1977). For a survey of adjustment cost models, see Rothchild (1971) and Harrison, (1985).

PART III

INTRODUCTION TO PART III

Past III consists of four chapters that deal with some theories in which the cycle is endogenously generated (see again the excerpt from Geoffrey Moore, (1977, p. 97) given in chapter 1). Chapter 8 is a systematic introduction to concepts and methods of nonlinear dynamics used in Part III. Chapter 9 is a reformulation of Kaldor's model suggested by Chang and Smyth (1971). The model is highly suggestive of what is involved in endogenously generated business cycles. Chapter 10 covers Benassy's non-Walrasian business cycle model, which is a very interesting generalization of the standard *IS-LM* Model. It can also be viewed as a logical extension of the New Keynesian approach of chapter 7, based on the representative agent. Chapter 11 deals with Goodwin's "growth cycle" model, the first published model to achieve successful integration of growth into the cycle model. The model explains a large number of the stylized facts of business cycles.

The merits of the three models are assessed in terms of criteria set out in chapters 2 and 3. The concluding chapter summarizes the results.

8

Introduction to Self-Sustained Oscillations

INTRODUCTION

So far in this book, business cycle theory has been explained entirely by exogenous factors: random demand shocks (Lucas), exogenous and unexplained productivity shocks (real business cycle theory), and rigidities of market structure that are exogenous to the cycle theory (New Keynesian). In part III we explore a selection of the most important business cycle theories in which the cycle does not rely on some exogenous factor but is shown to be endogenously generated. Such models rely in some way on aspects of the mathematical theory of oscillations, developed earlier by physicists and mathematicians to explain oscillating physical phenonema, such as a pendulum.

Section 8.1 reviews in a leisurely manner some introductory ideas in the theory of oscillations, particularly self-sustained oscillations. In the very first volume of the journal *Econometrica* the study of self-sustained oscillations for explaining business cycles was advocated. A key nonlinear differential equation is presented to show the qualitative nature of oscillations compared to a linear differential equation, but the full derivation of the equation is deferred to the next section, where the nonlinear equation is systematically built up, starting from Newton's Second Law of Motion. Physical examples are used to show how the nonlinear equation makes sense. In the final section, the important concept of limit cycle is explained, and two important theorems are stated without proof. Subsequent chapters in the book rely heavily on the methods and concepts developed here.

8.1 LINEAR AND NONLINEAR DIFFERENTIAL EQUATIONS

The simplest example of persistent cycles is sinusoidal representation of the motion of a pendulum; if the pendulum were in an ideal vacuum, so that there would be zero air resistance, then in theory the cyclical motion should persist forever, just as the orbits of the planets will persist practically forever. But a sinusoidal representation of business cycles lacks a theory, as well as conviction.

Consider a simple second order linear differential equation:

$$\ddot{x} + 2a\dot{x} + bx = 0, \quad b > a^2 \tag{8.1}$$

Here either the cyclical solution tends to zero when $a > 0$, and so the cycle peters out, or when $a < 0$, the amplitude of the cycle increases as time increases, so that it is explosive. In fact, this is a general characteristic of *all linear* differential equations. Let us rewrite equation (8.1) slightly, in which the variable y is now the deviation from a position of equilibrium:

$$\ddot{y} + \alpha\dot{y} + y = 0 \tag{8.2}$$

Consider three cases: [1] when $\alpha > 0$, $\alpha = 0$, or $\alpha < 0$. The solution to equation (8.2) consists of **harmonic oscillations** of decreasing, constant, or increasing amplitude, depending on the sign of the parameter α. If $\alpha > 0$, the amplitude of the cycle decreases so that the cycle peters out eventually. If $\alpha = 0$, we get a harmonic oscillation with a constant amplitude. If $\alpha < 0$, the cycle does not peter out as required, but unfortunately the amplitude increases so that eventually the cycle is destroyed. If, however, one could modify the equation so that cycles do not peter out but also do not become explosive, then the cycle would be made *self-sustaining*. Suppose one could introduce a positive resistance that *increases* with the amplitude of the oscillations, so that the cycle is 'tamed' – i.e., it persists without becoming explosive. Such an equation was discovered by B. van der Pol, and is thus known as the **Van der Pol equation:**

$$\ddot{y} + \alpha(y^2 - 1)\dot{y} + y = 0 \tag{8.3}$$

Here the coefficient of $\dot{y}$ is the required resistance where the resistance is a *nonlinear* function of the deviation from the position of equilibrium. To understand the dynamics of such a nonlinear resistance, consider figure 8.1 which shows the nature of the fluctuations for four different values of α.

In Figure 8.1(a), $\alpha = 0$; it shows that the oscillations are of constant amplitude – i.e., it is sinusoidal. With $\alpha = 0$, equation (8.3) reduces to equation (8.2), both showing oscillations of constant amplitude. However, when α is positive, we know that equation (8.2) would yield a damped cycle that will peter out, but this is not the case with equation (8.3), as shown in figure 8.1(b), where $\alpha = 0.1$. Increasing the value of α to $\alpha = 1$, the amplitude increases at first but quickly establishes a persistent but nonexplosive cycle, as shown in figure 8.1(c). Finally, when α is positive and large, the solution of equation (8.3) very rapidly reaches a constant amplitude, and a "shape" that repeats itself as time t increases, as shown in Figure 8.1(d). Indeed this figure is worth considering further. Instead of $t = 100$, let us re-produce it for 50 time periods in figure 8.1(e). As the shape repeats itself, we can easily produce its *phase portrait*, which is given in Figure 8.1(f). Notice how the phase portrait quickly converges to a bounded motion. Such bounded motion is called a *limit cycle* (see below for more on that concept).

It is intuitively clear that the greater the displacement from equilibrium, the greater is the restoring force, so that the faster the "shape" (or pattern) is restored. Second, a slight variation in the resistance changes the *periodicity* – i.e., time period required for it to return to the same position. The resistance may be said to *damp* the fluctuation. Third, the damping effect produces an asymmetrical cycle: the upturn is different from the downturn, unlike a sinusoidal cycle, which is perfectly symmetrical. Van der Pol called such oscillations "*relaxation oscillations.*" In a business cycle, too, the upturn or expansion is different from a contraction. Hence, business cycle fluctuations could in principle be identified with relaxation oscillations.

The potential value of using the Van der Pol equation to model economic crises, or business cycles, was recognized early by a Dutch economist, L. Hamburger (1934), who became acquainted with Van der Pol's work in 1928, when van der Pol presented his paper at the 1928 meeting of the Batavian Society of Logical Empirical Philosophy. In a note in *Econometrica*, Hamburger (1934) claims that as early as 1922, the then rector of the University of Amsterdam, a Professor J. K. A. Wertheim Salomonson, had delivered a speech highlighting the importance of the emerging mathematical theory of (nonsinusoidal) oscillations for explaining fluctuating economic phenomena. In 1930,

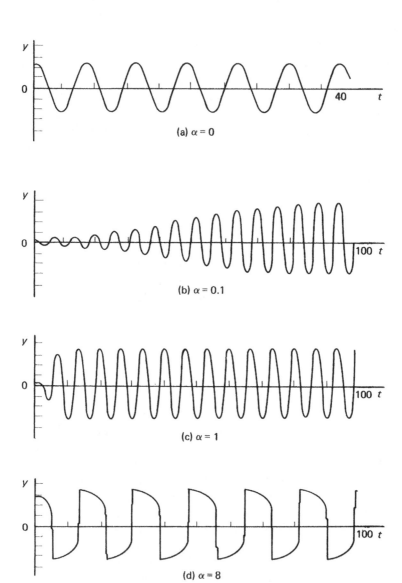

Figure 8.1   The Van der Pol Equation: $\alpha > 0$

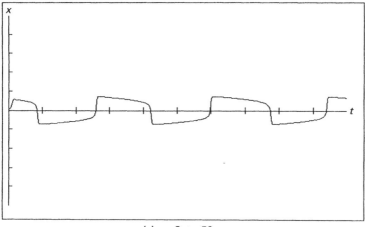

(e) $\alpha = 8$, $t = 50$

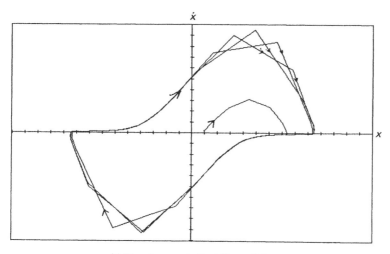

(f) The phase portrait of Figure 8.1e

Figure 8.1.e and Figure 8.1.f

Hamburger himself published an article on the subject in the Dutch journal *De Economist* (vol. 89, pp. 1–38). A French version of his paper appeared in Hamburger (1931).

At about the same time, A. Liénard and Ph. Le Corbeiller were also working on the theory of oscillations, although Lord Raleigh had essentially discovered the mathematical equivalent of the Van der Pol equation in 1883.[2] At a meeting of the Econometric Society in Lausanne, in September 1931, Le Corbeiller presented an account of the Van der Pol equation, and his remarks were published in the first volume of *Econometrica* in 1933.

Le Corbeiller (1933) argued that it was by chance that the theory of oscillations was developed by "telephone engineers" but the theorems were quite independent of their *specific* applications in mechanics, thermodynamics, or economics. He made a strong plea for a marriage of political economy and the new theory of oscillations in explaining fluctuations in prices as well as the business cycle.

He also made a very important distinction between a *forced* oscillation and a self-sustained oscillation. A forced oscillation has an unchangeable *periodic* cause, such as variations due to seasonal factors for example. However, self-sustained oscillation is governed by nonlinear controls and a mechanism that has inertia, viscosity and rigidity. These complications are as inevitable in political economy as they are in radio-engineering. A self-sustained oscillation acts as if the inertia, viscosity, and rigidity can be overcome by a compensating nonlinear mechanism. An important characteristic of relaxation oscillations is the presence of one nonlinearity per period, which ensures that turning points occur.

Hicks's (1950) business cycle model is a linear multiplier-accelerator model that is made nonlinear by two exogenously imposed nonlinearities, the ceiling and the floor. The Van der Pol equation shows that *one* endogenous nonlinearity is both necessary and sufficient to ensure that turning points occur.

8.2 THE LIÉNARD EQUATION

In this section the Van der Pol type of equation is built up systematically, and an appreciation of the equation with reference to physical examples will make the subsequent analysis easier to follow.

8.2.1 The laws of motion

Consider a body with a constant mass m that is concentrated at a point and whose motion is restricted to a single line, say the x axis. The body accelerates under the influence of a force. Otherwise it is at rest or in motion at a uniform velocity. If the line of motion is the x axis, then its position is indicated by $x(t)$, its velocity by $\dot{x}(t)$, and its acceleration by $\ddot{x}(t)$. If F is the sum of forces acting on a body, then its motion is given by the following second-order linear differential equation:

$$F = m\ddot{x} \qquad (8.4)$$

Next, suppose that this mass is at rest at $x = 0$ on a smooth, frictionless table along the x axis. This mass is attached to a spring, which is itself attached to a wall. The spring is neither stretched nor compressed when the mass is at rest. If it were stretched or compressed, we would expect the spring to behave as a force that tends to restore the mass back to its position of rest. Assume that the spring is an "ideal" spring with no mass of its own and that its restoring force is proportional to the distance the body is displaced from rest. Let this constant of proportionality be k. Then motion of the mass-spring is governed by

$$m\ddot{x} = -kx \qquad (8.5)$$

That is, when x is positive, so that the spring is stretched, then the restoring force is in the opposite direction. Hence the negative sign. When the spring is compressed (i.e., when x is negative), then the negative sign of k ensures that the restoring motion is to the right.

Suppose we now drop the assumption of a frictionless tabletop, and introduce some frictional resistance, which is a force that operates in the opposite direction. One example is *viscous damping*, which is associated with motion through a fluid medium such as air. Let this resistance be proportional to the velocity $\dot{x}$, and as it operates in the opposite direction, the resistance is $-k_1\dot{x}$. Obviously, the restoring force must be greater than the viscous damping force if there is to be movement after displacement. Therefore the equation of motion now becomes

$$m\ddot{x} = -kx - k_1\dot{x} \qquad (8.6)$$

The negative sign of k_1 indicates that if motion is to the right, so that $\dot{x} > 0$, then the resistance is to the left. If motion is to the left ($\dot{x} < 0$), then resistance is to the right.

Next let us *suspend* the mass-spring from the ceiling so that motion is along the y axis, and the positive direction is upward. If the mass were zero, then its position would be $y = 0$ (see figure 8.2). However, when mass is nonzero a gravitational force comes into play, which tends to pull the body downward, below $y = 0$, to the point y_0 where $y_0 < 0$. The downward pull is due to gravity, which is a force of per unit mass. For mass m, the gravitational force operating in the downward direction is $-mg$. Therefore with viscous damping as well as the gravitational force, the equation of motion is now given by

$$m\ddot{y} = -ky - k_1\dot{y} - mg \qquad (8.7)$$

The sign of the gravitational force is negative because it always acts in the negative y axis direction. Now divide equation (8.7) through by m and define $\alpha = k_1/m$ and $w^2 = k/m$. Then equation (8.7) becomes

$$\ddot{y} + \alpha\dot{y} + w^2y = -g \qquad (8.8)$$

Let $z = y + g/w^2$, and we get

$$\ddot{z} + \alpha\dot{z} + w^2z = 0 \qquad (8.9)$$

Note too that $\dot{y} = \dot{z}$ and $\ddot{y} = \ddot{z}$.

What is the position of rest for the spring-mass system? It is at the origin, so that $y = 0$, which implies that $z = 0$. But when $z = 0$, $y = -g/w^2$. Therefore the rest position in the vertical direc-

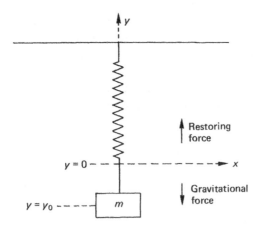

Figure 8.2   The Vertical Mass-Spring System

tion, when gravitational pull is in effect, is $y_0 = -g/w^2$, which is less than zero.

Equation (8.9) is the same as equation (8.2), where the coefficient of $\dot{y}$ is the damping effect.

If we generalize the damping effect and write it as a *function* $f(z)$, we then get Liénard's equation:[3]

$$\ddot{z} + f(z)\dot{z} + z = 0 \tag{8.10}$$

A special case of Liénard's equation is the van der Pol equation given above as equation (8.3) and repeated below with $z = x$:

$$\ddot{x} + \alpha(x^2 - 1)\dot{x} + x = 0 \tag{8.11}$$

However, note that while equation (8.2) is linear, the introduction of $f(z)$ as the coefficient of $\dot{z}$ (or $\dot{x}$) makes equations (8.3), as well as equations (8.10) or (8.11) above *nonlinear*. It is in fact the nonlinearity that leads to a nonexplosive cycle with a repeated pattern, as shown earlier in figure 8.1(d).

The idea of a "repeated pattern" is very important in business cycle theory. In the next subsection, a physical analog that generates a repeated pattern is given. It is known as the Kipp oscillator.

8.2.2 The Kipp oscillator

Figure 8.3 describes a simple hydraulic system that generates the main features of sustained cycles, which Van der Pol called "relaxation oscillations." A storage tank T is filled by a steadily flowing stream of water from faucet F. When the height of water in the tank is h_2, a syphon comes into operation through B and causes the level to drop to a height h_1. Air entering into the syphon at B breaks off the discharge, and the tank T begins to fill again until the height of the water reaches h_2.

If the behavior of filling and emptying is considered over time, we get figure 8.4. Here the period of oscillation is simply the sum of filling time T_F and emptying time T_E. The corresponding phase-plane diagram shows the repeated pattern. Such a repeated pattern is called a *limit cycle*. It is shown in figure 8.5. It is also important to note that a system may not *begin* in a limit cycle, but as time increases, it may *fall* into a limit cycle. Technically, the motion may begin anywhere but approach a limit cycle, as was illustrated earlier in figure 8.1(f). Thus a

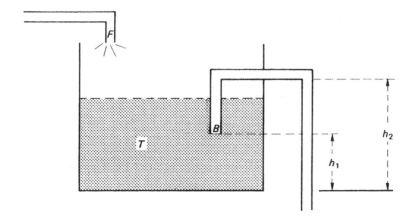

Figure 8.3   The Kipp Oscillator

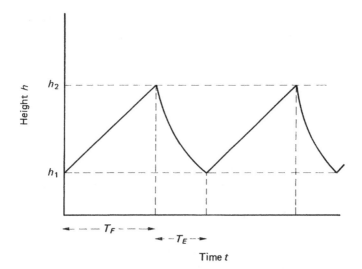

Figure 8.4   A Relaxation Oscillation

limit cycle is the *eventual* pattern that is established, usually as time increases. The limit cycle in the Kipp oscillator is shown in figure 8.5.

Finally note that maintained oscillations shown in figure 8.4 depend on certain *initial* conditions and parameters. For instance, initial air pressure in spout B (figure 8.3) must be the same as that on the water in the tank; the rate of inflow from F must not be so high that the

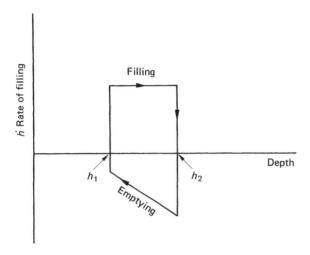

Figure 8.5 A Limit Cycle

inflow rate far exceeds the outflow rate so that the height of the water in tank T never drops below h_1. Initial parameters are the diameters of the two pipes, the density of the fluid in the tank, and so on.

The importance of the value of parameters has already been made clear in figure 8.1, which displays the Van der Pol equation for different values of α. The figure shows that $\alpha > 0$ is necessary for the behavior to approach a limit cycle. In figure 8.6, we return to consider what happens to the Van der Pol graph when $\alpha < 0$. The figure shows that for $\alpha < 0$, it can be shown that the limit cycle (when it exists) is unstable, i.e., it vanishes as time increases. Figure 8.6 shows the graph of two values of α: $\alpha = -0.1$ and $\alpha = -0.2$. The more negative the α, the more quickly the cycle disappears. Hence $\alpha > 0$ is a necessary condition for a stable limit cycle in the Van der Pol equation, where the origin (where $x = \dot{x} = 0$) is an unstable equilibrium, or a repelling center, as all paths move away from the center, as long as $\alpha > 0$. Note that the more negative the value of α, the more quickly the cycle disappears.[4]

8.3 EXISTENCE OF LIMIT CYCLES

The above section gave some idea of what a limit cycle is and under what conditions it exists in *one particular* equation: the Van der Pol

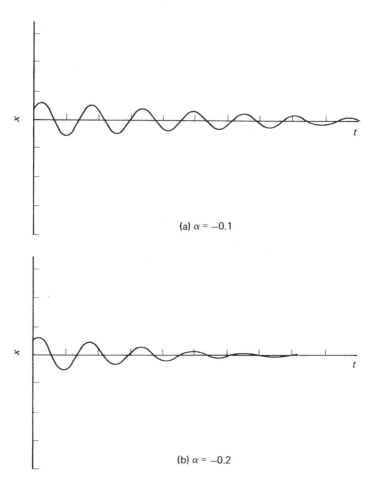

(a) $\alpha = -0.1$

(b) $\alpha = -0.2$

Figure 8.6   The Van der Pol Equation

Equation. It is useful to formalize the existence conditions for a slightly more general class of functions, beginning with a more rigorous definition of the concept of a limit cycle.

Modern texts (Beltrami, 1987) refer to the path of the system $\dot{x} = f(x)$, x in $\Re^2$ as an *orbit*. Call this orbit γ. Then the *positive limiting set* γ^+ is the set of points ρ in $\Re^2$, for which

$$||x(t_n) - \rho|| \to 0$$

as $n \to \infty$, where $\{t_n\}$ is an increasing sequence of time. A path or orbit that returns periodically to a point ρ is called a *cycle*, or a **closed orbit**.

Then any orbit γ is said to tend to a *limit cycle* Γ if $\gamma^+ = \Gamma$ and Γ is a nonconstant closed orbit.

A cycle γ is asymptotically stable if there is some open neighborhood Ω_0 of γ, such that every orbit that begins in Ω_0 stays in it and has γ as its limiting set. We now state (without proof) a weak form of the Poincaré-Bendixson Theorem for two-dimensional dynamical systems. The theorem is stated in two parts:

Theorem 8.3.1
(i) Let Ω be the set of orbits of the system $\dot{x} = f(x)$, $x \in \Re^2$. Let γ be an orbit that begins in Ω. Then its positive limiting set γ^+ is nonempty, and if it contains no equilibria of the system, then either γ is a cycle or γ^+ is a limit cycle.
(ii) If on the other hand Ω contains no cycle but does contain a single attracting point ρ, then $\gamma^+ = \rho$.

In order to illustrate the above theorem, consider figure 8.7 (a) and (b). In (a) there is an unstable equilibrium $\overline{x}$ in Ω which is repelling in the sense that all orbits in a neighborhood of $\overline{x}$ move away from it. Remove this point. The remaining set Ω without this point must contain a limit cycle Γ. Roughly speaking all orbits "inside" and "outside" eventually approach Γ, as time goes to infinity. On the other hand, in figure 8.7(b) $\overline{x}$ is a single attracting point; it contains no cycles, and every path in the neighborhood ends in $\overline{x}$, the stable equilibrium.

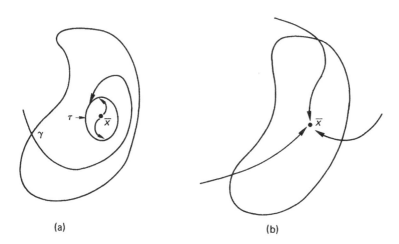

(a)   (b)

Figure 8.7   Illustration of Theorem 8.3.1

It is worth emphasizing that the Poincaré-Bendixson Theorem is valid only for two-dimensional systems. The behavior of higher order systems belongs to chaotic dynamics and is outside the scope of this book.

Having explained the meaning of a limit cycle, this chapter concludes with a statement of Liénard's Theorem, which applies to a class of nonlinear differential equations slightly more general than the Van der Pol equation.

Write equation (8.10) in a more general form as:

$$\ddot{x} + f(x)\dot{x} + g(x) = 0 \qquad (8.12)$$

We begin by giving two simple definitions of odd and even functions:

Definition 8.1
The function $f(x)$ is called an *odd function* if

$$f(-x) = -f(x)$$

Definition 8.2
The function $g(x)$ is called an *even function* if

$$g(-x) = g(x)$$

The reason why an "odd" function is so called is that the power series expansion of it at $x = 0$ has the form

$$f(x) = a_1x + a_2x^3 + a_3x^5 + \ldots$$

Similarly, an even function has a power series expansion at $x = 0$ of the form

$$g(x) = a_0 + a_2x^2 + a_4x^4 + \ldots$$

See, for example, Flanders, Korfhage, and Price (1979).

Theorem 8.3.2
Let the functions $f(x)$ and $g(x)$ satisfy the following conditions:

(i)   Both $f(x)$ and $g(x)$ are continuous and have continuous derivatives for all x;

(ii) $g(x)$ is an odd function such that $g(x) > 0$ for $x > 0$; and $f(x)$ is an even function;

(iii) the function

$$F(x) = \int_0^x f(x)dx$$

has exactly one positive zero at $x = a$, is negative for $0 < x < a$, is positive and nondecreasing for $x > a$, and $F(x) \to \infty$ as $x \to \infty$.

Then equation 8.12 (the Liénard equation) has a unique closed orbit, called a limit cycle Γ, surrounding the origin in the phase plane, and this limit cycle Γ is approached by every other orbit as $t \to \infty$. For a proof, see Simmons (1974, pp. 349–52).

It remains to show that the Van der Pol equation (equation 8.13 or equation 8.11) satisfies the requirements of Theorem 8.3.2 and so possesses at least one limit cycle. However, before we do that we can complete a physical interpretation of equation (8.12) in terms of the mass-spring system discussed in section 8.2: the function $g(x)$ diminishes the magnitude of the displacement of the mass, when disturbed. The assumption about $f(x)$ means that for small $|x|$ the motion is intensified, and for large $|x|$ the motion is retarded, so that oscillations are sustained. This is merely designed to understand the *role* played by $f(x)$ and $g(x)$; we know from section 8.2 that a real spring will not oscillate forever.

In the Van der Pol Equation, $f(x) = \alpha(x^2 - 1)$ and $g(x) = x$ which are both continuous and possess continuous derivatives. Furthermore, for $|x| < 0$, $f(x) = \alpha(x^2 - 1) < 0$ for $|x| > 0$, $f(x) = \alpha(x^2 - 1) > 0$

$$f(x)\big|_{x=a} = \alpha(a^2 - 1) = 0, \quad \text{where } a = 1$$

$$f(x)\big|_{x>a} = \alpha(x^2 - 1) > 0$$

$$f(x)\big|_{x<a} = \alpha(x^2 - 1) < 0$$

Note too that the area under the curve $f(x)$ is unbounded as $x \to \infty$ and for $x > a$ (*where* $a = 1$), it is nondecreasing (see figure 8.8). Hence all

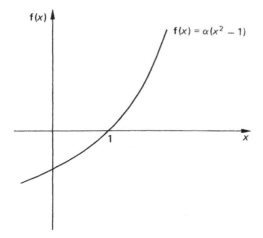

Figure 8.8   The function f(x) in the Van der Pol Equation

the requirements of Theorem 8.3.2 are satisfied, and the Van der Pol equation has at least one limit cycle, provided $\alpha > 0$.

CONCLUSION

The objective of this chapter was to provide a firm grasp of some key dynamical concepts important in the analysis of endogenous business cycle models. In some cases it will be shown that the business cycle model can be reduced to a Liénard – Van der Pol type of equation. Whether the economic justification for such an equation is convincing or not will also be a key question in appraising the validity of the models.

NOTES

1 Here α can be interpreted as resistance; see later in section 8.2.
2 Lord Raleigh's equation is

$$\ddot{y} + \alpha\left(\frac{\dot{y}^2}{3} - \dot{y}\right) + y = 0$$

Differentiate the above with respect to time to get

$$\dddot{y} + \alpha(\dot{y}^2\ddot{y} - \ddot{y}) + \dot{y} = \dddot{y} + \alpha(\dot{y}^2 - 1)\ddot{y} + \dot{y} = 0$$

Next define $x \equiv \dot{y}$, and the equation becomes

$$\ddot{x} + \alpha(x^2 - 1)\dot{x} + x = 0$$

Hence the Lord Raleigh equation and the Van der Pol equation are mathematically equivalent. However Lord Raleigh considered only the case where $\alpha < 1$.

3 See Minorsky, 1962, p. 102.
4 For some of the graphs in this Chapter, I have used PHASER, a computer program in Kocak (1989).

9

The Kaldor Model

INTRODUCTION

In this chapter, the concepts and methods of chapter 8 are put to use; it is shown that the analysis is considerably simplified if an appeal can be made to Theorems 8.3.1 and 8.3.2. If a nonlinear model can be reduced to the Liénard–Van der Pol equation, it is only necessary to check that the requirements of Theorem 8.3.2 are satisfied to guarantee the existence of cycles. It will also be shown that this approach makes it possible to focus on the *economic content* of the model in order to judge its merit.

Section 9.1 is an informal introduction to Kaldor's (1940) model. It enables us to concentrate on its most central proposition. In the following section the model is reformulated rigorously following Chang and Smyth (1971). It is shown that the Kaldor model can indeed be reduced to a Liénard–Van der Pol equation. As the cyclical fluctuations in the model depend on the nonlinear nature of the investment function, section 9.3 is a more detailed look at Kaldor's investment function. In the conclusion, there will be an attempt to assess the merits of the model.

9.1 AN INFORMAL STATEMENT OF THE MODEL

In his model Kaldor attempts to incorporate the insights of both Kalecki (1936–7) and Keynes (1936). In Keynesian theory the equality of savings (S) and investment (I) is a standard condition for equilibrium in the goods market. However, both I and S are functions of the level of economic activity x. If one or both functions were nonlinear, then the possibility of multiple equilibria at different levels of activity could be expected. This possibility is shown in figures 9.1 and 9.2. Note that multiple equilibria require that *either $I(x)$ or $S(x)$* be nonlinear (figure 9.2). This factor becomes important later on.

Kaldor offers an economic justification for a non-linear investment function $I(x)$: dI/dx will be low for very low levels of activity as well as for very high levels. For low x, I will be low because of excess capacity; for high levels of x, I will be low because of rising costs of construction, bottlenecks, and the high cost of borrowing. This would give investment the required sigmoid shape, shown in figures 9.1 and 9.2(b).

Similarly, it would be possible to argue that when x is low, savings would either be low or become negative in order to maintain consumption. At low x, employment too would be low so that more workers would rely on unemployment benefits that would be largely spent in order to maintain consumption. At high x, workers' incomes would be

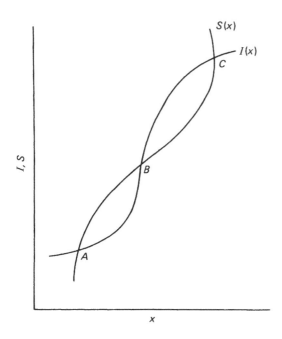

Figure 9.1 Nonlinear Savings and Investment

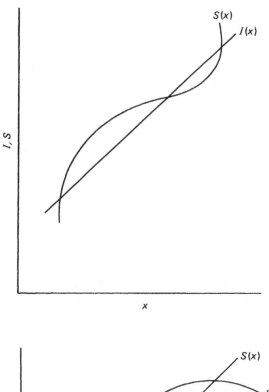

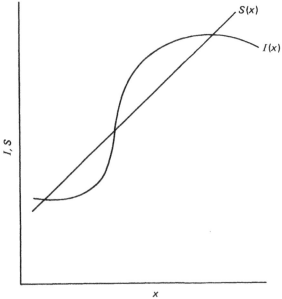

Figure 9.2   (a) Nonlinear Savings Function
              (b) Nonlinear Investment Function

higher than average, but higher prices would mean that the relative income distribution would shift in favor of profits, so that aggregate savings would be higher too.

Figure 9.1 shows three equilibria, A, B, and C. Both A and C are likely to be unstable equilibria. This is best understood with the aid of figure 9.3(a) to (f), where in (a) figure 9.1 is reproduced. The dynamics evolve from (a) to (b) to (c) to (d) to (e) and back to (a). Suppose x is high so that the equilibrium is at B. At B output is high and I is high too so that the capital shock (k) is high. But as incomes are high $S(x)$ will now shift upwards, and $I(x)$ will shift downwards as the accumulation of k will reduce profitable investment opportunities.

Although there will always be innovations that can be exploited, the cost factors put downward pressure on I. Therefore point B shifts down to the left as shown in figure 9.3(b). $I(x)$ continues to shift down and $S(x)$ to shift up, until the points B and C merge in figure 9.3(c). At this point *ex ante* savings are greater than investment, and a slight shock would curtail activity in such a way that the economy moves to point A. The momentum of falling x does not come to an end until A is reached, as shown in Figure 9.3 (d). During the downturn, the capital stock would not be expanding. Indeed, much needed replacement investment will also have been postponed.

Now the cost factors will be in favor of investment, both replacement and new investment. So $I(x)$ will shift up until A and C merge, this time in an expansion. This movement is shown in Figure 9.3 (e) to (f). In an expansion, savings rise so that $S(x)$ shifts up, and we are back at Figure 9.3(a). This constitutes the business cycle. It is disequilibrium in the goods market alone, when $S(x) \neq I(x)$, which drives the cycle, and although the cost factors are very important, they are not modeled explicitly. In the next section this model is formalized along lines suggested by Chang and Smyth (1971), although the exposition is different from theirs.

9.2 THE CHANG-SMYTH REFORMULATION

Let *ex ante* saving and *ex ante* investment be functions of income (y) and the capital stock (k):

$$I = I(y,k) \quad and \quad S = S(y,k)$$

and assume that $I_y, S_y, S_k > 0$, and $I_k < 0$.

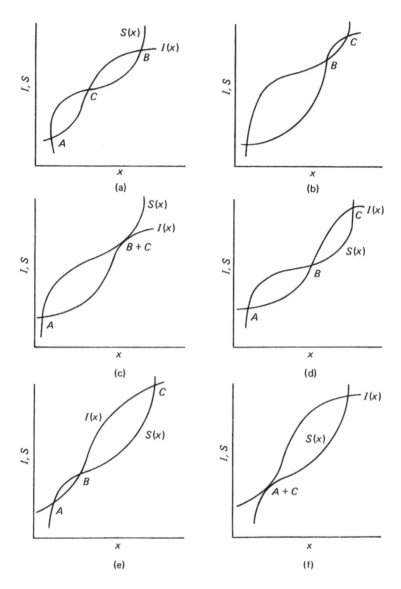

Figure 9.3   The Dynamics of the Kaldor Cycle

Income increases every time *ex ante* investment is greater than *ex ante* saving. Thus the time rate of change of income ($\dot{y}$) adjusts to the discrepancy between investment and saving at the speed ($1/\mu$). Formally,

$$\mu\dot{y} = I(y,k) - S(y,k) \qquad (9.1)$$

The investment leads to capital accumulation, but the rate of accumulation depends on realized investment. Therefore $\dot{k}$ is equal to the proportion δ of *ex ante* investment. However, as this factor of proportionality plays no role, we might as well set it to unity, i.e. $\delta = 1$. Hence

$$\dot{k} = \bar{I}(y,k) \qquad (9.2)$$

where $\bar{I}(y,k)$ is realized investment.

The savings and investment functions are assumed to be non-linear, but now they are functions of income (y), rather than the level of activity (x). Next we make a crucial assumption about the savings and investment functions.

Assumption A:

$$I_y > S_y \quad and \quad I_k > S_k$$

In words, assumption A states that investment is more responsive to both income and capital stock than savings are to income and capital stock.

Examining equation (9.1), we can write k as a function of y and $\dot{y}$

$$k = \psi(y, \dot{y}) \qquad (9.3)$$

or more generally we can write an implicit function $F(k, y, \dot{y}) = 0$ by looking at equation (9.1).

Using the implicit function rule, we have:

$$\frac{\partial k}{\partial y} = -\frac{F_y}{F_k} \quad and \quad \frac{\partial k}{\partial \dot{y}} = -\frac{F_{\dot{y}}}{F_k} \qquad (9.4)$$

It follows that

$$\frac{\partial k}{\partial y} = \psi_y = \frac{-(I_y - S_y)}{I_k - S_k} = \frac{S_y - I_y}{I_k - S_k} \qquad (9.5)$$

$$\frac{\partial k}{\partial \dot{y}} = \psi_{\dot{y}} = \frac{-\mu}{I_k - S_k} \qquad (9.6)$$

Now differentiate equation (9.3) with respect to time:

$$\dot{k} = \psi_y \dot{y} + \psi_{\dot{y}} \ddot{y} = \bar{I}(y, k) \tag{9.7}$$

Next substitute equations (9.5) and (9.6) into (9.7):

$$\left[\frac{S_y - I_y}{I_k - S_k} \right] \dot{y} + \left[\frac{-\mu}{I_k - S_k} \right] \ddot{y} = \bar{I}(y, k) \tag{9.8}$$

Simplifying, we have,

$$[S_y - I_y]\dot{y} + [-\mu]\ddot{y} = [I_k - S_k]\bar{I}(y, k)$$

or

$$\ddot{y} + \frac{1}{\mu}[I_y - S_y]\dot{y} = \frac{1}{\mu}[S_k - I_k]\bar{I}(y, k)$$

$$\ddot{y} + \frac{1}{\mu}[I_y - S_y]\dot{y} + \frac{1}{\mu}[I_k - S_k]\bar{I}(y, k) = 0 \tag{9.9}$$

Finally, we can eliminate k from equation (9.9) by substituting equation (9.3) – that is, $\bar{I}[y, \psi(y, \dot{y})]$ can be written $h(y, \dot{y})$. Therefore equation (9.9) becomes:

$$\ddot{y} + \frac{1}{\mu}[I_y - S_y]\dot{y} + \frac{1}{\mu}[I_k - S_k]h(y, \dot{y}) = 0 \tag{9.10}$$

Before comparing equation (9.10) to the generalized Liénard–Van der Pol equation, consider $h(y, \dot{y})$ further. Define $z \equiv h(y, \dot{y})$; taking the total differential

$$dz = h_y dy + h_{\dot{y}} d\dot{y}$$

Divide through by dy:

$$\frac{dz}{dy} = \frac{\partial h}{\partial y} + \frac{\partial h}{\partial \dot{y}} \frac{d\dot{y}}{dy}$$

If the *time rate* of change of income is unchanged by a change in income, then

$$\frac{d\dot{y}}{dy} = 0. \text{ Therefore}$$

$$\frac{dz}{dy} = \frac{dh}{dy} \quad and$$

$$\frac{dz}{dy} \gtrless 0 \quad as \quad \frac{dh}{dy} \lessgtr 0$$

$$and \quad h(y, \dot{y}) = 0 \quad when \quad y = 0 \tag{9.11}$$

Consequently equation (9.10) can be compared to the Liénard–Van der Pol equation

$$\ddot{y} + f(y)\dot{y} + g(y) = 0$$

where in equation (9.10)

$$f(y) = \frac{1}{\mu}[I_y - S_y]$$

and $f(y) > 0$ *iff* $I_y > S_y$, which is guaranteed by assumption A, and $f(y)$ and $g(y)$ are continuous by assumption. Note that $f(y) = 0$ *iff* $I_y = S_y$ – i.e., when $I(y, k)$ and $S(y, k)$ are zero when $y = 0$. Also the area under the curve $f(y)$ is unbounded, as $y \to \infty$, because $f(y)$ increases as y increases. Finally, in equation (9.10),

$$g(y) = \frac{1}{\mu}[I_k - S_k]h(y, \dot{y})$$

By assumption A, $g(y) > 0$ *iff* $I_k > S_k$ and $g(y) = 0$ when $h(y, \dot{y}) = 0$, by equation (9.11). Hence all the requirements of theorem 8.3.2 are satisfied.

We conclude that equation (9.1) has at least one limit cycle.

9.3 DISCUSSION

It is obvious from the above two sections that the nature of the savings and investment functions is crucial in the Kaldor model. Assumption A in section 9.2 is crucial; as stated above, assumption A states that investment is more responsive to changes in income and capital stock than is savings. The assumption is plausible, but still arbitrary: there appears to be no real economic justification for it. Yet without it there can be no cycles in the model, as reformulated above.

But the alternative in the literature (e.g. Ichimura [1943], or Sordi [1990]) is even less attractive. Ichimura writes:

$$I(y, k) = f(y) - mk$$

$$S(y, k) = sy + nk$$

What is the meaning of the above investment function? Investment is a flow and so is income, so that $f(y)$ is a flow, measured in dollars (say), but k is a stock. So how are we to interpret $f(y) - mk$? Suppose the stock k is large and is measured in dollars and m is some constant ($0 < m$, but possibly $m \geq 1$). If mk is large but the investment induced by income is smaller than mk, then it would appear that $I(y, k)$ would be negative!

Although the same problem does not arise with Ichimura's savings function, it also faces the same dimensionality problem, as the savings function is an addition of a flow (sy) and a stock (nk). For the same reason Sordi's (1990, p. 142) interpretation of mk as a negative intercept is also questionable. Therefore it makes no economic sense to write the investment and savings functions as done by Ichimura.

Another issue is the relationship of the change in capital stock $\dot{k}$) to realized investment. Kosubud and O'Neil (1972) write $\dot{k}$ as a linear combination of realized investment and savings. This is clearly unsatisfactory. It is a matter of definition that the change in the capital stock must be equal to the *realized* investment, where realized investment may be some fraction of desired or *ex ante* investment. Consequently, the original Chang and Smyth formulation has been retained in equation 9.1.

CONCLUSION

It has been shown that the Kaldor model can be reformulated as an endogenously sustained business cycle model in which a limit cycle exists: income fluctuates over time, provided assumption A holds. Assumption A is plausible, but there is no strong economic justification for it; it is not based on any observed regularity. The model is confined to the goods market only, and an important Keynesian dimension, namely the labor market, plays no role in it.

In the next chapter we consider a model with endogenously generated cycles, in which the influence of the labor market is brought in.

10

The Benassy Model

INTRODUCTION

The Benassy (1986, pp. 173–85) model is an important representative of the work of economists who call themselves "neo-Keynesians". The neo-Keynesians represent an approach that rejects the market-clearance assumption of the New Classical school, but they accept that important macro questions should be investigated from a *microeconomics* perspective. Consequently, their analysis begins with a representative agent. Like the New Keynesians, the neo-Keynesians assume a representative household and a representative firm. However, they claim to be "non-Walrasian" in the sense that they reject the mythical auctioneer. Without an auctioneer, it is necessary to face the problem of who sets the price. The non-Walrasian approach is thus open to different market structures. While a detailed exposition of the non-Walrasian approach is outside the scope of this book, the first section below provides a brief introduction. It also contains an informal statement of the Benassy business cycle model. In section 10.2 the model is formally stated, and it is shown that for the purposes of cycles the model can be reduced to the Liénard–Van der Pol equation, so that Theorem 8.3.2 can be applied, and it is shown that the requirements of the theorem are satisfied. It is also shown that the reformulation as a Liénard equation has advantages over the original formulation, particularly when it comes to interpreting the mathematics in terms of economics. It also helps to bring out the elegance of the model in that no special functional forms need to be assumed. It also highlights the particular market interactions that are proposed to be central in the business cycle.

10.1 INTRODUCTION TO NON-WALRASIAN ANALYSIS

At the very beginning, the non-Walrasian school took its lead from Clower (1965) and Leijonhufvud (1968) who had argued that Keynes's concept of *effective demand* must be distinguished from the Walrasian concept of demand, which they called notional demand. Notional demands become effective demands only if *all* agents (in the course of trading) achieve their desired demands. In that case Walrasian demand or notional demand is the same as the Keynesian concept of effective demand. But if the auctioneer is rejected, trade takes place in sequence, with each agent visiting one market, offering his or her commodities or labor and then going on to the next market. The agent's demand on the latter market depends on what she/he was able to sell on the first market. If her desired (notional or Walrasian) supplies were somehow constrained, so that the agent was unable to sell all she desired, then the sales constraint she encountered will now constrain what she can buy on her visits to other markets. Consequently, agents' effective demands will not equal their Walrasian *ex ante* desired demands. Clower claimed that Keynes's effective demand was of this type.

In the presence of an auctioneer, such quantity constraints cannot occur; all proposed trades that lead to demand and supply imbalances are *not* allowed. It is only when the auctioneer has found an equilibrium price for *every* commodity that trade takes place. In a non-Walrasian model without an auctioneer, agents will often be quantity constrained so that both goods *and* labor markets may fail to clear.

In a macro context the focus is not n markets for n goods, but typically one is concerned with a goods market, a labor market, and a money market. However, the money market has its own characteristics, where equilibrium on the money market is satisfactorily described by the usual LM curve. Therefore it is the goods and the labor markets that need to be considered further.

With two markets, there are four possible cases since each market can be in excess demand or in excess supply. In figure 10.1, the columns represent excess supply of goods E_G^s and excess demand for goods, E_G^D. The rows represent excess supply of labor, E_L^s and excess demand for labor E_L^D. The four possible combinations are marked K, C, R and F, for the Keynesian, Classical, Repressed Inflation, and the Fourth Regimes, respectively. Each regime is considered in detail next.

	E_G^S	E_G^D
E_L^S	K	C
E_L^D	F	R

Figure 10.1   The Four Regimes

10.1.1   The Keynesian regime

In the Keynesian regime (K), there is excess supply of both goods and labor. As *actual* transactions are constrained by the lesser of demand or supply, the "short" side of the market dominates. Hence transactions are demand determined in this regime. All the traditional Keynesian results and policies apply in this regime.

Let household consumption C be a function $C(y,p,\tau)$, where y is income, p is the price level, and τ is the tax rate. Then it is reasonable to suppose that $C_y > 0, C_p < 0, C_t < 0$. Assuming investment is zero, and g is government expenditure, then aggregate expenditure AE is

$$y^k = AE(p, g, \tau)$$

where the superscript k indicates the Keynesian Regime. All the traditional Keynesian multipliers can be verified. For instance,

$$\frac{\partial y^k}{\partial g} = \frac{1}{1 - c_y} > 0 \quad for \quad 0 < C_y < 1$$

and so on (see Benassy, 1986, p.69).

In particular, note that in this regime, a decrease in the price level increases consumption, which increases AE, and so increases y^k. Therefore a fall in p increases employment. This result depends on the assumption that the propensity to consume is identical for wage income and profit income, and therefore that total consumption does not depend on the distribution of real income y between wages and profits. If the marginal propensity to consume is higher for wage income than for profit income (which will occur if the representative firm distributes only a part of a period's profits), then the consumption function will depend positively on wages, w, and an increase in w will increase employment and income.

10.1.2 The classical regime

In this regime, there is excess demand for goods and excess supply of labor. The representative household is constrained on both markets, but the firm faces no binding quantity constraint: it will thus carry out its Walrasian employment and sales plan.

In this regime Keynesian measures, such as an increase in g or a decrease in τ will only increase excess demand on the goods market. Therefore Keynesian measures will not work; only a reduction in the real wage will increase production and employment, and reduce the excess supply of labor.

10.1.3 Repressed inflation regime

In this regime there is excess demand in both the goods and the labor markets. The household is quantity constrained on the goods market by the amount of production, and the representative firm is constrained by the inelastic supply of labor.

As long as the economy is in the repressed inflation regime, no government policies will have an effect on employment. An increase in government spending will crowd out private consumption completely and increase the excess demand for goods.

10.1.4 The fourth regime

In this regime, there is an excess supply of goods and an excess demand for labor. The firm is quantity constrained in how much it can sell, and it is also constrained in how much labor it can buy. This case is not very interesting because in the absence of inventories, an excess supply of goods is incompatible with an excess demand for labor: the firm that cannot sell its output would not demand more labor.

10.1.5 A taxonomy of regimes

It should be clear from the above that it is the level of employment ℓ and sales y which determine each regime, as well as the parameters, p, w, and g. Therefore it should be possible to find actual realized ℓ (call it ℓ^r) and realized y (y^r) as a function of the exogenous parameters p, w, g, and τ.

Let y_0 represent the Walrasian level of income –i.e., income when all desired demands and desired supplies are fulfilled. Let the downward-sloping demand curve for labor be the inverse of the marginal product of labor, $F'^{-1}(\ell)$. The profit-maximizing firm will hire labor up to the point where the marginal product of labor is equal to the real wage w/p. Therefore the demand for labor can be written as

$$F[F'^{-1}(w/p)]$$

Consequently realized income is constrained by the *minimum* of y_0, the demand for labor, and aggregate expenditure:

$$y^r = \min \, [AE(p, \, g, \, \tau), \, F[F'^{-1}(w/p)], \, y_0] \tag{10.1}$$

$$\ell^r = F^{-1}(y^r) \tag{10.2}$$

As p, g, and τ are parameters, the regime depends only on the real wage w/p, and y^r, realized income or sales. Consequently, the three regimes can be represented in a two-dimensional diagram (figure 10.2) in $(w/p, y^r)$ space. The downward-sloping curve is demand for labor. Walrasian equilibrium y_0 corresponds to full employment ℓ_0. That is,

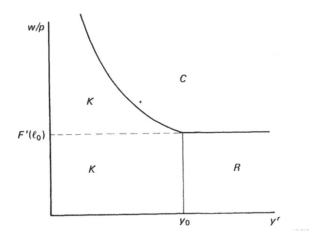

Figure 10.2 The Three Regimes

at y_0 neither the goods market nor the labor market is constrained. In the Keynesian region (K), $w/p \leqslant F'(\ell)$, and $\ell < \ell_0$. In the Classical region (C), the real wage is too high, $w/p > F'(\ell)$. Here only a lower real wage will help as it will reduce the excess supply of labor by expanding production and that will also reduce excess demand for goods. The region R represents a region where output *cannot* be increased to reduce the excess demand for goods because labor is in inelastic supply. Only increases in prices can ration the available supply of goods.

The taxonomy of the three regimes is useful as it suggests the possibility that business cycles may be represented as being 'switches' between regimes. A depression is clearly in the K region whereas a boom may be either in C or R. But the theory developed so far cannot show how the transitions between regimes occur and why they occur. The crucial question is how do the goods and labor markets *interact* to produce cycles? How does excess demand or supply in one market affect the other in such a way as to lead to the switches? In other words, what governs the dynamics? These issues are explored in the next section, where Benassy's business cycle model is formulated.

We also reformulate Benassy's model as a Liénard equation, and show that such a reformulation improves on Benassy's original presentation. In particular, the arbitrary assumption made by Benassy to show existence of cycles, has no sensible economic interpretation. We show that this assumption is not necessary. All that is necessary is that output falls as wages rise, and that output rises nonlinearly as expected demand rises. These two assumptions are sufficient to guarantee cycles.

10.2 THE BUSINESS CYCLE MODEL

The non-Walrasian approach summarized above makes an important statement: in the absence of the auctioneer, the Walrasian equilibrium (y_0) can be achieved fortuitously only; the most likely outcome is a non-Walrasian equilibrium, which is by definition an equilibrium with quantity constraints on the goods or the labor markets. With an all-knowing, benevolent auctioneer, the constraints do not occur as the auctioneer can change prices costlessly *before* trading is allowed. The most glaring consequence of the lack of an auctioneer is shown in macroeconomics; the macroeconomy lurches from one non-Walrasian equilibrium to another, or from one *short-run* non-Walrasian equilibrium to another. Benassy demonstrates this by incorporating the standard *IS-LM* analysis into a dynamic non-Walrasian adjustment path, which is cyclical. As would be expected in a model in which agents are quantity constrained, the driving element in the cycle is unstable quantity dynamics that originate in the dynamic adjustment of the capital stock through investment, and in the dynamic adjustment of demand expectations. The damping or stabilizing factors are the effects of the price level on demand and wage movements along a Phillips curve, which tend to bring the system back toward the long-run equilibrium.

10.2.1   The short-run equilibrium

Assume that in the short run the money wage w is fixed and the price level is flexible. The *IS* curve is derived in the usual way to reflect equilibrium on the goods market:

$$y = C(y, p) + I(x, r, p) \qquad (10.3)$$

where y is income, p is the price level, x is expected demand, and r is the rate of interest. The *LM* curve is given by a fixed money supply $\bar{m}$, and there is no government. The *LM* curve is

$$L(y, r, p) = \bar{m} \qquad (10.4)$$

All functions are continuously differentiable and have continuous partial derivatives with the following signs:

$$C_y > 0, \ C_p < 0, \ I_x > 0, \ I_r < 0$$
$$L_y > 0, \ L_p > 0, \qquad L_r < 0$$
$$and \quad 0 < C_y < 1$$

In addition, consumption is positive at zero income – that is, $C(0, p) > 0$ for all finite values of p. This constitutes the demand side. Next, consider the supply side.

The firm is not quantity constrained at all; its demand for labor is equal to its notional demand and as a result the short-run supply of goods is equal to its notional supply. The firm has a short run production function with the usual neoclassical properties. Thus for a given stock of capital, the production function is

$$y = F(\ell) \tag{10.5}$$

where ℓ is labor, and where $F'(\ell) = dF/d\ell$, and $F'' = d^2F/d\ell^2$. The firm maximizes profits π, subject to the production function:

$$\text{Max } \pi = pF(\ell) - w\ell$$

$$\frac{\partial \pi}{\partial \ell} = pF'(\ell) - w = 0 \Rightarrow \frac{w}{p} = F'(\ell) \tag{10.6}$$

Given that $F'' < 0$ for all ℓ, we can use the inverse function rule to write.

$$\ell = F'\left(\frac{w}{p}\right) \equiv \phi(w,p) \tag{10.9}$$

Then differentiating (10.6) we have

$$\frac{\partial(w/p)}{\partial w} = \frac{1}{p} = \frac{dF'(\ell)}{d\ell} \cdot \frac{\partial \ell}{\partial w}$$

$$= F''(\ell)\frac{\partial \phi(w,p)}{\partial w} = F''(\ell)\phi_w \tag{10.8}$$

and

$$\frac{\partial(w/p)}{\partial p} = \frac{-w}{p^2} = \frac{\partial F'(\ell)}{\partial \ell} \cdot \frac{\partial \ell}{\partial p}$$

$$= F''(\ell)\frac{\partial \phi(w,p)}{\partial p} = F''(\ell)\phi_p \tag{10.9}$$

Equation (10.8) implies

$$\phi_w = \frac{1}{pF''(\ell)} < 0 \tag{10.10}$$

and equation (10.9) implies

$$\phi_p = \frac{-w}{p^2F''(\ell)} > 0 \tag{10.11}$$

Hence the short-run production function is

$$y = F[F'^{-1}(w/p)] = F[\phi(w,p)] \equiv S(w,p) \qquad (10.12)$$

and

$$\frac{\partial y}{\partial w} = \frac{\partial F}{\partial \phi} \cdot \frac{\partial \phi}{\partial w} \equiv S_w < 0 \quad \text{(from equation (10.10))} \qquad (10.13)$$

$$\frac{\partial y}{\partial p} = \frac{\partial F}{\partial \phi} \cdot \frac{\partial \phi}{\partial p} \equiv S_p > 0 \quad \text{(from equation (10.11))} \qquad (10.14)$$

To summarize, the short-run *IS-LM* model is described by the following three equations:[1]

$$y = C(y, p) + I(x,r) \qquad (10.3)$$

$$y = S(w, p) \quad , \quad S_w < 0, \quad S_p > 0 \qquad (10.12)$$

$$L(y, r, p) = \overline{m} \qquad (10.4)$$

The three equations determine the short-run equilibrium values of y, r, and p, for given values of x and w. Thus the solution of y is of the form:

$$y = H(x, w) \qquad (10.15)$$

Next we show (1) that $dy/dx = H_x$ is positive, and that (2) $dy/dw = H_w$ is negative. We need both these results to show the existence of cycles. We begin by writing the three equations in implicit form:

$$\left.\begin{array}{l} y - C(y, p) - I(x, r) = F_1(y, r, p; x, w) = 0 \\ y - S(w, p) = F_3(y, r, p; x, w) = 0 \\ L(y, r, p) - \overline{m} = F_2(y, r, p; x, w) = 0 \end{array}\right\} \qquad (10.16)$$

Now totally differentiate both sides of these three equations to obtain:

$$\left[\frac{\partial F_i}{\partial y}\right] dy + \left[\frac{\partial F_i}{\partial r}\right] dr + \left[\frac{\partial F_i}{\partial p}\right] dp \qquad (10.17)$$

$$= -\left\{\left[\frac{\partial F_i}{\partial x}\right] dx + \left[\frac{\partial F_i}{\partial w}\right] dw\right\}, \quad i = 1, 2, 3$$

It is easy to evaluate[2] each partial derivative in equation (10.17) for $F_1(.)$, $F_2(.)$ and $F_3(.)$.

These partial derivatives can be neatly arranged as a matrix:

$$\left.\begin{array}{rcl}(1 - C_y) \, dy - I_r - C_p dp &=& I_x dx \\ dy \qquad - S_p dp &=& S_w dw \\ L_y dy + L_r + L_p dp &=& 0\end{array}\right\} \qquad (10.18)$$

The Jacobian (Chiang, 1984, p. 184) of the matrix is

$$|\mathcal{J}| = \begin{vmatrix} (1 - C_y) & -I_r & -C_p \\ 1 & 0 & -S_p \\ L_y & L_r & L_p \end{vmatrix}$$

$$= (1 - C_y)(0 + L_r S_p) + I_r(L_p + S_p L_y) + (-C_p L_r)$$
$$= \underbrace{(1 - C_y)L_r S_p}_{(-)} + \underbrace{I_r(L_p + S_p L_y)}_{(-)} - \underbrace{C_p L_r}_{(-)}$$
$$\qquad\quad (-) \qquad + \qquad (-) \qquad + (-)$$

$$\therefore \ |\mathcal{J}| < 0$$

Now assuming $dw = 0$, we can write (10.18) as:

$$\left.\begin{bmatrix} (1 - C_y) & -I_r & -C_p \\ 1 & 0 & -S_p \\ L_y & L_r & L_p \end{bmatrix} \begin{bmatrix} \dfrac{\partial y}{\partial x} \\[2mm] \dfrac{\partial r}{\partial x} \\[2mm] \dfrac{\partial p}{\partial x} \end{bmatrix} = \begin{bmatrix} I_x \\ 0 \\ 0 \end{bmatrix}\right\} \qquad (10.19)$$

from which we can obtain $\partial y/\partial x$, using Cramer's rule:

$$\frac{\partial y}{\partial x} = \frac{\partial H(x, w)}{\partial x} = z_x = \begin{vmatrix} I_x & -I_r & -C_p \\ 0 & 0 & -S_p \\ 0 & L_r & L_p \end{vmatrix} / |\mathcal{J}| \qquad (10.20)$$

$$= \frac{I_x L_x S_p}{|\mathcal{J}|} > 0$$

$$H_x > 0 \qquad (10.20a)$$

Similarly, assuming that $dw \neq 0$, and $dx = 0$, we can find:

$$\frac{\partial y}{\partial w} = \frac{\partial H(x, w)}{\partial w} = H_w = \begin{vmatrix} 0 & -I_r & -C_p \\ S_w & 0 & -S_p \\ 0 & L_r & L_p \end{vmatrix} \Big/ |\mathcal{J}|$$

$$= \frac{-S_w(-I_r L_p + C_p L_r)}{|\mathcal{J}|} = \frac{(+)}{(-)}$$

That is,

$$H_w < 0 \qquad (10.21)$$

We can summarize this subsection by stating that the equilibrium solutions of the short-run *IS-LM* are obtainable for *given* values of the parameters w, the money wage rate, and the expected demand x. Over the long run, the solution will depend on how w and x vary. This is investigated in the next subsection.

10.2.2 Dynamics and long-run equilibrium

The short-run equilibrium discussed above could be an equilibrium with full employment [$y_0 = F(\ell_0)$] or an equilibrium with unemployment [$y = F(\ell)$ where $y < y_0$ and $\ell < \ell_0$]. In the analysis of the dynamics, Benassy assumes a Phillips curve that has the characteristic that wage increases become infinite as y approaches y_0. Therefore full employment *can never be attained by assumption*. As a result, there is now more structure on the supply side.

We begin by repeating equation (10.12), which was:

$$y = F[F'^{-1}(w/p)] = F[\phi(w,p)] = S(w,p) \qquad (10.12)$$

We now add a Phillips curve given by equation (10.22) (see figure 10.3):

$$\dot{w} = \varphi(u), \quad \varphi' < 0 \qquad (10.22)$$

As before let ℓ_0 be the inelastic labor supply. Then the unemployment u is given by:

$$u = \ell_0 - F^{-1}(y) \qquad (10.23)$$

From figure 10.3, it is clear that

$$\lim_{u \to 0} \varphi(u) = +\infty$$
$$\varphi(\bar{u}) = 0$$

That is, the firm is never constrained in the labor market; as ℓ_0 is never obtained, it is workers who are constrained on how much labor they can sell.

Substituting equation (10.23) into (10.22), we can obtain the inverse of figure 10.3, shown in Figure 10.4.

$$\dot{w} = \varphi(u) = \varphi(\ell_0 - F^{-1}(y)) = G(y) \quad \text{where} \quad G'(y) > 0 \tag{10.24}$$

Also,

$$\lim_{y \to y_0} G(y) = \lim_{y \to y_0} \varphi \, [\ell_0 - F^{-1}(y)] = +\infty$$

$$G(\bar{y}) = \varphi[\ell_0 - F^{-1}(\bar{y})] = 0 = \varphi(\bar{u}) = 0$$

This completes the analysis of the supply side. Benassy adds one final equation to the demand side: Let expected demand adjust to actual demand y with a speed of adjustment equal to θ:

$$\dot{x} = \theta(y - x) \tag{10.25}$$

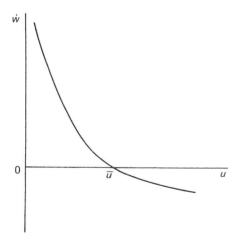

Figure 10.3   The Phillips Curve

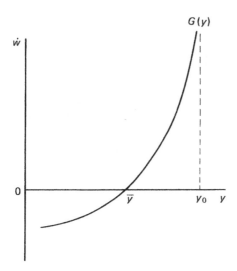

Figure 10.4   The Inverse of the Phillips Curve

Therefore the full dynamics of the system is summarized by the following two equations:

$$\dot{w} = G(y) \tag{10.24}$$

$$\dot{x} = \theta(y - x) \tag{10.25}$$

$$where\ y = H(x, w) \tag{10.15}$$

Let the triple $(y^\star, x^\star, w^\star)$ be the long run equilibrium values of the variables. From figures 10.3 and 10.4, $\dot{w} = 0$ implies $u = \bar{u}$, and $y = \bar{y}$, so that in the long-run equilibrium

$$y^\star = x^\star = \bar{y} = \bar{x}$$

Substituting into equation (10.15), we find that w must be $w^\star$:

$$H(\bar{y}, w^\star) = \bar{y}$$

To find the conditions required for the existence of limit cycles, totally differentiate equation (10.15) and divide both sides by dt:

$$dy = H_x dx + H_w dw$$

$$\frac{dy}{dt} = H_x \frac{dx}{dt} + H_w \frac{dw}{dt}$$

$$\dot{y} = H_x \dot{x} + H_w \dot{w} \tag{10.26}$$

Next, consider equation (10.25):

$$\dot{x} = \theta y - \theta x, \text{ and } y = \frac{1}{\theta}\dot{x} + x \tag{10.27}$$

$$\ddot{x} = \theta \dot{y} - \theta \dot{x},$$

$$\frac{1}{\theta}\ddot{x} + \dot{x} = \dot{y} \tag{10.28}$$

Before proceeding, linearize equation (10.24) by taking a Taylor series expansion around the equilibrium $\bar{y}$ and by ignoring everything except the first term:

$$\dot{w} = G'(\bar{y}) \ (y - \bar{y}) \tag{10.29}$$

and note that from equation (10.27),

$$\bar{y} = \frac{1}{\theta}\dot{x} + \bar{x} \tag{10.30}$$

We are now ready to proceed. First substitute (10.27), (10.28) and (10.29) into (10.26):

$$\frac{1}{\theta}\ddot{x} + \dot{x} = H_x[\theta y - \theta x] + H_w G'(\bar{y})(y - \bar{y}) \tag{10.31}$$

and eliminate all y in the above expression:

$$\frac{1}{\theta}\ddot{x} + x = H_x \left[\theta\left(\frac{1}{\theta}\dot{x} + x\right) - \theta x \right] + H_w G'(\bar{x}) \left[\left(\frac{1}{\theta}\dot{x} + x\right) - \left(\frac{1}{\theta}\dot{x} + \bar{x}\right) \right]$$

$$= H_x \dot{x} + H_w G'(\bar{x})(x - \bar{x})$$

$$\ddot{x} = \theta(H_x - 1)\dot{x} + \theta H_w G'(\bar{x})(x - \bar{x})\big|_{x \neq \bar{x}}$$

$$\ddot{x} - \theta(H_x - 1)\dot{x} - \Theta H_w G'(\bar{x})(x - \bar{x}) = 0$$

$$\text{or } \ddot{x} + \theta(1 - H_x)\dot{x} - \theta H_w G'(\bar{x})(x - \bar{x}) = 0 \qquad (10.32)$$

Equation (10.32) is, of course, the desired Liénard equation of the form,

$$\ddot{x} + f(x)\dot{x} + g(x) = 0$$

Comparing equation (10.32) with the latter, gives:

$$f(x) = \theta(1 - H_x) \qquad (10.33)$$

$$g(x) = -\theta H_w G'(\bar{x})(x - \bar{x})|_{x \neq \bar{x}} \qquad (10.34)$$

In what follows, as θ is a positive constant, we can set it to equal 1 without loss of generality.

In figure 10.5 we sketch the function $f(x)$. Clearly, it has only one root. It is also unbounded, so that its integral $F(s)$

$$F(s) \equiv \int_0^{H_x} f(s)ds = \infty$$

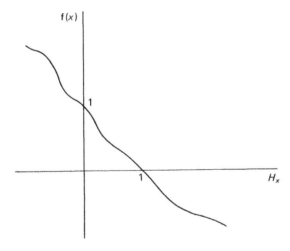

Figure 10.5   Sketch of $f(x)$

Next we check for $g(x)$. Recall that $H_w < 0$, and $G'(\bar{y}) = G'(\bar{x}) > 0$ (see figure 10.4). Therefore $g(x) > 0$, as shown in figure 10.6. It is positive for all $x > \bar{x}$.

We conclude that all the requirements of Theorem 8.3.2 are met. Therefore, there is at least one limit cycle in the Benassy model.

The reformulation of the model in this section improves on the original exposition by Benassy. In the original, Benassy linearizes the dynamic system in order to study the properties of a long-run equilibrium which has to be unstable in order to guarantee the existence of cycles in the model. Benassy (1986, p. 183) therefore assumes that the Trace T of the linearized system is positive. That is, cycles exist only if it is assumed that

$$T = \theta(H_x - 1) + \varphi'(\bar{y})H_w > 0 \qquad (10.35)$$

In the formulation given above, this assumption is *not* necessary. A stable and unique cycle is guaranteed by equation (10.32). In this formulation, the long run equilibrium is a bounded stable motion, not a particular level of output.

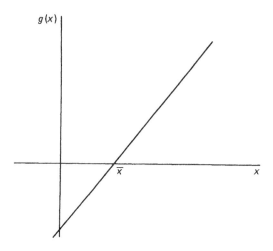

Figure 10.6 Sketch of g (x)

10.3 AN ECONOMIC INTERPRETATION OF EQUATION (10.32)

In the above section, it was shown that Benassy's assumption, given in inequality (10.35), is not necessary to establish the existence of cycles, if the model is expressed as a Liénard equation. However the Liénard equation yields $f(x)$ and $g(x)$ shown in equations (10.33) and (10.34) respectively. What is the economic meaning of these two latter equations?

First, note that, being nonlinear, the Benassy model does not depend on any particular speed of adjustment θ as long as θ is positive, which is required in the model. But a negative speed of adjustment makes no sense anyway.

Second, no special functional forms or "shapes" of the investment, consumption, or other functions are assumed. Even the *IS* curve does not have to be downward-sloping. Only the firm's production function, for a given capital stock, is of the usual neoclassical type, showing diminishing returns to labor.

Third, the structure of the model is very sparse indeed: only three equations – that is, equations (10.24), (10.25) and (10.15) – describe the dynamics of the model. There are no transcendental expressions, no exogenous shocks. The model is very elegant.

Fourth, in analogy with the mass-spring example of chapter 8 (see page 145–7), the restoring force is $g(x)$. Setting aside the speed of adjustment θ, only two components determine this restoring force. It is necessary that H_w be negative so that $g(x)$ be positive. The negative H_w was established in equation (10.21): it makes good economic sense that output (of the single firm) falls as wages rise. Thinking in terms of the mass-spring example, when output increases above equilibrium, *cost factors reduce output*, in the direction of equilibrium.

Finally, consider the most essential factor required to sustain the oscillations, namely $f(x)$. This is the damping force which increases the oscillation for small x and damps it (reduces it) for large x. To understand the economic meaning of $f(x)$, differentiate equation (10.33) with respect to x:

$$f'(x) = -\theta H_{xx} < 0 \tag{10.36}$$

$$\Rightarrow H_{xx} < 0 \ because \ \theta > 0$$

In figure 10.7 we sketch $y = H(x)|_{dw=0}$ – that is, $y = H(x, w)$ when w is a constant. It is clear that

$$\frac{\partial y}{\partial x}\bigg|_{dw=0} = H_x > 0 \quad and \quad H_{xx} < 0$$

Thus with respect to expected demand x, output is an increasing function of x but it increases at a decreasing rate. Hence output is a nonlinear function of expected demand.

To summarize, if $y = H(x, w)$ and $H_x > 0$, then $H_{xx} < 0$ and $H_w < 0$ are both necessary and sufficient to establish the existence of limit cycles. That is all that is necessary if the model is first expressed as a Liénard equation.

Over the cycle, output rises in response to an increase in demand, but wage cost increases lead to an upper turning point in the business cycle; the fall in output reduces wage increases, which again stimulates output. This is the interaction of the labor market and the goods market. Thus we have answered the question posed toward the end of section 10.1.5 (page 171).

The model suppresses the capital stock altogether although investment is a component of demand and the investment must be adding to the capital stock. It concentrates on the integral relationship between

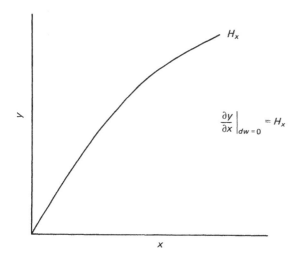

Figure 10.7   Sketch of H_x

output, employment and wages; but as the series of short-run equilibria are intersections of the *IS* and *LM* curves, the interest rate would be procyclical, as illustrated in figure 10.8. However, as output increases toward full-employment y_0, wage rate increases approach infinity, so that y_0 is never reached.

Just as the model suppresses the influence of the capital stock, it also suppresses the long-run relationship between output y and price level p. But for the short run the influence of p is explicit in the model. Consider *IS-LM* again:

$$y = C(y, p) + I(x, r, p)$$
$$L(y, r, p) = \overline{m}$$

Just as we did before, we can write the solution in y of the above system in terms of two parameters, this time x, and p. Let the solution based on these parameters be $y = k(x, p)$. It is then easy to show that

$$k_p = \frac{(C_p + I_p)L_r - I_r L_p}{(1 - C_y)L_r + L_y I_r} \quad < 0 \quad \text{or} \tag{10.37}$$

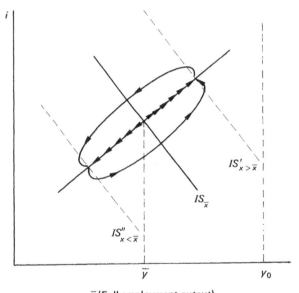

$\overline{y}$ (Full employment output)

Figure 10.8   Business Cycles in the Benassy Model

$$k_p = \frac{C_p + I_p - I_r L_p / L_r}{(1 - C_y) + L_y I_r / L_r} < 0 \qquad (10.37)$$

That is, both output and demand must be in the *opposite* direction when prices rise, through three channels. Price has a negative influence on consumption and investment because $C_p < 1, I_p < 0$ are in the numerator. There is also an indirect negative effect on investment via the interest rate and the demand for money.

However, our interest is in the long-run dynamics, and here the relationship between y and p is not explicit. If we were to extrapolate from the short run, we get an inverse relationship between y and p, which is exactly the opposite of what we observe over time and over the actual cycle. Therefore it would be wrong to extrapolate in a microeconomic fashion.

There are some obvious mathematical limitations: the Poincaré-Bendixson theorem (see Theorem 8.3.1) is confined to two-dimensional systems. One possible way of correcting the (y, p) relationship is to use a markup equation that Benassy (1986, p. 91) uses elsewhere and write it in its inverse form:

$$p = \gamma \xi(w), \gamma > 1 \qquad (10.38)$$

This would make the price level a function of a markup on wage costs. Then prices would rise with wages and with output. This would make the price level procyclical, as observed. Strictly speaking this is not shown in the long-run dynamics of the business cycle model, but the dimensionality problem means that the model builder must select the most crucial variables that generate the cycle, and then leave some or other cyclical variables dependent on one or the other of the crucial variables. We shall do this again in the next chapter, for the same reason – namely, that the Poincaré-Bendixson Theorem is given for two-dimensional systems only. For more than two dimensions it may be necessary to resort to gradient methods and chaotic dynamics.

CONCLUSION

In this chapter we derived the Liénard equation from Benassy's dynamical equations of his model. Doing it this way one can avoid a purely mathematical assumption that Benassy made in order to guarantee the existence of cycles. Benassy's assumption lacked a credible economic interpretation. It was shown that if output is an increasing function of expected demand, but increases at a decreasing rate, and if output decreases with increasing wages, then a limit cycle can be obtained in the Liénard equation of the model. The model is elegant and has a number of advantages not shared by other models, especially those that are dependent on outside shocks. In principle even the price level can be made procyclical in the model.

Two weaknesses of the model should be mentioned. First, it is a representative agent model, with one firm. This firm adjusts output to demand at a constant speed. If there were a *distribution* of firms, whose adjustment speeds were different and were time variable, so that different firms adjusted their output at different times and at different speeds, the cycle might well disappear.

Second, the model does not incorporate *growth* of income in spite of the fact that investment takes place. As has been stated before, growth and cycle are inextricably linked. A model that integrates both growth and cycle is the subject of the next chapter.

Notes

1 To find the slope of *IS*, take the total differential of (10.3) and (10.12):

$$dy = C_y dy + C_p dp + I_x dx + I_r dr \qquad (10.3a)$$

$$dy = S_w dw + S_p dp \qquad (10.12a)$$

In the short run w and x are fixed so that $dw = dx = 0$

$$\therefore dp = \frac{1}{S_p} dy$$

Substitute this into (10.3a) and divide through by dy:

$$\left. \frac{dr}{dy} \right|_{IS} = \frac{1 - C_y - (C_p/S_p)}{I_r}$$

which is negative only if $C_y + C_p/S_p < 1$, since $I_r < 0$. Similarly, for the slope of *LM*:

$$L_y dy + L_r dr + L_p dp = 0$$

$$\frac{dr}{dy}\bigg|_{LM} = \frac{-(L_y + L_p/S_p)}{L_r} > 0$$

Section 10.2.1 largely follows Sordi's (1990) excellent exposition, but section 10.2.2 is different from her approach.

2 For the first equation $F_1(.)$:

$$1\,dy - C_y dy = \frac{\partial F_1}{\partial y}\,dy; \quad -I_r dr = \frac{\partial F_1}{\partial r}\,dr$$

$$-C_p dp = \frac{\partial F_1}{\partial p}\,dp$$

Add them up and equate to r.h.s. of (10.17) for $i = 1$:

$$(1 - C_y)\,dy - I_r dr - C_p dp = \frac{\partial F_1}{\partial x}\,dx + \frac{\partial F_1}{\partial w}\,dw$$

$$= I_x dx + 0 \quad \text{or}$$

$$(1 - C_y)\,dy - I_r dr - C_p dp = I_x dx \qquad (10.17a)$$

For the second equation $F_3(.)$:

$$1 dy = \frac{\partial F_3}{\partial y}; \quad 0 = \frac{\partial F_3}{\partial r}\,dr; \quad -S_p dp = \frac{\partial F_3}{\partial p}\,dp$$

Add them up and equate to r.h.s. of (10.17) for $i = 3$:

$$1 dy - S_p dp = \frac{\partial F_3}{\partial x}\,dx + \frac{\partial F_3}{\partial w}\,dw$$

$$dy - S_p dp = 0 + S_w dw$$

$$dy - S_p dp = S_w dw \qquad (10.17b)$$

For the last equation $F_2(.)$:

$$L_y dy + L_r dr + L_p dp = 0 \qquad (10.17c)$$

because the l.h.s. of the third equation of (10.16) has no x or w; consequently

$$\frac{\partial F_3}{\partial x} \, dx = 0 \text{ and } \frac{\partial F_3}{\partial w} \, dw = 0 \ .$$

Arrange equations (10.17a,b,c) to get (10.18).

11

The Goodwin Growth Cycle Model

INTRODUCTION

In this chapter a business cycle model of Goodwin (1967) that incorporates growth is reviewed. Its distinguishing feature is that it was the first model that incorporated both growth *and* cycle. It puts income distribution at the center of the explanation of the business cycle. The model has received wide recognition as perhaps the most important business cycle model since Schumpeter. Four Nobel Laureates in economics have admired Goodwin's work (Velupillai, 1990). Of the four, we shall quote only two here: Richard Stone said (Vellupillai, 1990, p. 64):

Of Richard Goodwin's many ingenious and insightful contributions to economics, a particular favourite of mine is his note "A Growth Cycle," which was presented at the First World Congress of the Econometric Society in 1965 and later appeared as . . . Goodwin (1967).

Robert M. Solow said (Velupillai, 1990, p. 34):

(It) is five pages long. It does its business clearly and forcefully and stops. It contains no empty calories.

Section 11.1 is an informal statement of the model, followed in section 11.2 by a formal derivation. As the model leads to two partial nonlinear differential equations that are *coupled*, there is no explicit solution. However, a graphical solution showing limit cycles is easy to grasp, following Volterra's technique. Section 11.3 is a numerical simulation carried out by Blatt (1983). Section 11.4 is an extension of the model with the incorporation of money and prices. The final section offers a critical assessment of the model.

11.1 THE GOODWIN MODEL: AN INFORMAL STATEMENT

Goodwin identifies the dynamics of the labor market as the governing mechanism behind the business cycle. While most economists deal with total output only, Goodwin focuses on its dual, namely value added. Since net output is also equal to value added, the two main divisions of value added are wages and profits (assuming all interest can be lumped in with profits). That is, national income is divided into the share of wages, and the share of profits. The share of wages depends on the phase in the business cycle. In the expansion phase, the share of wages rises both through rising wages and rising employment. The higher this share, the *lower* the profit share. But the profit share is the main determinant of gross investment, and employment growth depends on it. Hence the lower the profit share, the slower the growth of employment, so that the ratio of people employed in the labor force (i.e., the employment ratio) falls. New job creation falls as investment falls, and the labor force grows through natural increase and through workers displaced by labor saving technical innovations. The growth in the unemployed puts downward pressure on wages. As wage growth falls, profits rise. This spurs investment and employment growth. In the neighborhood of full employment, wage increases put downward pressure on profits, so that at the peak of the cycle profits per unit of sales decline. The decline in profits then leads to a downturn. The cycle is repeated.

Throughout the cycle, wages and income grow; in the downturn, income falls but usually not to the same level in real terms as the previous trough in income. In this way we see cyclical fluctuations around the *post factum* growth trend, although the growth trend does not exist independently of the cycle. As is shown below, a number of comovements can be shown to exist, especially when the model is extended to include money.

11.2 A FORMAL STATEMENT

The assumptions of the model are as follows:

(A1) Assume steady technological progress due to which labor productivity increases through better capital equipment. Thus the ratio of output $y(t)$ to labor $\ell(t)$ employed goes up steadily:

$$a(t) = \frac{y(t)}{\ell(t)} = a_0 e^{at} \qquad (11.1)$$

That is, $a(t)$ is the growth rate of labor productivity, and a is a constant.

(A2) The labor force $n(t)$ grows at a steady rate β

$$n(t) = n_0 e^{\beta t} \qquad (11.2)$$

(A3) The fraction of the labor force employed is the *employment ratio* $\lambda(t)$, where

$$\lambda(t) \equiv \frac{\ell(t)}{n(t)} \qquad (11.3)$$

When $\lambda = 1$, there is full-employment, which is never reached, as in the model of chapter 10.

(A4) The real wage is $w(t)$, and labor's share of output is

$$\frac{w(t) \; \ell(t)}{y(t)} = \omega(t) \qquad (11.4)$$

(A5) The capital stock is

$$K(t) = vy(t) \qquad (11.5)$$

(A6) The proportionate growth rate of wages is a function of labor-market tightness, i.e.

$$\frac{\dot{w}}{w} = f(\lambda) \qquad (11.6)$$

(A7) Workers consume all their wages and firms invest all their profits.

From the above assumptions, Goodwin derives three fundamental coupled differential equations. Notice that the assumptions are mainly innocuous definitions. The only *economic* hypotheses are A5 and A6, where the latter is the Phillips curve. In A5 v is the accelerator coefficient; its numerical value does not affect the qualitative character of the model, as long as $v > 0$, which is reasonable.

The three *final* differential equations of the model are first stated and then derived. The final equations are:

$$\dot{y} = \frac{1 - \omega}{v} y \tag{11.7}$$

$$\dot{\lambda} = \lambda \left[\frac{1 - \omega}{v} - a - \beta \right] \tag{11.8}$$

$$\dot{\omega} = \omega[f(\lambda) - a] \tag{11.9}$$

11.2.1   Derivations

Derivation of Equation (11.7)

By A7, firms invest their entire share of output which is $[1 - \omega(t)]y(t)$:

$$\text{Investment} = \dot{K} = [1 - \omega(t)]y(t)$$

Differentiate equation (11.5) with respect to time and equate with the above

$$\dot{K} = v\dot{y}(t)$$

$$[1 - \omega(t)]y(t) = v\dot{y}(t)$$

$$\therefore \dot{y}(t) = \frac{1 - \omega(t)}{v} y \qquad \qquad \square$$

which completes the derivation of equation (11.7).

Derivation of Equation (11.8):

First note that from equation (11.2),

$$\frac{1}{n}\frac{dn}{dt} = \beta \tag{11.10}$$

and from equation (11.1)

$$\frac{1}{a}\frac{da}{dt} = a \qquad (11.11)$$

The above turn out to be very useful below. From equation (11.1),

$$\ell(t) = y(t).[a(t)]^{-1}$$

$$\dot{\ell}(t) = \frac{1}{a}\dot{y} - \frac{1}{a^2}y\dot{a}$$

Using (11.11), we have

$$\dot{\ell}(t) = \frac{1}{a}[\dot{y} - ay(t)] \qquad (11.12)$$

From equation (11.3),

$$\dot{\lambda} = \frac{1}{n}\dot{\ell} - \frac{\ell}{(n^2)}\dot{n}$$

$$= \frac{1}{n}[\dot{\ell} - \ell\beta] \quad (using\ (11.10)) \qquad (11.13)$$

Substitute (11.12) into (11.13):

$$\dot{\lambda} = \frac{1}{n}\left[\frac{1}{a}\dot{y} - y(t) - \ell\beta\right]$$

$$= \frac{1}{n}\left[\frac{1}{a}\left(\frac{1-\omega}{v}\right)y - y - \ell\beta\right]$$

$$= \frac{1}{n}\left[\frac{1}{a}\left(\frac{1-\omega}{v}\right)a\ell - a\ell - \ell\beta\right]$$

$$= \frac{\ell}{n}\left[\frac{1-\omega}{v} - a - \beta\right]$$

$$\dot{\lambda} = \lambda\left[\frac{1-\omega}{v} - a - \beta\right] \qquad \square$$

Derivation of Equation (11.9):

From the definition in equation (11.4),

$$w(t) = \omega(t)\frac{y(t)}{\ell(t)} = \omega(t) \cdot a(t)$$

Utilizing (11.6), we have:

$$\dot{w} = a\dot{\omega} + \dot{a}\omega = f(\lambda)w$$

$$\therefore \quad \frac{\dot{a}\omega + a\dot{\omega}}{\omega a} = f(\lambda)$$

$$\frac{\dot{a}}{a} + \frac{\dot{\omega}}{\omega} = f(\lambda)$$

$$a + \frac{\dot{\omega}}{\omega} = f(\lambda) \qquad \text{[using 11.11]}$$

$$\dot{\omega} = \omega[f(\lambda) - a] \qquad\qquad \square$$

One final interesting observation, which will be useful for the numerical simulation of the next section: recall that the share of the firms is $1 - \omega$. The rate of return on the capital stock K should be Profits/Capital, or

$$\frac{Profits/y}{K/y} = \frac{1 - \omega}{v}$$

Hence the proportionate rate of growth of output $\dot{y}/y$ is nothing but profits [see 11.7], which are all invested.

11.2.2　The existence of limit cycles

In this section the nature of cycles in the model is established using a technique due to Volterra; it is also the technique used by Goodwin. However, some preliminary preparation is necessary.

Substitute equation (11.1) into (11.4):

$$\frac{w}{a} = \omega \tag{11.14}$$

and define

$$u \equiv \frac{w}{a}$$

an expression which can be substituted into equation (11.8):

$$\frac{\dot{\lambda}}{\lambda} = \frac{1-\omega}{v} - (a+\beta) = \frac{1}{v} - \frac{\omega}{v} - (a+\beta)$$

$$= \frac{1}{v} - (a+\beta) - \frac{w}{av}$$

$$= \frac{1}{v} - (a+\beta) - \frac{u}{v} \quad \text{or}$$

$$\dot{\lambda} = \left[\frac{1}{v} - (a+\beta) - \frac{u}{v}\right]\lambda \tag{11.15}$$

Next consider a linear approximation to the Phillips curve given in equation (11.6). That is, let

$$\frac{\dot{w}}{w} = f(\lambda) = -\gamma + m\lambda$$

and substitute into equation (11.9):

$$\frac{\dot{\omega}}{\omega} = [f(\lambda) - a] = -\gamma + m\lambda - a$$

$$= -(\gamma + a) + m\lambda$$

Substitute equation (11.14) on l.h.s.:

$$\dot{u} = [-(\gamma + a) + m\lambda]u \tag{11.16}$$

Let us simplify the notation. Define $s \equiv 1/v - (a + \beta)$ and $b \equiv 1/v$ in equation (11.15) and let $c \equiv \gamma + a$ in equation (11.16):

$$\dot{\lambda} = (s - bu)\lambda \qquad\qquad (11.17)$$

$$\dot{u} = -(c - m\lambda)u \qquad\qquad (11.18)$$

We can eliminate time by considering the ratio of the two equations:

$$\frac{\partial \lambda / \partial t}{\partial u / \partial t} = \frac{\lambda(s - bu)}{-u(c - m\lambda)} \quad \text{or}$$

$$\frac{\partial \lambda}{\partial u} = \frac{\lambda(s - bu)}{-u(c - m\lambda)}$$

$$-u(c - m\lambda)d\lambda = \lambda(s - bu)du$$

Which can be expressed as:

$$\frac{-u(c - m\lambda)d\lambda}{\lambda} = \frac{(s - bu)du}{u}$$

Integrate both sides:

$$\int \frac{-u(c - m\lambda)\, d\lambda}{\lambda} = \int \frac{(s - bu)du}{u}$$

$$-c\log \lambda + m\lambda + \log A = s\log u - bu$$

$$\lambda^{-c}e^{m\lambda}A = u^{s}e^{-bu} \qquad\qquad (11.19)$$

where the constant of integration $A = \lambda_0^c u_0^s e^{-m\lambda_0 - bu_0}$ in terms of the initial values of λ and u.

Although we cannot solve equation (11.9) explicitly either for λ or for u, we can determine the nature of their relationship graphically as done by Volterra. To this end, equate the left and right sides of (11.19) to two new variables h and z and then plot the graphs C_1 *and* C_2 of the functions

$$h = \lambda^{-c}e^{m\lambda}A \quad and \quad z = u^{s}e^{-bu} \qquad\qquad (11.20)$$

in figure 11.1. Since $z = h$ by equation (11.19), in the third quadrant there is a 45 degree line OL. In the second quadrant plot z as a function of u, and in the fourth quadrant plot h as a function of λ. To the maximum of the curve C_1 at D, there correspond two points D' and D'' (via OL) on C_2, and these points determine the bounds between which λ may vary. These bounds yield the points P and P' on curve C_3. Similarly, the minimum value of h given by B on C_2 maps onto B' and B'' on C_1, and these points determine the bounds of the variable u (the wage share) and give points Q_1 and Q_2 on curve C_3

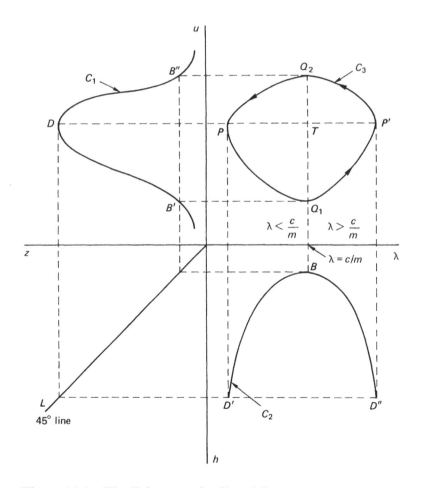

Figure 11.1 The Existence of a Closed Curve

It should be obvious that the "depth" of curve C_2 is given by the constant A in equation (11.20); as the curve C_2 shifts down in the fourth quadrant, the limits set by P and P' get closer, so that a new closed curve inside C_3 is obtained. In fact varying the value of the constant A yields a family of closed curves around the point T. The curve C_3 shrinks to the point T, when the minimum value of h equals the maximum value of z.

We may conclude that varying the initial conditions would generate different closed curves of the sort obtained in figure 11.1. A family of four closed curves for four different initial conditions is shown in figure 11.2. for the pair of equations 11.17 and 11.18 (usually called **predator-prey equations**).

What is the direction of motion of the curve C_3 in figure 11.1?

Let $\lambda = \dfrac{c}{m}$ in equation (11.18):

$$\frac{\dot{u}}{u} = -\left[c - m \left(\frac{c}{m} \right) \right] = 0 \qquad (11.21)$$

$$\therefore \text{ when } \lambda < \frac{c}{m}, \quad \frac{\dot{u}}{u} < 0$$

That is, labor's share is falling. That occurs to the left of the imaginary line $Q_2 T Q_1 B$. When $\lambda > c/m$, $\dot{u}/u > 0$ which occurs to the right of the

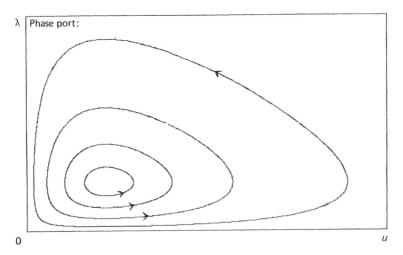

Figure 11.2 A Family of Closed Curves

line. Thus as λ increases, the *direction* of *u must* be from P to Q_1 to P'. Therefore the motion is anticlockwise, as shown in figure 11.1.

The economic meaning is as follows: in an expansion phase (from P to Q_1) employment expands as profits increase; profits are at a maximum at Q_1, when the employment ratio is c/m. However, the expansion leads to an increase in employment beyond $\lambda = c/m$, and from Q_1, profits start to fall, as the share of labor rises. Profits are lowest at Q_2, and only a fall in employment reduces the bargaining strength of labor. But expansion does not occur until labor's bargaining strength is very low at P, when employment starts to expand again.

The limit cycle C_3 is, of course, an idealization; if all the underlying parameters remain constant, the cycle in u *and* λ will repeat itself exactly, but, of course, output and real wages continue to rise from cycle to cycle; any parameter that distorts the shape of C_1 or of C_2, or any factor that shifts either curve will generate a new corresponding C_3 curve. But what affects C_3 will also affect the nature of the growth cycle of output. Whether output actually decreases or merely rises less rapidly will depend on the severity of the cycle. For a mild cycle, the growth rate may decrease but not become negative, but in other cases there may be a sharp fall. However, the increases will predominate over decreases as the time average of profits is positive, and hence so also is that of $\dot{y}/y$.

In the long run, employment grows at the same rate as the labor supply, and although the long-run share of labor is constant, the fact that output is growing implies rising (real) wages. The fruits of technological progress accrue as profits, but profits lead to expansion, and expansion forces wages up and the profit rate down: that is the "Malthusian Iron Law of Profits." This is because firms or capitalists always invest and increase the capital stock. On the other hand, labor enjoys a rent, because the long-run supply of labor is not a function of wages. Thus labor is the ultimate beneficiary of technical change.

The next section is a numerical illustration of the model.

11.3 A NUMERICAL ILLUSTRATION

Table 11.1 contains a numerical illustration of the Goodwin model due to Blatt (1983). The time period may be a quarter or it may be a year, depending on the period chosen. Note that the length of the limit cycle is about nine periods, when both the share of labor and the employ-

Table 11.1 The Goodwin Business Cycle: A Numerical Illustration

Rate of growth of labor productivity $a = 0.015$
Rate of growth of labor force $\beta = 0.020$
Accelerator coefficient $v = 3.0$
Phillips curve crosses zero at $\lambda_p = 0.96$;
  goes to -0.04 for $\lambda = 0$

Equilibrium values are: $\bar{\lambda} = 0.966$ (employment ratio)
  $\bar{\omega} = 0.895$ (labor's share)

Starting values are: $\lambda(0) = 0.966$; $\omega(0) = 0.750$

Time t	Employment ratio λ	Labor's share ω	Current rate of return (in percent)	Index of output	Index of real wage
0.00	0.966	0.750	8.33	1.000	1.000
0.50	0.988	0.791	6.96	1.041	1.063
1.00	0.982	1.040	−1.33	1.053	1.408
1.50	0.957	1.055	−1.84	1.044	1.439
2.00	0.933	1.038	−1.26	1.036	1.426
2.50	0.912	1.015	−0.51	1.031	1.405
3.00	0.896	0.991	0.30	1.030	1.382
3.50	0.884	0.967	1.11	1.034	1.358
4.00	0.875	0.943	1.91	1.042	1.334
4.50	0.870	0.919	2.71	1.054	1.311
5.00	0.868	0.896	3.48	1.070	1.287
5.50	0.869	0.873	4.24	1.091	1.264
6.00	0.874	0.851	4.97	1.117	1.241
6.50	0.882	0.830	5.68	1.147	1.219
7.00	0.894	0.809	6.36	1.182	1.198
7.50	0.908	0.790	7.01	1.222	1.178
8.00	0.925	0.772	7.60	1.268	1.160
8.50	0.946	0.757	8.11	1.319	1.146
8.943	0.966	0.750	8.33	1.368	1.144
Average	0.912	0.895	3.50	−	−

Notes

1 Output declines for a short period, between $t = 1$ and $t = 3$.
2 Wages rise rapidly initially and decline steadily after $t = 1.50$.
3 The rate of return equals $(1 - \omega)/v = (1 - \omega)/3$ and is given for convenience. It
  is negative when $\omega(t)$ exceeds unity. But it is positive on the average.
4 Since we start with $\lambda(0) = \bar{\lambda}$, the starting value of ω is the true minimum over
  the entire cycle.
5 The average value of λ differs from $\bar{\lambda}$ but the average of ω equals $\bar{\omega}$

Source: Blatt (1983)

ment ratio return to the starting values. But, of course, output and real wages continue to rise.

The average value of the share of labor (ω) over the full cycle is 0.895, which is also the equilibrium value of (ω). The motion over the cycle is unsymmetrical: the rate of return on capital declines for three time periods, but rises for about six periods. Hence the expansion is longer than a contraction. When the rate of return is negative but rising, unemployment increases but after $t = 5.0$ to $t = 9$, unemployment falls (λ increases), until λ peaks again at $t = 5.0$ (remember that the cycle is repeated), but employment falls as the rate of return falls.

Notice that there are no exogenous shocks; the cycle is self-sustained.

11.4 THE GOODWIN MODEL WITH MONEY AND PRICES

Many attempts have been made to extend the Goodwin model; some of these are contained in Goodwin *et al.* (1984). A very recent example is Asada (1989) in Semmler (1989). Perhaps the most interesting is the one by Di Matteo (1984), which extends the model by incorporating money and prices.

Di Matteo's model has the following equations:

$$I = y - \left(\frac{w}{p}\right)\ell + \sigma K \left(\frac{\dot{\theta}}{\theta} - \mu \frac{\dot{y}}{y}\right) \tag{11.22}$$

$$\frac{\dot{p}}{p} = \frac{\varepsilon}{(1 + \varepsilon)} \left[\frac{\dot{w}}{w} - a\right] \tag{11.23}$$

$$\frac{\dot{w}}{w} = -\gamma + \phi\lambda \tag{11.24}$$

$$S = S(y) \tag{11.25}$$

$$p(I - S] + \eta(M^d - M) = 0 \tag{11.26}$$

$$M^d = F(p, y, r) \tag{11.27}$$

In equation (11.22) p is the price level, σ is a constant, $\dot{\theta}/\theta$ is the proportionate growth rate of money, and μ is the income elasticity of money demand. For the sake of the present exposition, assume that $\mu = 1$, to simplify.

Equation (11.23) is the price equation, where the price level rises if the growth rate of wages exceeds the productivity growth rate, as was shown in chapter 2, equation (2.2). Equation 11.24 is the linearized Phillips Curve. The next three equations are quite standard. Equation (11.27) is the money demand equation. All other equations remain the same as before.

First, an expression for $\dot{y}/y$ is derived by substituting equation (11.22) into $\dot{K} = v\dot{y}$, where $\dot{K} \equiv I$:

$$y - \left(\frac{w}{p}\right)\ell + \sigma K\left(\frac{\dot{\theta}}{\theta} - \frac{\dot{y}}{y}\right) = v\dot{y}$$

$$y - \left(\frac{w}{p}\right)\ell + \sigma vy\frac{\dot{\theta}}{\theta} - \sigma v\dot{y} = v\dot{y}$$

$$\left(1 - u + \sigma v\frac{\dot{\theta}}{\theta}\right)y = (1 + \sigma)v\dot{y}$$

$$\therefore \quad \frac{\dot{y}}{y} = \frac{1 - u + \sigma v\frac{\dot{\theta}}{\theta}}{v(1 + \sigma)} \tag{11.28}$$

Note that without money ($\sigma = 0$), equation (11.28) reduces to equation (11.7). The equation corresponding to equation (11.8) is:

$$\frac{\dot{\lambda}}{\lambda} = \frac{1 - u + \sigma v\frac{\dot{\theta}}{\theta}}{v(1 + \sigma)} - (a + \beta) \tag{11.29}$$

The share of labor is u as before, but the share of profits is now

$$\left(1 - u + \sigma v\frac{\dot{\theta}}{\theta}\right)$$

and the rate of profit or the rate of return is

$$\frac{\dfrac{Profits}{y}}{\dfrac{K}{y}} = \frac{1 - u + \sigma v \dfrac{\dot{\theta}}{\theta}}{v(1 + \sigma)}$$

For $\sigma = 0$, we get back to the original expressions (that is, equations 11.7 and 11.8). It is still possible to derive expressions for equations corresponding to equations (11.17) and (11.18), except that the constants s, c, b, and m have more parameters determining them.[1] Consequently, we get the same closed orbit of figure 11.1, which has been reproduced in figure 11.3. In this figure, as before $\dot{u} = 0$, $\dot{\lambda} = 0$, $\Rightarrow \lambda = c/m$. The point T corresponds to the natural rate of growth of $\dot{y}/y = a + \beta$. That is, it is equal to productivity growth plus the growth rate of the labor force. It corresponds to $\dot{p}/p = 0$ for all t, but with employment below full employment.

In figure 11.3, at P, the employment ratio λ is below its average (λ_{ave}). The unemployment means that labor is in a weak bargaining position. Therefore money wages increase at a rate less than the productivity rate (see equation 11.23)). Therefore as u falls, the profits increase from P to Q_1, but as λ increases, income increases too. From equation (11.23), we can see that $\dot{p}/p < 0$ – that is, the inflation rate is negative. But at Q_1,

$$\frac{\dot{w}}{w} = a \Rightarrow \frac{\dot{p}}{p} = 0.$$

P to Q_1 is the recovery phase.

Starting from Q_1, λ expands at an increasing rate. Thus Q_1 to P' is a rapid expansion phase; here $\dot{w}/w > a$ so that $\dot{p}/p > 0$, but at a slower rate than the difference between $\dot{w}/w$ and a. As prices increase at a lower rate than wages, profitability slows down as u increases, until at P' profits are at their long-run average. The decline in profitability continues, which reduces investment and therefore employment falls. From P' to Q_2 is an early phase of the recession, during which $\dot{w}/w > a$ so that $\dot{p}/p > 0$. Beyond Q_2, employment has fallen below its long-run average, and now the bargaining power of labor is low, so that $\dot{w}/w < a$ and $\dot{p}/p < 0$. The depth of the recession is not reached until P, when employment is at its lowest. The trough of the cycle is at P, its peak at P'. This establishes a *complete* cycle in output, employment, and profits. Note, too, that inflation is procyclical. It is worth emphasizing that here is an *integral relationship between output, employ-ment, inflation, and profits*, something that has not been encountered in any of the models considered so far in this book.

The savings-investment relationship over the same cycle might also be worth considering. This is not so straightforward – see equation (11.26). At point P in figure 11.3, if the money market is in equilibrium, then savings equal investment at both P and P', whereas $I > S$ in the segment Q_1P' – that is, in the rapid expansion phase. The investment is being financed partly by loans, through the process of credit creation by the banking system, as Schumpeter (1939) astutely observed decades earlier. In the segment $P'Q_2$, investment falls short of savings ($I < S$). It must also be a phase of loan contraction, as firms repay loans and put a premium on liquidity.[2] We would thus expect inside money to be procyclical.

The model says nothing about the determination of interest rates. If we were to adopt the *classical* (anti-Keynesian) mechanism, then whenever the demand for savings exceeds its supply ($I > S$), the interest rate would rise. However, the model is compatible with the

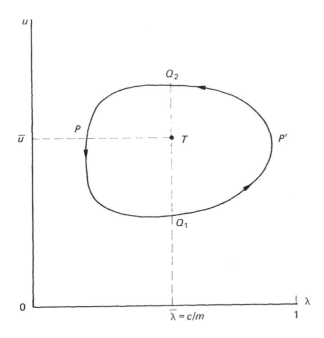

Figure 11.3   The Closed Curve $PQ_1P'Q_2$

endogenous money supply view (see for example, B. Moore, [1988]), since the bulk of the money supply is inside money. The endogenous money supply view would make the rate of interest procyclical, but not because of the adoption of a classical mechanism.[3]

The above analysis is based on the assumption that the income elasticity of money demand μ is set to equal 1. When $\mu \neq 1$, there is a multiplicative parameter μ in the denominator of both equations (11.28) and (11.29). Apart from this, the introduction of nominal variables do not significantly affect the qualitative nature of the cycle, which is determined by *real* factors, u and λ.

Although money does not change the cycle, Di Matteo (1984, p. 19) mentions two requirements that must be satisfied if the money side is to be consistent with the real side of the economy. First, over the long run, the real rate of interest must not exceed the rate of profit, as debts must be paid out of profits. Second, the real rate of interest must not deviate too far from the long run rate of profit. If the real interest rate exceeded the rate of profit, there would be no incentive to invest; firms would do better to earn interest with their surpluses by *postponing* investment. If the real rate of interest were too far below the rate of profits, liquidity would fall as savings would be held in the form of assets that appreciate in value (old masters, antiques, etc.).[4]

A temporary high real rate of interest will have the effect of reducing investment and therefore reducing employment, which will have the effect of curbing the bargaining power of labor, as postponed investment will lower λ. This suggests a possible role played by a central bank, which ostensibly cuts the money supply and raises the real interest rate in order to fight inflation, but in effect the action reduces the bargaining power of labor.

The role of monetary policy deserves a brief treatment. A natural Keynesian countercyclical monetary policy suggested by this model is:

$$\frac{\dot{\theta}}{\theta} = \gamma(\bar{\lambda} - \lambda) - \delta(\bar{u} - u) \tag{11.30}$$

which has the effect of expanding the money supply in the contraction $(Q_2 P Q_1)$ and contracting it in the expansion $(Q_1 P'(Q_2))$, see figure 11.4.[5] However as $\dot{\theta}/\theta$ is largely endogenous money, the effectiveness of monetary policy is limited: in the expansion phase, contracting the money supply by traditional methods will curb the expansion[6] – that is, it will "shave off" the corner around the point P', as shown by the dotted curve in figure 11.4. Indeed, if the contraction in money supply

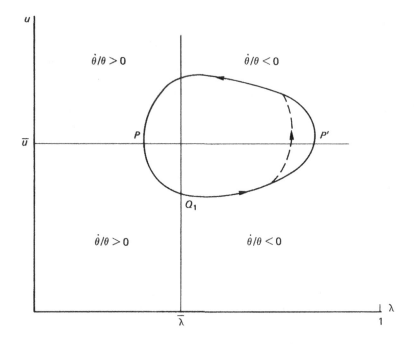

Figure 11.4 The Goodwin Model with Money

is severe enough, the dotted curve can be pushed further to the left; such credit crunches are not unknown.[7] In a contractionary phase of the business cycle, the central bank can increase outside money, but this could simply lead to excess reserves, and the banking system could use part or all of the excess reserves in a manner that does not expand investment and employment.[8] For this reason, monetary policy has been likened to a string: you can pull on it, but not push it. Its response is thus asymmetrical.

11.5 An Assessment

It has been stated that the extended Goodwin Model not only incorporates growth with cycle, so that the *growth cycle* is one phenomenon, but also offers an integral relationship between output, employment, inflation, and money. All the main stylized facts, discussed in chapter 2, emerge together in this model. We now make a more stringent test: does the model explain actually observed business cycles? What are some of its limitations?

Perhaps the second question is easier than the first, and it is natural to begin with that. The Goodwin model assumes that productivity grows at a steady rate. In reality, productivity itself is also procyclical. Therefore it might be more appropriate to make productivity also a function of income. The employment ratio and the wage share are both dimensionless ratios, by definition, and one cannot object to that. In fact, it is a positive advantage to work with dimensionless variables. The only other assumption deals with the Phillips curve.

What is the economic justification of the Phillips curve? One could give a number of answers – that it is an empirical reality, that it is the aggregate supply curve of labor, and so on.

Why should the real wage rise as employment increases? Both Goodwin (1967) and Brody (1990, p. 92) suggest that labor enjoys a rent, a rent of scarcity, because labor is reproducible only after a gestation lag. But there are two kinds of lags: a short training period required to get the best out of the worker, say about two months, and a longer period required to 'reproduce' the worker, through nurturing, education and training from birth to the time the worker is deployable in the production process. This period can be anything from 16 to 24 years, or an average of 20 years. Then the slope coefficient of the (linearized) Phillips curve, which is m in equation (11.16), can be interpreted as the lag, either a short-run lag, or a long lag: it can be shown that the period of the cycle is T, where

$$T = 2\pi m^{-\frac{1}{2}} v^{\frac{1}{2}}$$

If we take $v = 3$ (as we did in the numerical illustration), then $m = 1/6$ of a year (two months), or $m = 20$ years, for the long-run lag.

When $m = 1/6$, a cycle is equal to

$$2\pi \sqrt{\left(3 \times \frac{1}{6}\right)}$$

which is approximately 4.4 years, a figure remarkably close to the average of the cycle calculated by Zarnowitz and his colleagues at the NBER (see chapter 2).

On the other hand, if $m = 20$ years, then $T = 2\pi\sqrt{3 \times 20} = 49$ years. Thus 49- or 50-year cycles would be observed if there were absolute scarcity of labor. This can be safely dismissed, as evidence on Kondratiev cycles is very flimsy. In any case, if the age distribution of labor is roughly normally distributed, then absolute scarcity of labor will not hinder industry, as the number of workers retiring would be about equal to new young entrants into the labor force. Hence the most persuasive interpretation for the rising wage as the employment ratio increases is the short-run training lag, or gestation period. This is the most plausible economic interpretation of the slope coefficient of the (linearized) Phillips curve.

We come now to the first question posed earlier. As Solow (1990, p. 38) has argued, the original Goodwin model neglects aggregate demand and assumes that $S = I$. That is, that aggregate demand is equal to aggregate output ($C + I = y$). Thus the model adopts Say's Law. However, it should be noted that Keynes was wrong in attacking Say's Law, because Say's Law permits *any* level of output as an equilibrium; it takes an additional assumption about the clearing of the labor market to guarantee full employment. Quite correctly there is, of course, no such additional assumption in Goodwin. Nevertheless, the model *is* silent about aggregate demand.[9] Solow, a leading New Keynesian, argues that the short-run (three or four year cycle) fluctuations seem to be dominated by exogenous and endogenous fluctuations in aggregate demand.

Solow computed the phase diagram in the (λ, u) plane for U.S. data for the period 1947 to 1986, reproduced in figure 11.5. Note that his v is the employment ratio (our λ), which is on the vertical axis. This means that the direction of motion is now clockwise. The figure shows a very messy limit cycle, which does not seem to corroborate the Goodwin cycle, at least for U.S. data. But, as Solow points out, there are three distinct closed curves: the first eight observations are followed by a displacement and then the next 20 observations give a closed orbit. This is followed by a large and long-lasting displacement followed by another closed curve. The displacements suggest that the *center* of the limit cycles (i.e., the point T in figure 11.1) is shifting in the north-west direction. This may be *prima facie* evidence of a decrease in fluctuations (Di Matteo, 1984, p. 20) due to a smaller amplitude. On the other hand the most recent observations (the last eight) suggest a shift in the center toward the south, indicating an increase in the amplitude of the fluctuations. This must include the 1981–82 recession, the most severe since the Great Depression (at least until 1992). In any case Solow is right: his phase diagram gives only weak empirical support to the Goodwin model, and as he suggests,

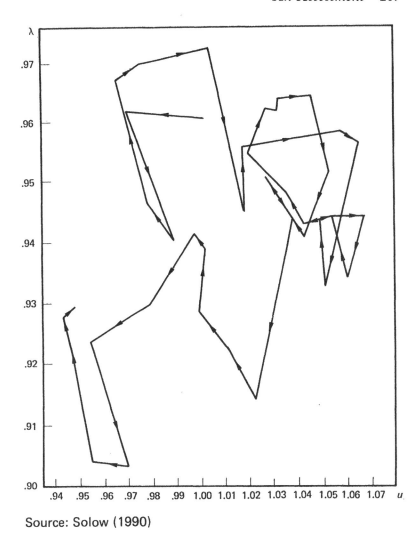

Source: Solow (1990)

Figure 11.5 Solow's Computed Closed Curve (clockwise motion)

more empirical work, including work on the effects of money in shifting the center, is warranted.

In spite of the weak empirical support, Solow acknowledges the following:

(1) There are periods or episodes in which employment is rising because real wages are relatively low and the resulting high profits have led to increased investment and production.

(2) These alternate with periods or episodes in which real wages are relatively high compared with productivity, and the profit-driven impetus to faster-than-average growth is blunted.
(3) The alternation of these episodes is *endogenous*, induced by the real-wage Phillips curve.

Solow [1990, p. 38] concludes:

My feeling is that the model does capture something real. At least I can think of episodes that seem to conform to that pattern . . . It is no contradiction to say that the everyday business cycle marches to a different drumbeat.

CONCLUSION

It was shown that in the Goodwin model the cycle is endogenously generated, and the cycle and trend are integrated, producing a growth cycle. Neither the trend nor the cycle can be independently analyzed. The model reflects all the main stylized facts of business cycles considered in chapter 2, as it explains the motion of output, employment, inflation and money in *one* consistent framework. The governing mechanism of the business cycle is the fluctuation in profits and the employment ratio: above average profits (i.e., lower labor share) lead to the growth of employment, but high employment pushes up wages, which reduces profits. The reduction in profits reduces investment, which reduces employment. The fall in employment reduces the bargaining strength of labor, which thereby reduces the growth rate of (real) wages. But lower wage growth then leads to an increase in profits, which in turn stimulates employment. That is the qualitative character of the business cycle. It was shown that money (mainly of the inside variety) can be incorporated into the model. Indeed, inside money is by far the largest component of total money supply.

A numerical illustration showed how over the cycle output and real wages continue to grow, and how in about nine time periods the cycle in the wage share and employment ratio is repeated while output and real wages continue to grow in the *next* cycle.

An economic interpretation, due to Brody, of the slope coefficient of the linearized Phillips curve is offered. Using it, the model suggests a cycle of about four years. Solow's computed phase diagram for U.S. data shows limited but incomplete support for the Goodwin cycle. In the history so far of business cycle theory, the Goodwin model must be seen as a remarkable achievement.

NOTES

1 It can be shown that in this model,

$$s = \frac{\left[\dfrac{1}{v} + \sigma\theta - (1 + \sigma)\right](a + \beta)}{1 + \sigma}$$

$$b = \frac{1}{v(1 + \sigma)}, \quad c = \frac{(\varepsilon + a)}{(1 + \varepsilon)}$$

$$m = \frac{\theta}{(1 + \varepsilon)}$$

2 For further details, see Di Matteo (1984).
3 This is a vast subject and is beyond the scope of this book. See P. Earl (1990), Wray (1990), and Rogers (1989).
4 There may also be capital flight.
5 The stability analysis is omitted here; however, Di Matteo (1984, p. 21) claims that if δ is high enough the model becomes unstable and diverges monotonically, irrespective of the value of γ. But if $\delta < smc/\sigma$, then the system is stable, provided $\gamma > 0$.
6 That is, through open-market operations, changing reserve requirements of the commercial banks, etc.
7 The 1981–82 Great Recession was partly caused by a severe credit crunch, ostensibly to fight inflation but directed at wage inflation.
8 The banking sector could use its excess cash to speculate in foreign currency markets and commodity exchanges, where the prospects of short-term speculative gain are often better than interest earned from long-term investment projects. This subject too is vast and outside the scope of this book (but see chapter 7, section 7.1.5). For a detailed treatment, see Susan Strange's (1986) aptly titled book, *Casino Capitalism*.
9 Peter Skott (1989), however, has incorporated Keynesian demand into a Goodwin-like model. It is not discussed here for reasons of space. But it is also an interesting model, although (a) there is no money in the model and (b) the cycle variables are the capital output ratio and the employment ratio.

12

General Conclusions

The objective of this book has been to evaluate the main approaches to the study of the theory of business cycles. As stated earlier, this book is *not* a review or survey of all the theories.

This book defines the "main approaches" to be the following:

(1) The New Classical approach
(2) The New Keynesian approach
(3) The endogenous cycle approach

In chapter 2, ten empirical regularities (stylized facts) associated with modern business cycles were stated, together with the empirical evidence. It was then shown that the first nine can also be consistently derived as properties of a simple static macro model. In the absence of agreed methods of confirmation, corroboration, and refutation in economics, the stylized facts provide a benchmark to assess the merits of business cycle theories. The most important of these stylized facts is the *integral relationship of output, inflation, and unemployment over time,* shown in figure 2.1, Chapter 2. However, before that criterion can be applied, one must be satisfied that the mathematical model of business cycles contains *no redundant* mathematics, – that is, mathematics that have no economic content (chapter 3). Lastly, the model must identify the most crucial interactions through the *governing mechanism,* which, in principle, must be testable and falsifiable. These three criteria can then be applied to the main approaches of business cycle theory.

12.1 THE NEW CLASSICAL APPROACH

The New Classical approach has essentially two kinds of models, the monetary misperceptions models of Lucas and Barro, and the real business cycle models of Kydland, Prescott, Long, Plosser, King, and others. The central ideas of the real business cycle theory can be found in Lucas, who has subsequently expressed his approval of real business cycle theory in his Yrjö Jahnsson lectures, although at the same time his estimates show that in terms of loss of consumption the (American) business cycle is a minor problem: the utility gain (for his representative agent) from smoothing out the business cycle would be negligibly small.

The misperceptions approach to business cycles has serious shortcomings. Tobin argued that informational asymmetry in the misperceptions model has to be of a special kind that leads to positive correlations between output and prices, whereas Okun delivered the mortal blow: if there are assumed to be extensive contingent markets, why is there no market in information? This missing market represents a profit-making opportunity. Hence the misperceptions model is *not* an equilibrium account. Misperceptions are also not compatible with rational expectations, for with the latter, systematic misperceptions cannot occur. (Incidentally, this contradiction is not present in Friedman's 1968 model.)

The model relies on the unwarranted assumption that cyclical growth is decomposable into a trend component and a cyclical component. Finally the model contains what we called (in chapter 3) "redundant mathematics," that is mathematics with no corresponding *economic* interpretation. The cyclical component has a weight λ, which is between zero and 1. This weight has no economic interpretation. Nor is it endogenously derived: it is a *deus ex machina*.

In terms of the stylized facts, the model establishes comovement in output, prices, and money – which means that money and prices are procyclical. No other stylized fact is reflected in the model. The governing mechanism of the cycle is misperceptions about prices caused by money supply growth.

The internal inconsistencies of the model fail to account for the business cycle, and also fail to preserve the policy ineffectiveness propositions.

Real business cycle (RBC) theory was meant to remedy the defects of the misperceptions approach and to recreate, as it were, an equilibrium account of the cycle that would make policy intervention redundant.

In an RBC model, all households are alike, which is equivalent to *one*, representative household. This representative agent maximizes her utility intertemporally. The intertemporal general equilibrium has of course no cyclical feature. Even with a random productivity shock in the production function (to which the representative agent has access), there is no business cycle, as there is no comovement of any of the variables and no persistent autocorrelation of output. In order to incorporate these features the shock is given a first order autoregressive form, AR(1). When the exogenous shock is AR(1), consumption and capital stock become AR(2) processes. Again, as in the Lucas model, output is decomposed into a permanent and a cyclical component; the latter can be shown to be nothing but an infinite sum of past random shocks. Thus the cyclical component exists only because of the assumed lag structure of capital and of the shocks. When money is incorporated (with yet another shock), several stylized facts are replicated: money, output, and real wages are procyclical; output variations persist over many periods; nominal variables are more correlated than their corresponding real variables. The exogenous shock has no satisfactory economic interpretation; it is in fact redundant mathematics. But matters do not end there, for the shock is given a particular lag structure, which compounds the redundant mathematics. The governing mechanism is precisely this shock with the particular lag structure.

12.2 THE NEW KEYNESIAN APPROACH

The New Keynesian approach attacked the New Classical results by showing that the assumptions of complete market clearance through (perfect) competition do not hold in the modern (U.S.) economy. In the view of the New Keynesians, it is precisely because prices do not adjust instantaneously due to changing demand and supply conditions, and because firms are not perfectly competitive, operating at minimum average costs, that business cycles occur. In particular, the New Keynesians wish to demonstrate that underemployment equilibrium can be an outcome of rational (profit-maximizing) behavior. This makes an expansion a special case, just as Keynes had postulated. A necessary concomitant is that interventionist policies are necessary and desirable following a downturn.

In order to demonstrate the above propositions, New Keynesians adopt the same representative agent assumption used by Friedman and by the New Classical economists. But unlike the New Classicals, they undertook a wide-ranging theoretical and empirical analysis of the U.S. economy, into the nature of product, labor, and financial markets; into mechanisms that determine price setting in the absence of a mythical auctioneer; and into the consequent aggregate demand failures and coordination failures. Some of the most fascinating results are obtained about the nature of the U.S. economy, which is characterized by monopolistic competition. There is considerable price rigidity and excess capacity in the product markets. The labor market is characterized by efficiency wages, labor hoarding, and staggered contracts that make the real wage above market equilibrium, and a real wage that adjusts slowly to changing conditions. The financial markets are characterized by vast numbers of paper transactions of a speculative nature that have nothing to do with financing the *real* sector of the economy. Thus in the hands of New Keynesians, we see a full integration of market structure with macroeconomics. In such a sluggish real economy, even small "menu costs" could impart a rigidity that *to the firms themselves* has a cost that is of second order only, whereas to the economy as a whole the rigidity results in large welfare losses, as the economy gets stuck at an underemployment equilibrium.

New Keynesians are less concerned about explaining the stylized facts; to them the "business cycle" is the underemployment equilibrium, the recession, and not just the associated welfare losses; each recession leaves the economy's capital stock lower than it would have been. Consequently, the loss is an entire growth *path* that is lost forever and can never be made good. Any and *every* recession imposes such huge social costs.

The governing mechanism of the cycle (which is synonymous with recession) is the oligopolistic nature of the economy. I have not seen any work by a New Keynesian that advocates making the economy less oligopolistic and more "competitive," perhaps because achieving the abstract ideals of perfect competition would be pure fantasy; but what we do see is the advocacy of judicious use of monetary and fiscal policy to achieve the traditional goals of full employment with some degree of price stability.

12.3 ENDOGENOUS CYCLE MODELS

The endogenous cycle approach offers one important lesson: that business cycles are inherent to a free enterprise economy, a lesson that Schumpeter tried to drive home much earlier. The Benassy model has much in common with the New Keynesian approach; it is a representative agent model and it admits an imperfectly competitive market structure, in which transactions occur in disequilibrium, because there is no auctioneer to guide traders. The model displays the appropriate integral relationship between output, employment, prices, and wages. Thus the main stylized facts are reflected in the model. But the model does *not* incorporate growth into the cycle. In the model, investment takes place and the capital stock increases, but income does not grow.

However, the model does incorporate the usual *IS-LM* analysis into a dynamic non-Walrasian adjustment path, which turns out to be cyclical. As agents are quantity constrained, the cycle reflects the adjustment of the capital stock to demand expectations that are unknown without a coordinator. When output is expanding, high wage costs lead to an upper turning point, and a fall in output leads to reduced wages, and reduced wages lead to the lower turning point in the cycle. The governing mechanism is the interaction of the goods and labor markets.

The final model considered is the Goodwin model, which integrates growth with the cycle and explains *all* but one of the set of ten stylized facts. The assumptions of the model are sparse indeed. It shows that the share of labor (or one minus the share of labor, which is profits) and the employment ratio fluctuate; in the expansion, employment and the share of labor increase, but near full employment the high wages depress profits, which depresses investment and thus leads to a fall in employment. The fall in employment eventually raises profits so that another cycle starts again.

The Benassy and Goodwin models both focus our attention on the labor market. In a boom wage growth is high and prices rise. The central bank becomes concerned about inflation, and imposes a credit crunch (see the quotation from Eckstein and Sinai, given on p. 116), and a downturn is precipitated by the actions of the central bank.

The Goodwin model explicitly puts the issue of income distribution at the center of the explanation of the business cycle. Countries that have tried some form of cooperative agreement on wage increases have fared better in controlling the cycle. The Japanese economy, too, has weathered many a cycle in spite of its heavy reliance on exports by achieving fairly smooth growth in comparison to the U.S. economy. I believe they have achieved it with a greater degree of agreement on wage growth, and with lower interest rates. Lower interest rates are feasible if inflation is low. In other words, such countries have some form of a tacit incomes policy. An income policy may be the answer to reducing the ravages of business cycles and the consequent stop-go policies that accompany it. But that is not the subject of this book.

References

Adelman, I. and Adelman, F.L. (1959) 'The dynamic properties of the Klein-Goldberger model," *Econometrica* 27 (4), 596–625.

Akerlof, G. (1969) "Relative wages and the rate of inflation," *Quarterly Journal of Economics* 83, 353–74.

Akerlof, G. (1970) "The market for lemons: qualitative uncertainty and the market mechanism," *Quarterly Journal of Economics* 84 (3), 488–500.

Akerlof, G. (1984) "Gift exchange and efficiency wage theory: four views," *American Economic Review* 74, 79–83.

Akerlof, G. and Yellen, J. (1985) "A near-rational model of the business cycle, with wage and price inertia," *Quarterly Journal of Economics* 100 supp., 823–38. In Mankiw and Romer, *op. cit.* vol. 1.

Akhand, H. (1991) "Policy credibility and inflation in a wage setting game," *Canadian Journal of Economics*, forthcoming.

Angeles, P.A. (1981) *Dictionary of Philosophy*. New York: Harper and Row.

Arrow, K.J. and Kurz, M. (1970) *Public Investment, the Rate of Return, and Optimal Fiscal Policy*. Baltimore: Johns Hopkins Press.

Arrow, K.J. (1989) "Von Neumann and the existence theorem for general equilibrium," in Dore, M.H.I. ed. *John Von Neumann and Modern Economics*. Oxford: Oxford University Press.

Asada, T. (1989) "Monetary stabilization policy in a Keynes-Goodwin model of the growth cycle," in Semmler, W., ed. *Financial Dynamics and Business Cycles: New Perspectives*. Armonk, New York: M.E. Sharpe.

Ashton, T.S. (1959) *Economic Fluctuations in England, 1700–1800*. Oxford: Clarendon Press.

Ball, L., Mankiw, N.G. and Romer, D. (1988) "The new Keynesian economics and the output-inflation trade-off," *Brookings Papers on Economic Activity* 1, 1–65. In Mankiw and Romer, *op. cit.* vol. 1.

Barro, R.J. (1972) "A theory of monopolistic price adjustment," *Review of Economic Studies* 39 (1), 17–26.

Barro, R.J. (1976) "Rational expectations and the role of monetary policy," *Journal of Monetary Economics* 2 (1), 1–32.

Barro, R.J. (1980) "Federal deficit policy and the effects of public debt shocks," *Journal of Money, Credit and Banking* 12 (4 part II), 747–61.

Barro, R.J. (1981) *Money, Expectations and Business Cycles*. New York: Academic Press.

Barro, R.J. (1987) *Macroeconomics*, 2nd ed. New York: Wiley.

Barro, R.J., ed. (1989) *Modern Business Cycle Theory*. Cambridge, Mass: Harvard University Press.

Barro, R.J. and Grossman, H. (1971) "A general disequilibrium model of income and employment," *American Economic Review* 61, 82–93.

Bellman, R. (1957) *Dynamic Programming*. Princeton: Princeton University Press.

Beltrami, E. (1987) *Mathematics for Dynamic Modeling*. New York: Academic Press.

Benassy, J.-P. (1976) "The disequilibrium approach to monopolistic price setting and general monopolistic equilibrium," *Review of Economic Studies* 43, 69–81.

Benassy, J.-P. (1986) *Macroeconomics: An Introduction to the Non-Walrasian Approach*. Orlando: Academic Press.

Bernanke, B.S. (1983) "Nonmonetary effects of the financial crisis in the propagation of the great depression," *American Economic Review* 73, 257–76. Reprinted in Mankiw and Romer, *op. cit.* vol.2.

Bertola, G. and Caballero, R.J. (1990) "Kinked adjustment costs and aggregate dynamics," *NBER Macroeconomics Annual 1990*, 237–88.

Beveridge, S. and Nelson, C.R. (1981) "A new approach to decomposition of economic time series into permanent and transitory components with particular attention to measurement of the 'business cycle,'" *Journal of Monetary Economics* 7, 151–74.

Bils, M. (1985) "The cyclical behavior of marginal cost and price," working paper no. 30, University of Rochester.

Birkhoff, G. and MacLane, S. (1966) *A Survey of Modern Algebra*. New York: Macmillan.

Blackorby, C. and Schworm, W.E. (1988) *The Implications of Additive Community Preferences in a Multi-consumer Economy*. University of British Columbia Department of Economics: Discussion Paper no.88–20.

Blanchard, O. (1986) "The wage price spiral," *Quarterly Journal of Economics* 101, 543–65.

Blatt, J.M. (1983) *Dynamic Economic Systems: A Post-Keynesian Approach*. Armonk: M.E.Sharpe.

Blinder, A. (1987) "Credit rationing and effective supply failures," *Economic Journal* 97, 327–52.

Bodkin, R. (1969) "Real wages and cyclical variations in employment: a re-examination of the evidence," *Canadian Journal of Economics* 2, 353–74.

Brock, W.A. and Mirman, L.J. (1972) "Optimal economic growth and uncertainty: the discounted case," *Journal of Economic Theory*, 4, 479–515.

Brody, A. (1970) *Proportions, Prices and Planning*. Amsterdam: North Holland.

Brody, A. (1990) "Observations concerning the growth cycle," in Velupillai, *op. cit.*

Bulow, J., Geanakoplos, J. and Klemperer, P. (1985) "Multimarket oligopoly: strategic substitutes and complements," *Journal of Political Economy* 93, 488–511.

Bulow, J. and Summers, L. (1986) "A theory of dual labor markets with application to industrial policy, discrimination and Keynesian unemployment," *Journal of Labor Economics* 4, 376–414.

Burns, A.F. and Mitchell, W.C. (1946) "Measuring business cycles," *Studies in Business Cycles*, no.2. New York: National Bureau of Economic Research.

Caballero, R.J. (1991) *A Fallacy of Composition*. National Bureau of Economic Research, Working Paper Series no.3735.

Cagan, P. (1965) *Determinants and Effects of Changes in the Stock of Money, 1875–1960*. New York: Columbia University Press for the National Bureau of Economic Research.

Campbell, J.Y. and Mankiw, N.G. (1987) "Permanent and transitory components in macroeconomic fluctuations," *American Economic Review, Papers and Proceedings*, 77 (2), 111–7.

Caplin, A.S. and Spulber, D.F. (1987) "Menu costs and the neutrality of money," *Quarterly Journal of Economics* 102, 703–25. In Mankiw, N.G. and Romer, D., *op. cit.* vol. 1.

Carlton, D.W. (1983) "Equilibrium fluctuations when price and delivery lags clear the market," *Bell Journal of Economics* 14, 562–72.

Carlton, D.W. (1986) "The rigidity of prices," *American Economic Review* 76, 637–658.

Carlton, D.W. (1989) "The theory and facts of how markets clear: Is industrial organization useful for understanding macroeconomics?," ch. 15 in Schmalensee, R. and Willig, R., eds., *Handbook of Industrial Organization*. A revised version appears in ch. 21 of Carlton, D.W. and Perloff, J. *Modern Industrial Organization*. Glenview, Ill.: Scott-Foresman, 1990.

Chang, W.W. and Smyth, D.J. (1971) "The existence and persistence of cycles in a non-linear model: Kaldor's 1940 model re-examined," *Review of Economic Studies* 38, 37–44.

Charles River Associates (1986) *Natural Gas Procurement Experience with Spot vs. Contract Pricing in Analogous Commodity Markets*.

Chiang, A.C. (1974) *Fundamental Methods of Mathematical Economics*; 2nd ed. New York: McGraw-Hill.

Clark, P. (1987) "The cyclical component of U.S. economic activity," *Quarterly Journal of Economics* 102 (4), 797–814.

Clower, R.W. (1965) "The Keynesian counter-revolution: A theoretical appraisal" in Hahn, F.H. and Brechling, F.P.R., eds., *The Theory of Interest Rates*. London: Macmillan.

Cochrane, J.H. (1986) *How Big Is the Random Walk in GNP?* University of Chicago Working Paper.

Cornwall, J. (1987) "Total factor productivity," in *The New Palgrave: A Dictionary of Economics*, vol.4. New York: Stockton Press.

Cooper, R. and John, A. (1988) "Coordinating coordination failures in Keynesian models," *Quarterly Journal of Economics* 103, 441–63. In Mankiw and Romer, *op. cit.* vol. 2.

Cournot, A.A. ([1938] 1927) *Researches into the Mathematical Principles of the Theory of Wealth* (trans. Nathaniel T.Bacon). New York: Macmillan.

Cuthbertson, K. and Taylor, M.P. (1987) *Macroeconomic Systems*. Oxford: Basil Blackwell.

Dalziel, P. (1990) "Market power, inflation and income policies," *Journal of Post-Keynesian Economics* 12 (3), 424–38.

Darnell, A.C. and Evans, J.L. (1990) *The Limits of Econometrics*. Aldershot, Hants: Edward Elgar.

David, P.A. (1988) "Path-dependence: putting the past in the future of economics," Stanford University, Technical Report no. 533, Institute for Mathematical Studies in the Social Sciences, Mimeo.

Davidson, P. (1972) *Money and the Real World*. London: Macmillan.

Debreu, G. (1959) *Theory of Value: An Axiomatic Analysis of Economic Equilibrium*. New York: John Wiley.

Desai, M. (1984) "An econometric model of the share of wages in national income: UK 1885–1965", in Goodwin, R.M., Kruger, M. and Vercelli, A., eds. *Non-Linear Models of Fluctuating Growth*, Lecture Notes in Economics and Mathematical Systems no. 228. Berlin: Springer-Verlag.

DeVany, A. and Saving, T. (1977) "Product quality, uncertainty and regulation: the trucking industry," *American Economic Review* 67 (4), 583–94.

Diamond, P. (1982) "Aggregate demand management in search equilibrium," *Journal of Political Economy* 90, 881–94. In Mankiw, and Romer, *op. cit.* vol. 2.

Di Matteo, M. (1984) "Alternative monetary policies in a classical growth cycle," in Goodwin, R.M., Kruger, M. and Vercelli, A., eds. *Nonlinear Models of Fluctuating Growth*. New York: Springer-Verlag.

Domowitz, I., Hubbard, R.G. and Peterson, B.C. (1986a) "Business cycles and the relationship between concentration and price-cost margins," *Rand Journal of Economics* 17 (1), 1–17.

Domowitz, I., Hubbard, R.G. and Peterson, B.C. (1986b) "Intertemporal stability of the concentration-margins relationship," *Journal of Industrial Economics* 35 (1), 1–22.

Domowitz, I., Hubbard, R.G. and Peterson, B.C. (1986c) "Oligopoly super-games: some empirical evidence." Unpublished paper.

Dore, M.H.I. (1977) *Dynamic Investment Planning*. London: Croom Helm.

Dore, M.H.I. (1984–85) "The concept of equilibrium," *Journal of Post Keynesian Economics* III (2), 193–206.

Dore, M.H.I. (1988–89) "The Use of Mathematics in Social Explanation," *Science and Society* 52, (4), (Winter) 456–69.

Dore, M.H.I. (1989a) "The legacy of John von Neumann," in Dore, M.H.I., Chakravarty, S. and Goodwin, R., eds. *John von Neumann and Modern Economics*. Oxford: Clarendon Press.

Dore, M.H.I., ed. (1989b) *John Von Neumann and Modern Economics*. Oxford: Oxford University Press.

Dunlop, J. (1938) "The movement of real and money wage rates," *Economic Journal* 48, 413–34.

Durlauf, S.N. (1991a) *Nonergodic Economic Growth*. NBER Working Paper no. 3719. Cambridge, Mass: NBER.

Durlauf, S.N. (1991b) *Path Dependence in Aggregate Output*: NBER Working Paper no. 3718. Cambridge, Mass: NBER.

Durlauf, S.N. (1991c) "Multiple equilibria and persistence in aggregate fluctuations," *American Economic Review* 81 (2), 70–74.

Earl, P.E. (1990) *Monetary Scenarios: A Modern Approach to Financial Systems*. Aldershot, Hants: Edward Elgar.

Eckstein, O. and Sinai, A. (1986) "The mechanisms of the business cycle in the postwar era," in Gordon, R., ed. *The American Business Cycle: Continuity and Change*. Chicago: University of Chicago Press for NBER.

Eichenbaum, M. (1990) "Real business cycle theory: wisdom or whimsy?" *Federal Reserve Bank of Chicago Working Paper Series* 90/13.

Encaoua, D. and Geroski, P. (1984) "Price dynamics and competition in five countries," working paper no. 8414, University of Southampton.

Fisher, I. (1923) "The business cycle is largely a *Dance of the Dollar*," *Journal of the American Statistical Association* 18, 1024–8.

Flanders, H., Korfhage, R.R., and Price, J.J. (1974) *A Second Course in Calculus*. New York: Academic Press.

Friedman, M. (1955) "Leon Walras and his economic system: A review article," *American Economic Review* 45 (5), 900–9.

Friedman, M. (1957) *A Theory of the Consumption Function*. Princeton: Princeton University Press.

Friedman, M. (1959) *A Program of Monetary Stability*. New York: Fordham University Press.

Friedman, M. (1968) "The role of monetary policy," *American Economic Review* 58 (1), 1–17

Friedman, M. (1969) *Optimum Quantity of Money and Other Essays*. London: Macmillan.

Friedman. M. and Schwartz, A.J. (1963) *A Monetary History of the United States, 1867–1960*. Princeton: Princeton University Press.

Friedman, M. and Schwartz, A.J. (1970) *Monetary Statistics of the United States*. New York: Columbia University Press for the National Bureau of Economic Research.

Friedman, M. and Schwartz, A.J. (1982) *Monetary Trends in the United States and the United Kingdom: Their Relation to Income, Prices and Interest Rates 1867–1975*. Chicago: University of Chicago Press.

Gabisch, G. and Lorenz, H.–W. (1989) *Business Cycle Theory: A Survey of Methods and Concepts;* 2nd ed. New York: Springer-Verlag.

Garretsen, H. and Janssen, M.C.W. (1989) "Two fallacies of composition in a Keynesian OLG model," University of Groningen Research Memorandum no. 317.

Geary, P. and Kennan, J. (1982) "The employment-real wage relationship: An international study," *Journal of Political Economy* 90, 854–71.

Georgescu-Roegen, N. (1951) "The aggregate linear production function and its application to von Neumann's economic model," in Koopmans, T.C., ed. *Activity Analysis of Production and Allocation*. New York: John Wiley.

Geweke, J. (1985) "Macroeconomic modelling and the theory of the representative agent", *American Economic Review*, Papers and Proceedings, 75 (2), 206–10.

Glasner, D., ed. (1992 forthcoming) *Encyclopedia of Business Cycles, Panics, Crises and Depressions*. New York: Garland Publishing.

Godley,W. (1984) "Notes for a talk in Luxembourg on October 3rd,1984." Cambridge: Cambridge University Department of Applied Economics, mimeo.

Golub, S.S. (1983) *International Financial Markets, Oil Prices and Exchange Rates*. Ph.D. diss.. Yale University.

Goodwin, R.M. (1953) "The problem of trend and cycle," *Yorkshire Bulletin of Economic and Social Research*. In Goodwin, R.M. (1982) *Essays in Economic Dynamics*. London: Macmillan.

Goodwin, R.M. (1967) "A growth cycle," in Feinstein, C.H. ed., *Socialism, Capitalism and Economic Growth: Essays Presented to Maurice Dobb*. Cambridge: Cambridge University Press.

Goodwin, R.M. (1982) *Essays in Economic Dynamics*. London: Macmillan.

Goodwin, R.M., Kruger, M. and Vercelli, A., eds. (1984) *Nonlinear Models of Fluctuating Growth*. New York: Springer-Verlag.

Gordon, R. (1983) "A century of evidence on wage and price stickiness in the United States, the United Kingdom and Japan," in Tobin, J., ed. *Macroeconomics, Prices and Quantities: Essays in Memory of Arthur M. Okun*. Washington, D.C.: Brookings Institution, 85–134.

Gordon, R., ed. (1986) *The American Business Cycle: Continuity and Change*. Chicago: Chicago University Press for NBER.

Gould, J. (1978) "Inventories and stochastic demand: equilibrium models of the firm and industry", *Journal of Business* 51 (1), 1–42.

Graaff, J. de V. (1967) *Theoretical Welfare Economics*. Cambridge: Cambridge University Press.

Gurley, J. and Shaw, E. (1955) "Financial aspects of economic development," *American Economic Review* 45, 515–38.

Hahn, F.H. (1971) "Professor Friedman's views on money: A review article," *Economica* NS 38 (149), 61–80.

Hahn, F.H. (1982) "Stability," in Arrow and Intriligator eds., *Handbook of Mathematical Economics*, vol. 2. Amsterdam: North-Holland.

Hall, R.E. (1975) "The rigidity of wages and the persistence of unemployment," *Brookings Papers on Economic Activity* 2, 301–35.

Hall, R.E. (1986) "Market structure and macroeconomic fluctuations", *Brookings Papers on Economic Activity*, No. 2, pp. 285–322. In Mankiw and Romer, *op. cit.* vol. 1. 1991.

Hamburger, L. (1931) "Analogie des fluctuations economiques et des oscillations de relaxation," *Supplement aux Indices du Mouvement des Affaires* 9, 3–36.

Hamburger, L. (1934) "Note on economic cycles and relaxation-oscillations," *Econometrica* 2, 112.

Hansen, G.D. (1985) "Indivisible labor and the business cycle," *Journal of Monetary Economics* 16 (3), 309–28.

Harrison, J.M. (1985) *Brownian Motions and Stochastic Flow Systems*. New York: John Wiley and Sons.

Harrod, R.F. (1936) *The Trade Cycle: An Essay*. Oxford: Oxford University Press.

Hayek, F. (1933) *Monetary Theory and the Trade Cycle*. New York: Augustus M. Kelley, 1975.

Hendry, D.F. and Ericsson, N.R. (1991) "An econometric analysis of U.K. money demand in *Monetary Trends in the United States and the United Kingdom* by Milton Friedman and Anna J. Schwartz," *American Economic Review* 81 (1), 8–38.

Hercowitz, Z. and Sampson, M. (1986) *Growth and Employment Fluctuations*. Working paper.

Hicks, J.R. (1950) *A Contribution to the Theory of the Trade Cycle*. Oxford: Clarendon Press.

Hodgson, G. (1986) "Behind methodological individualism," *Cambridge Journal of Economics* 10, 211–24.

Hoover, K.D. (1988) *The New Classical Macroeconomics*. Oxford: Basil Blackwell.

Howitt, P. (1984) "Information and coordination: a review article," *Economic Inquiry* 22, 429–46.

Howitt, P. and McAffee, R.P. (1988) "Stability of equilibria with externalities," *Quarterly Journal of Economics* 103, 261–78.

Ichimura, S. (1943) "Toward a general nonlinear macrodynamic theory of economic fluctuations," in Kurihara, K.K., ed. *Post-Keynesian Economics*. London: Allen and Unwin.

Kakutani, S. (1941) "A generalization of Brouwer's fixed-point theorem," *Duke Mathematical Journal*, 8(3), 457–59.

Kaldor, N. (1940) "A model of the trade cycle," *Economic Journal* 50, 78–92.

Kaldor, N. (1959) "Economic growth and the problem of inflation – Parts 1 and 2," *Economica* 26, 212–26 and 287–98. Reprinted in *Essays on Economic Policy*, vol. 1. New York: Holmes and Meier, 1964.

Kalecki, M. (1936–7) "A theory of the business cycle," *Review of Economic Studies* 4 (2), 77–97.

Keane, M., Moffitt, R. and Runkle, D. (1988) "Real wages over the business cycle: Estimating the impact of heterogeneity with micro data," working paper no.87–10, Brown University.

Keynes, J.M. (1936) *The General Theory of Employment, Interest and Money*. In Keynes, *Collected Writings, Vol. VII*, 1973. London: Macmillan, for the Royal Economic Society.

Keynes, J.M. (1972) *Essays in Persuasion*, vol. IX of the collected writings of J.M. Keynes, edited by E. Johnson and D. Moggridge. London: Macmillan.

King, R.G., and Plosser, C.I. (1984) "Money, credit and prices in a real business cycle," *American Economic Review* 74 (3), 363–80

King, R.G., Plosser, C.I. and Rebelo, S.T. (1988) "Production, growth and business cycles. I: the basic neoclassical model," *Journal of Monetary Economics* 21 (2/3), 309–42.

Kocak, H. (1989) *Differential and Difference Equations through Computer Experiments*. 2nd ed. New York: Springer-Verlag.

Koopmans, T.C. (1940) "The degree of damping in business cycles," *Econometrica* 9, 79–89.

Koopmans, T.C. (1941) "The logic of economic business-cycle research", *Journal of Political Economy* 49 (2), 157–81.

Koopmans, T.C. (1949) "The economic approach to business fluctuations," *American Economic Review, Papers and Proceedings* 39 (3), 64–72.

Koopmans, T.C. (1964) "Economic growth at a maximal rate," *Quarterly Journal of Economics* 78, 355–94. In Sen, A., ed. *Growth Economics*. Harmondsworth: Penguin Books, 1970.

Kosobud, R.F. and O'Neil, W.D. (1972) "Stochastic implications of orbital asymptotic stability of a nonlinear trade cycle model," *Econometrica* 40, 69–86.

Krueger, A.B. and Summers, L.H. (1988) "Efficiency wages and the interindustry wage structure," *Econometrica* 56, 259–93. In Mankiw and Romer, *op. cit.* vol. 2. 1991.

Lang, S. (1968) *Linear Algebra*. Reading, Mass: Addison-Wesley.

Leamer, E.E. (1983) "Let's take the con out of econometrics," *American Economic Review* 73, 31–43.

Le Corbeiller, P. (1933) "Les systemes autoentretenus et les oscillations de relaxation," *Econometrica* 1, 328–32.

Leijonhufvud, A. (1968) *On Keynesian Economics and the Economics of Keynes: A Study in Monetary Theory*. New York: Oxford University Press.

Leijonhufvud, A. (1981) *Information and Coordination: Essays in Macroeconomic Theory*. Oxford: Oxford University Press.

Long, J.B., Jr., and Plosser, C.I. (1983) "Real business cycles," *Journal of Political Economy* 91 (1), 39–69.

Lucas, R.E. (1972) "Expectations and the neutrality of money," *Journal of Economic Theory* 4, 103–24.

Lucas, R.E. (1973) "Some international evidence on output-inflation tradeoffs," in Lucas (1981a) *op. cit.* Reprinted from *American Economic Review* 63 (3), 326–34.

Lucas, R.E. (1975) "An equilibrium model of the business cycle," in Lucas (1981a) *op. cit.*

Lucas, R.E. (1976) "Econometric policy evaluation: A critique," in Lucas (1981a) *op. cit.* Reprinted from Brunner, K. and Meltzer, A.H., eds. *The Phillips Curve and Labor Markets.* Carnegie-Rochester Conference Series on Public Policy, vol. 1. Amsterdam: North Holland.

Lucas, R.E. (1977) "Understanding business cycles," in Lucas (1981a) *op. cit.* Reprinted from Brunner, K. and Meltzer, A.H., eds. *Stabilization of the Domestic and International Economy.* Carnegie-Rochester Conference Series on Public Policy, vol. 5, Spring. Amsterdam: North Holland.

Lucas, R.E. (1981a) *Studies in Business Cycle Theory.* Oxford: Basil Blackwell.

Lucas, R.E. (1981b) "Tobin and monetarism: A review article," *Journal of Economic Literature* 19 (2), 558–67.

Lucas, R.E. (1987) *Models of Business Cycles: Yrjö Jahnsson Lectures, May 1985.* Oxford: Basil Blackwell.

Lucas, R.E. and Prescott, E.C. (1971) "Investment under uncertainty," *Econometrica*, 39 (September), 659–82.

Lucas, R.E. and Sargent, T.J., eds. (1981), *Rational Expectations and Econometric Practice.* London: Allen and Unvin.

Maital, S. and Benjamini, Y. (1980) "Inflation as prisoner's dilemma", *Journal of Post Keynesian Economics* 2 (4), 459–81.

Mankiw, N.G. (1985) "Small menu costs and large business cycles: A macroeconomic model of monopoly," *Quarterly Journal of Economics* 100 (2), 329–33. In Mankiw and Romer, *op. cit.*

Mankiw, N.G. and Romer, D., eds. (1991) *New Keynesian Economics.* Cambridge, Mass: MIT Press.

Mankiw, N.G., Rotemburg, J. and Summers, L.H. (1985) "Intertemporal substitution in macroeconomics," *Quarterly Journal of Economics* 100 (1), 225–51.

McCallum, B.T. (1989) "Real business cycle models," in Barro, R.J. ed. *Modern Business Cycle Theory.* Cambridge, Mass: Harvard University Press.

Minorsky, N. (1962) *Nonlinear Oscillations.* New York: Van Nostrand.

Moore, B.J. (1988) *Horizontalists and Verticalists: The Macroeconomics of Credit Money.* Cambridge: Cambridge University Press.

Moore, G. (1977) "Business cycles: Partly exogenous, mostly endogenous," *Social Science Quarterly* 58 (1), 96–103.

Moore, G. and Zarnowitz, V. (1986) "The development and role of the

National Bureau of Economic Research's Business Cycle Chronologies," in Gordon, R.J., ed. *The American Business Cycle*. Chicago: University of Chicago Press.

Muth, J.F. (1961) "Rational expectations and the theory of price movements." Reprinted in Lucas, R.E. and Sargent, T.J., eds. (1981) *Rational Expectations and Econometric Practice*. London: Allen and Unwin.

Neftci, S. (1978) "A time-series analysis of the real wages-employment relationship", *Journal of Political Economy* 86, 281–91.

Nelson, C.R. and Plosser, C.I. (1982) "Trends and random walks in macroeconomic time series," *Journal of Monetary Economics* 10 (September), 139–62.

Neumann, J. von (1937) "Über ein Ökonomisches Gleichungssystem und eine Verallgemeinerung des Brouwerschen Fixpunktsatzes", *Ergebnisse eines Mathematischen Kolloquiums* 8; first English translation as "A Model of General Economic Equilibrium," *Review of Economic Studies* 13 (1946–6), 1–9.

Oi, W.Y. (1962) "Labor as a quasi-fixed factor," *Journal of Political Economy* 70, 538–55.

Oi, W.Y. (1983) "The fixed employment costs of specialized labor," in Triplett, J.E., ed. *The Measurement of Labor Costs*. Chicago: University of Chicago Press.

Okun, A.M. (1980) "Rational expectations-with-misperceptions as a theory of the business cycle," *Journal of Money, Credit and Banking* 12 (4, part 2), 817–25

Pagan, A. (1987) "Three econometric methodologies: a critical appraisal", *Journal of Economic Surveys* 1, 3–24.

Patinkin, D. (1956, 1965) *Money, Interest and Prices*, 1st ed. 1956, 2nd ed. 1965. New York: Harper and Row.

Prescott, Edward C. (1986) "Theory ahead of business cycle measurement," in Brunner, K. and Meltzer, A.H., (eds.) *Real Business Cycles, Real Exchange Rates and Actual Policies*. Carnegie-Rochester Conference Series on Public Policy, vol. 25, Autumn. Amsterdam: North Holland. Reprinted in *Federal Reserve Bank of Minneapolis Quarterly Review* 10 (4), Fall, 9–22.

Raisian, J. (1983) "Contracts, job experience and cyclical labor market adjustments," *Journal of Labor Economics* 1, 152–70.

Rogers, C. (1989) *Money, Interest and Capital*. Cambridge: Cambridge University Press.

Rogerson, R. (1988) "Indivisible labor, lotteries and equilibrium," *Journal of Monetary Economics* 21 (1), 3–16.

Romer, Paul M. (1989) "Capital accumulation in the theory of long-run growth," in Barro (1989) *op.cit.*

Rosen, S. (1974) "Hedonic prices and implicit markets: product differentiation in pure competition," *Journal of Political Economy* 82 (1), 34–55.

Rotemberg, J. (1987) "The new Keynesian microeconomic foundations," *NBER Macroeconomic Annual*, 69–114.

Rothchild, M. (1971) "On the cost of adjustment," *Quarterly Journal of Economics* 85 (4), 605–22.

Salop, S. (1979) "A model of the natural rate of unemployment," *American Economic Review* 69, 117–25.

Sargan, J.D. (1964) "Wages and prices in the U.K.: A study in economic methodology." In Hart, P.E., Mills, G. and Whitaker, J.K., eds., *Econometric Analysis for National Economic Planning*. London: Butterworth.

Sargent, T.J. (1973) "Rational expectations, the real rate of interest and the natural rate of unemployment," *Brookings Papers on Economic Activity* 2, 429–72.

Sargent, T.J. (1978) "Estimation of dynamic labor demand schedules under rational expectations," *Journal of Political Economy* 86, 1009–44.

Sargent, T.J. (1979) *Macroeconomic Theory*. New York: Academic Press.

Sargent, T.J. (1987) *Dynamic Macroeconomic Theory*. Cambridge, Mass: Harvard University Press.

Sargent, T.J. and Wallace, N. (1975) "Rational expectations, the optimal monetary instrument, and the optimal money supply rule," *Journal of Political Economy* 83, 241–54.

Scheinkman, J.A. and Weiss, L. (1986) "Borrowing constraints and aggregate economic activity," *Econometrica* 54, 23–45.

Schumpeter, J.A. (1939) *Business Cycles*. New York: McGraw-Hill.

Semmler, W., ed. (1989) *Financial Dynamics and Business Cycles: New Perspectives*. Armonk, New York: M.E. Sharpe.

Shapiro, C. and Stiglitz, J.E. (1984) "Equilibrium unemployment as a worker-discipline device," *American Economic Review* 74, 433–44. In Mankiw, N.G. and Romer, D., *op. cit.* vol. 2. 1991.

Sheehan, R.G. and Grieves, R. (1982) "Sunspots and cycles: a test of causation," *Southern Economic Journal*, (January), 775–7.

Sheshinski, E. and Weiss, Y. (1977) "Inflation and costs of price adjustment," *Review of Economic Studies* 44 (2), 287–303.

Sheshinski, E., and Weiss, Y. (1983) "Optimum pricing policy under stochastic inflation," *Review of Economic Studies* 50 (3), 513–29.

Shiller, R.J. (1981) "Do stock prices move too much to be justified by subsequent changes in dividends?" *American Economic Review*, 70: 421–36.

Simmons, G.F. (1972) *Differential Equations: with Applications and Historical Notes*. New York: McGraw-Hill. Also published by Tata McGraw-Hill, India: New Delhi, 1974.

Sims, C.A. (1972) "Money, income and causality," In Lucas and Sargent (1981) *op. cit.* Reprinted from *American Economic Review* 62 (4), 540–52.

Skott, P. (1989) *Conflict and Effective Demand in Economic Growth*. Cambridge: Cambridge University Press.

Solow, R.M. (1990) "Goodwin's growth cycle: reminiscence and rumination," in Velupillai, K., *op. cit.*

Sordi, S. (1990) *Teorie del ciclo economico*. Bologna: Editrice Bologna.

230 *References*

Spanos, A. (1986) *Statistical Foundations of Econometric Modelling.* Cambridge: Cambridge University Press.
Sraffa, P. (1960) *Production of Commodities by Means of Commodities.* Cambridge: Cambridge University Press.
Stigler, G. and Kindahl, J. (1970) *The Behavior of Industrial Prices.* National Bureau of Economic Research, General Series, 90. New York: Columbia University Press.
Stock, J.H. and Watson, M. W. (1986) *Testing for Common Trends.* Harvard University Working Paper.
Stock, J.H. and Watson, M.W. (1988) "Variable trends in economic time series," *Journal of Economic Perspectives* 2 (3), 147–74.
Strange, S. (1986) *Casino Capitalism.* Oxford: Basil Blackwell.
Tarshis, L. (1939) "Changes in real and money wage rates," *Economic Journal* 49, 150–4.
Tobin, J. (1972) "Inflation and unemployment," *American Economic Review* 62 (1), 1–18.
Tobin, J. (1980) "Are new classical models plausible enough to guide policy?" *Journal of Money, Credit and Banking* 12 (4, part 2), 788–99
Tobin, J. (1984) "On the efficiency of the financial system," *Lloyd's Bank Review*, No. 153, pp. 1–15; In Tobin (1987) *Policies for Prosperity.* Cambridge, Mass: MIT Press.
Velupillai, K., ed. (1990) *Nonlinear and Multisectoral Macrodynamics: Essays in Honour of Richard Goodwin.* New York: New York University Press.
Watson, M. W. (1986) "Univariate detrending methods with stochastic trends," *Journal of Monetary Economics* 18, 49–75.
Weintraub, E.R. (1961) *Classical Keynesianism, Monetary Theory and the Price Level.* Westport, Conn: Greenwood Press.
Weintraub, E. R. (1979). *Microfoundations: the Compatibility of Microeconomics and Macroeconomics.* Cambridge: Cambridge University Press.
Weiss, A. (1980) "Job queues and layoffs in labor markets with flexible wages", *Journal of Political Economy* 88, 526–38.
Wray, L.R. (1990) *Money and Credit in Capitalist Economies: The Endogenous Money Approach.* Aldershot, Hants: Edward Elgar.
Yellen, J. (1984) "Efficiency-wage models of unemployment," *American Economic Review* 74, 200–5. In Mankiw and Romer, *op. cit.* vol. 2.
Zarnowitz, V. (1962) "Unfilled orders, price changes and business fluctuations," *Review of Economics and Statistics* 44 (4), 367–94.
Zarnowitz, V. (1973) *Orders, production and investment.* New York: National Bureau of Economic Research.
Zarnowitz, V. (1981) "Business cycles and growth: some reflections and measures." In Muckl, W.J. and Ott, A.E., eds. *Wirtschaftstheorie und Wirtschaftspolitik: Gedenkenschrift fur Erich Preiser.* Passau: Passavia Universitatsverlag.

Zarnowitz, V. and Moore, G.H. (1986) "Major changes in cyclical behavior." In Gordon, R.J., ed. *The American Business Cycle: Continuity and Change.* Chicago: University of Chicago Press.

Zarnowitz, V. (1992). *Business Cycles: theory history, indicates, and forecasting.* NBER Studies in Business Cycles, vol 27. Chicago: The University of Chicago Press.

Index of Subjects

Name Index

Printed and bound by CPI Group (UK) Ltd, Croydon, CR0 4YY

16/04/2025

14658548-0002